Post-Scarcity Anarchism

Murray Bookchin

WORKING CLASSICS SERIES
3

Post-Scarcity Anarchism

ISBN: 9781904859062
LCCN: 2004115247

AK Press
370 Ryan Ave. #100
Chico, CA 95973
USA
www.akpress.org
akpress@akpress.org

AK Press
33 Tower St.
Edinburgh EH6 7BN
Scotland
www.akuk.com
ak@akedin.demon.co.uk

Interior layout and design by Christopher Nelson
Cover design by Enamel Media
Printed in the USA

CONTENTS

To the memory of
Josef Weber and Allan Hoffman

Introduction to the First Edition

We normally live completely immersed in the present—to such a degree, in fact, that we often fail to see how much our own social period differs from the past—indeed from a mere generation ago. This captivity to the contemporary can be very insidious. It may shackle us unknowingly to the most reactionary aspects of tradition, be they obsolete values and ideologies, hierarchical forms of organization, or one-sided modes of political behavior. Unless our roots in contemporary life are broadened by a rich perspective, they may easily distort our understanding of the world as it really is, as well as its rich potentialities for the future.

For the world is changing profoundly, more profoundly than many of us seem to recognize. Until very recently, human society developed around the brute issues posed by unavoidable material scarcity and their subjective counterpart in denial, renunciation and guilt. The great historic splits that destroyed early organic societies, dividing man from nature and man from man, had their origins in the problems of survival, in problems that involved the mere maintenance of human existence.* Material scarcity provided the historic rationale for the development of the patriarchal family, private property, class domination and the state; it nourished the great divisions in hierarchical society that pitted town against country, mind against sensuousness, work against play, individual against society, and, finally, the individual against himself.

Whether this long and tortuous development could have followed a different, more benign, course is now irrelevant. The development is largely behind us. Perhaps like the mythic apple, which, once bitten, had to be consumed completely, hierarchical society had to complete its own bloody journey before its demonic institutions could be exorcised. Be that as it may, our position in that historic drama differs fundamentally from that of anyone in the past. We of the twentieth century are literally the heirs of human history, the legatees of man's age-old effort to free himself from drudgery and material insecurity. For the first time in the long succession of centuries, this century—and this one alone—has elevated mankind to an entirely new level of technological achievement and to an entirely new vision of the human experience.

* By "organic societies" I mean forms of organization in which the community is united by kinship ties and by common interests in dealing with the means of life. Organic societies are not yet divided into the classes and bureaucracies based on exploitation that we find in hierarchical society.

We of this century have finally opened the prospect of material abundance for all to enjoy—a sufficiency in the means of life without the need for grinding, day-to-day toil. We have discovered resources, both for man and industry that were totally unknown a generation ago. We have devised machines that automatically make machines. We have perfected devices that can execute onerous tasks more effectively than the strongest human muscles, that can surpass the industrial skills of the deftest human hands, that can calculate with greater rapidity and precision than the most gifted human minds. Supported by this qualitatively new technology, we can begin to provide food, shelter, garments, and a broad spectrum of luxuries without devouring the precious time of humanity and without dissipating its invaluable reservoir of creative energy in mindless labor. In short, for the first time in history we stand on the threshold of a post-scarcity society.

The word "threshold" should be emphasized here for in no way has the existing society realized the post-scarcity potential of its technology. Neither the material "privileges" that modern capitalism seems to afford the middle classes nor its lavish wasting of resources reflects the rational, humanistic, indeed unalienated, content of a post-scarcity society. To view the word "post-scarcity" simply as meaning a large quantity of socially available goods would be as absurd as to regard a living organism simply as a large quantity of chemicals.* For one thing, scarcity is more than a condition of scarce resources: the word, if it is to mean anything in human terms, must encompass the social relations and cultural apparatus that foster insecurity in the psyche. In organic societies this insecurity may be a function of the oppressive limits established by a precarious natural world; in a hierarchical society it is a function of the repressive limits established by an exploitative class structure. By the same token, the word "post-scarcity" means fundamentally more than a mere abundance of the means of life, it decidedly includes the kind of life these means support. The human relationships and psyche of the individual in a post-scarcity society must fully reflect the freedom, security and self-expression that this abundance makes possible. Post-scarcity society, in short, is the fulfillment of the social and cultural potentialities latent in a technology of abundance.

* Hence the absurdity of Tom Hayden's use of the expression "post-scarcity" in his recent book, *The Trial.* Hayden's fear that the youth culture might slip into "post-scarcity hedonism" and become socially passive suggests that he has yet to understand fully the meaning of "post-scarcity" and the nature of the youth culture.

Capitalism, far from affording "privileges" to the middle classes, tends to degrade them more abjectly than any other stratum in society. The system deploys its capacity for abundance to bring the petty bourgeois into complicity with his own oppression—first by turning him into a commodity, into an object for sale in the marketplace; next by assimilating his very wants to the commodity nexus. Tyrannized as he is by every vicissitude of bourgeois society the whole personality of the petty bourgeois vibrates with insecurity. His soporifics—commodities and more commodities—are his very poison. In this sense there is nothing more oppressive than "privilege" today, for the deepest recesses of the "privileged" man's psyche are fair game for exploitation and domination.

But by a supreme twist of dialectical irony, the poison is also its own antidote. Capitalism's capacity for abundance—the soporific it employs for domination—stirs up strange images in the dream world of its victims. Running through the nightmare of domination is the vision of freedom, the repressed intuition that what-is could be otherwise if abundance were used for human ends. Just as abundance invades the unconscious to manipulate it, so the unconscious invades abundance to liberate it, The fore-most contradiction of capitalism today is the tension between what-is and what-could-be—between the actuality of domination and the potentiality of freedom. The seeds for the destruction of bourgeois society lie in the very means it employs for its self-preservation: a technology of abundance that is capable of providing for the first time in history the material basis for liberation. The system, in a sense, is in complicity against itself. As Hegel put it in another context: "The struggle is too late; and every means taken makes the disease worse..."[1]

If the struggle to preserve bourgeois society tends to be self-vitiating, so too is the struggle to destroy it. Today the greatest strength of capitalism lies in its ability to subvert revolutionary goals by the ideology of domination. What accounts for this strength is the fact that "bourgeois ideology" is not merely bourgeois. Capitalism is the heir of history, the legatee of all the repressive features of earlier hierarchical societies, and bourgeois ideology has been pieced together from the oldest elements of social domination and conditioning—elements so very old, so intractable, and so seemingly unquestionable, that we often mistake them for "human nature." There is no more telling commentary on the power of this cultural legacy than the extent to which the socialist project itself is permeated by hierarchy, sexism and renunciation. From these elements come all the social enzymes that catalyze the everyday relationships of the bourgeois world—and of the so-called "radical movement."

Hierarchy, sexism and renunciation do not disappear with "democratic centralism," a "revolutionary leadership," a "workers' state," and a "planned economy." On the contrary, hierarchy, sexism, and renunciation function all the more effectively if centralism appears to be "democratic," if leaders appear to be "revolutionaries," if the state appears to belong to the "workers," and if commodity production appears to be "planned." Insofar as the socialist project fails to note the very existence of these elements, much less their vicious role, the "revolution" itself becomes a facade for counterrevolution. Marx's vision notwithstanding, what tends to "wither away" after this kind of "revolution" is not the state but the very consciousness of domination.

Actually, much that passes for a "planned economy" in socialist theory has already been achieved by capitalism; hence the capacity of state capitalism to assimilate large areas of Marxist doctrine as official ideology. Moreover, in the advanced capitalist countries, the very progress of technology has removed one of the most important reasons for the existence of the "socialist state"—the need (in the words of Marx and Engels) "to increase the total of productive forces as rapidly as possible."[2] To loiter any longer around the issues of a "planned economy" and a "socialist state"—issues created by an earlier stage of capitalism and by a lower stage of technological development—would be sectarian cretinism. The revolutionary project must become commensurate with the enormous social possibilities of our time, for just as the material pre-conditions of freedom have expanded beyond the most generous dreams of the past, so too has the vision of freedom. As we stand on the threshold of a post-scarcity society, the social dialectic begins to mature, both in terms of what must be abolished and what must be created. We must bring to an end not only the social relations of bourgeois society, but also the legacy of domination produced by long millennia of hierarchical society. What we must create to replace bourgeois society is not only the classless society envisioned by socialism, but the non-repressive utopia envisioned by anarchism.

Until now we have been occupied primarily with the technological capabilities of bourgeois society, its potential for supporting a post-scarcity society, and the tension this creates between what-is and what-could-be.

Let there be no mistaken notion that this tension floats in some vague fashion between theoretical abstractions. The tension is real, and it finds daily expression in the lives of millions. Often intuitively, people begin to find intolerable the social, economic and cultural conditions that were passively accepted only a decade or so ago. The growth of the black liberation movement over the past ten years (a movement that has heightened every sensibility of black people to their oppression) is explosive evidence of this development. Black liberation is being joined by women's liberation, youth liberation, children's liberation and gay liberation. Every ethnic group and virtually every profession is in a ferment that would have seemed inconceivable a mere generation ago. The "privileges" of yesterday are becoming the "rights" of today in almost dizzying succession among students, young people generally, women, ethnic minorities, and, in time, among the very strata on which the system has traditionally relied for support. The very concept of "rights" is becoming suspect as the expression of a patronizing elite which bestows and denies "rights" and "privileges" to inferiors. A struggle against elitism and hierarchy as such is replacing the struggle for "rights" as the main goal. It is not *justice* any longer that is being demanded, but rather *freedom*. Moral sensibilities to abuses—even the most minor abuses by earlier standards—are reaching an acuity that would have seemed inconceivable only a few years ago.

The liberal euphemism for the tension between actuality and potentiality is "rising expectations." What this sociological phrase fails to reveal is that these "expectations" will continue to "rise" until utopia itself is achieved. And for good reason. What goads the "expectations" into "rising"—indeed, into escalating with each "right" that is gained—is the utter irrationality of the capitalist system itself. When cybernated and automatic machinery can reduce toil to the near vanishing point, nothing is more meaningless to young people than a lifetime of toil. When modern industry can provide abundance for all, nothing is more vicious to poor people than a lifetime of poverty. When all the resources exist to promote social equality, nothing is more criminal to ethnic minorities, women and homosexuals than subjugation. These contrasts could be extended indefinitely, covering all the issues that have produced the social agony of our era.

In attempting to uphold scarcity, toil, poverty and subjugation against the growing potential for post-scarcity leisure, abundance and freedom, capitalism increasingly emerges as the most irrational, indeed the most artificial, society in history. The society now takes on the appearance of a totally *alien* (as well as alienating) force. It emerges as the "other," so to speak, of humanity's deepest desires and impulses. On an ever-greater scale, potentiality begins to determine and shape one's everyday view of actuality, until a point is reached where everything about the society—including its most "attractive" amenities—seems totally insane, the result of a massive social lunacy.

Not surprisingly, subcultures begin to emerge which emphasize a natural diet as against the society's synthetic diet, an extended family as against the monogamous family, sexual freedom as against sexual repression, tribalism as against atomization, community as against urbanism, mutual aid as against competition, communism as against property, and, finally, anarchism as against hierarchy and the state. In the very act of refusing to live by bourgeois strictures, the first seeds of the utopian lifestyle are planted. Negation passes into affirmation; the rejection of the present becomes the assertion of the future within the rotting guts of capitalism itself. "Dropping out" becomes a mode of dropping in—into the tentative, experimental, and as yet highly ambiguous, social relations of utopia. Taken as an end in itself, this lifestyle is not utopia; indeed, it may be woefully incomplete. Taken as a means, however, this lifestyle and the processes leading to it are indispensable in remaking the revolutionary, in awakening his sensibilities to how much must be changed if the revolution is to be complete. The lifestyle is indispensable in preserving the integrity of the revolutionary, in providing him with the psychic resources to resist the subversion of the revolutionary project by bourgeois values.

The tension between actuality and potentiality, between present and future, acquires apocalyptic proportions in the ecological crisis of our time. Although a large part of this book will deal with environmental problems, several broad conclusions should be emphasized. Any attempt to solve the environmental crisis within a bourgeois framework must be dismissed as chimerical. Capitalism is inherently anti-ecological. Competition and accumulation constitute its very law of life, a law which Marx pungently summarized in the phrase, "production for the sake of production." Anything, however hallowed or rare, "has its price" and is fair game for the marketplace. In a society of this kind, nature is necessarily treated as a mere resource to be plundered and exploited. The destruction of the natural world, far from being the result of mere hubristic blunders, follows inexorably from the very logic of capitalist production.

The schizoid attitude of the public toward technology—an attitude that mingles fear with hope—should not be dismissed lightmindedly. This attitude expresses a basic intuitive truth the same technology that could liberate man in a society organized around the satisfaction of human needs must inevitably destroy him in a society organized around "production for the sake of production." To be sure, the Manichean dualism imputed to technology is not a feature of technology as such. The capacities of modern technology to create or destroy are simply the two faces of a common social dialectic—the negative and positive features of hierarchical society. If there is any truth to Marx's claim that hierarchical society was "historically necessary" in order to "dominate" nature, we should never forget that the concept of "dominating" nature emerged from the domination of man by man. Both men and nature have always been the common victims of hierarchical society. That both are now faced with ecological extinction is evidence that the instruments of production have finally become too powerful to be administered as instruments of domination.

Today, as we stand at the end of hierarchical society's development, its negative and positive aspects can no longer be reconciled. Not only do they stand opposed to each other irreconcilably, they stand opposed to each other as mutually exclusive wholes. All the institutions and values of hierarchical society have exhausted their "historically necessary" functions. No longer is there any social rationale for property and classes, for monogamy and patriarchy, for hierarchy and authority, for bureaucracy and the state. These institutions and values, together with the city, the school and the instrumentalities of privilege, have reached their historical limits. In contrast to Marx, we would have little quarrel with Bakunin's view that the institutions and values of hierarchical society were *always* a "historically necessary evil." If Bakunin's verdict seems to enjoy a moral superiority over Marx's today, this is because the institutions have finally lost their moral authority.*

* Hence the reactionary aspect of the socialist project, which still retains the concepts of hierarchy, authority and the state as part of humanity's postrevolutionary future. By implication this project also retains the concepts of property ("nationalized") and classes ("proletarian dictatorship"). The various "orthodox" Marxists (Maoists, Trotskyists, Stalinists and the hybridized sects that combine all three tendencies) mediate the negative and positive features of the overall social development ideologically—*precisely* at a time when they have never been more irreconcilable objectively.

By the same token, the coming revolution and the utopia it creates must be conceived of as wholes. They can leave no area of life untouched that has been contaminated by domination.* From the revolution there must emerge a society that transcends all the splits of the past; indeed, one must emerge that offers every individual the feast of a many-sided, rounded and total experience.

In describing this utopia as "anarchism," I might have also used an equivalent expression—"anarcho-communism." Both terms denote a stateless, classless, decentralized society in which the splits created by propertied society are transcended by new, unalienated human relationships. An anarchist or anarcho-communist society presupposes the abolition of private property, the distribution of goods according to individual needs, the complete dissolution of commodity relationships, the rotation of work, and a decisive reduction in the time devoted to labor. As this description stands, however, we have little more than the anatomy of a free society. The description lacks an account of the physiology of freedom—of freedom as the process of communizing. The description, in effect, lacks those subjective dimensions that link the remaking of society to the remaking of the psyche.

Anarchists have probably given more attention to the subjective problems of revolution than any other revolutionary movement. Viewed from a broad historical perspective, anarchism is a libidinal upsurge of the people, a stirring of the social unconscious that reaches back, under many different names, to the earliest struggles of humanity against domination and authority. Its commitment to doctrinal shibboleths is minimal. In its active concern with the issues of everyday life, anarchism has always been preoccupied with lifestyle, sexuality, community, women's liberation and human relationships. Its central focus has always been the only meaningful goal social revolution can have—the remaking of the world so that human beings will be ends in themselves and human life a revered, indeed a marvelous, experience. For most radical ideologies, this goal has been peripheral. More often than not, these ideologies, by emphasizing abstractions over people, have reduced human beings to a *means*—ironically in the name of "the People" and "Freedom."

* Hence the revolutionary core of the women's liberation movement, which has brought the very syntax and musculature of domination into public view. In so doing, the movement has brought everyday life itself, not just abstractions like "Society," "Class," and "Proletariat," into question. Here I must apologize for using terms like "man," "mankind," and "humanity" and the masculine gender in this book. In the absence of substitutes for "people" and "individuals" my wording would have become awkward. Our language must also be liberated.

The difference between socialists and anarchists reveals itself not only in conflicting theories but also in conflicting types of organization and praxis. I have already noted that socialists organize into hierarchical bodies. By contrast, anarchists base their organizational structures on the "affinity group"—a collective of intimate friends who are no less concerned with their human relationships than with their social goals. The very mode of anarchist organization transcends the traditional split between the psyche and the social world. If the need arises, there is nothing to prevent the affinity groups from coordinating into fairly large movements (the Spanish anarchists, for example, built a nationwide federation of thousands out of this nuclear form). The movements, however, have the advantage that control over the larger organization lies always with the affinity groups rather than with the coordinating bodies. All action, in turn, is based on voluntarism and self-discipline, not on coercion and command. Praxis, in such an organization, is liberatory in the personal as well as in the social arena. The very nature of the group encourages the revolutionary to revolutionize himself.

This liberatory approach to praxis is carried still further in the anarchist conception of "direct action." Generally, direct action is regarded as a tactic, as a method of abolishing the state without recourse to state institutions and techniques. Although the foregoing interpretation is correct as far as it goes, it hardly goes far enough. Direct action is a basic revolutionary strategy, a mode of praxis intended to promote the individuation of the "masses." Its function is to assert the identity of the particular within the framework of the general. More important than its political implications are its psychological effects, for direct action makes people aware of themselves as individuals who can affect their own destiny.*

Finally, anarchist praxis also emphasizes spontaneity—a conception of praxis as an inner process, not an external, manipulated process. Its critics notwithstanding, this concept does not fetishize mere undifferentiated "impulse." Like life itself, spontaneity can exist on many different levels; it can be more or less permeated by knowledge, insight and experience. In a free society, the spontaneity of a three-year-old would hardly be of the same order as that of a thirty-year-old. Although both would be free to

* I should add here that the slogan "Power to the people" can only be put into practice when the power exercised by social elites is dissolved into the people. Each individual can then take control of his daily life. If "Power to the people" means nothing more than power to the "leaders" of the people, then the people remain an undifferentiated, manipulatable mass, as powerless after the revolution as they were before. In the last analysis, the people can never have power until they disappear as a "people."

develop without restraint, the behavior of the thirty-year-old would be based on a more defined and more informed self. By the same token, spontaneity may be more informed in one affinity group than in another, more seasoned by knowledge and experience.

But spontaneity is no more an organizational "technique" than direct action is merely an organizational tactic. Belief in spontaneous action is a part of a still larger belief—the belief in spontaneous development. Every development must be free to find its own equilibrium. Spontaneity, far from inviting chaos, involves releasing the inner forces of a development to find their authentic order and stability. As we shall see in the articles that follow, spontaneity in social life converges with spontaneity in nature to provide the basis for an ecological society. The ecological principles that shaped organic societies reemerge in the form of social principles to shape utopia. But these principles are now informed by the material and cultural gains of history. Natural ecology becomes social ecology. In utopia man no more returns to his ancestral immediacy with nature than anarcho-communism returns to primitive communism. Whether now or in the future, human relationships with nature are always mediated by science, technology and knowledge. But whether or not science, technology and knowledge will improve nature to its own benefit will depend upon man's ability to improve his social condition. Either revolution will create an ecological society, with new ecotechnologies and ecocommunities, or humanity and the natural world as we know it today will perish.

Every revolutionary epoch is a period of convergence when apparently separate processes collect to form a socially explosive crisis. If our own revolutionary epoch often seems more complex than earlier ones, this is because the processes that have been collecting together are more universal than they have ever been in the past. Our point of departure has no comforting historical precedents on which to rely. Earlier revolutionary epochs at least dealt with familiar institutional categories—the family, religion, property, toil and the state were taken for granted, even if their forms were challenged.* Hierarchical society had not exhausted these categories. Its development into more commanding and comprehensive social relations was still unfulfilled.

* This situation did not change with the Russian Revolution or the "socialist" revolutions that have occurred since then. The institutional categories have not disappeared; at most the names have changed.

In our time, however, this development has reached the point of saturation. There is no future for hierarchical society to claim, and for us there are the alternatives only of utopia or social extinction. So heavily are we laden with the debris of the past and so pregnant are we with the possibilities of the future that our estrangement with the world reaches the point of anguish. Past and future superimpose themselves on each other like latent images emerging in a double exposure. The familiar is there, but, like the psychedelic posters whose letters take the form of writhing human limbs, it blends elusively with the strange. A slight shift in position and the given reality is inverted completely. Learning to live appears to us the only mode of survival, play the only mode of work, the personal the only mode of the social, the abolition of sex roles the only mode of sexuality, tribalism the only mode of the family, sensuality the only mode of rationality. This interweaving of the old and new, with its incredible inversions, is not the usual "doublespeak" of the established order; it is an objective fact, which reflects the vast social changes that are in birth.

Every revolutionary epoch, moreover, not only brings together apparently separate processes but also converges them on a specific locus in time and space where the social crisis is most acute. In the seventeenth century this center was England; in the eighteenth and nineteenth, France; in the early twentieth, Russia. The center of the social crisis in the late twentieth century is the United States—an industrial colossus that produces more than half of the world's goods with little more than five percent of the world's population. Here is the Rome of world capitalism, the keystone of its imperial arch, the workshop and marketplace of its commodities, the den of its financial wizardry, the temple of its culture, and the armory of its weapons. Here, too, is the center of the world counterrevolution—and the center of the social revolution that can overthrow hierarchical society as a world-historical system.

To ignore the strategic position of the United States, both historically and internationally would reveal an incredible insensitivity to reality. To fail to draw all the implications of this strategic position and act upon them accordingly would be negligence of criminal proportions. The stakes are too great to allow for obscurantism. America, it must be emphasized, occupies the most advanced social terrain in the world. America, more than any other country, is pregnant with the most important social crisis in history. Every issue that bears on the abolition of hierarchical society and on the construction of utopia is more apparent here than elsewhere. Here lie the resources to annul and transcend what Marx called the "pre-history" of humanity. Here, too, are the contradictions that produce the most advanced form of revolutionary struggle. The decay of the American institutional structure results not from any mystical "failure of nerve" or from imperialist adventures in the Third World, but primarily from the over-ripeness of America's technological potential. Like hanging fruit whose seeds have matured fully, the structure may fall at the lightest blow. The blow may come from the Third World, from major economic dislocations, even from premature political repression, but fall the structure must, owing to its ripeness and decay.

In a crisis of this magnitude, the core problems of hierarchical society can be reached from *every* facet of life, be they personal or social, political or ecological, moral or material. Every critical act and movement erodes the domestic and imperial edifice. To repel any expression of discontent with sectarian harangues, borrowed from entirely different arenas and eras of social conflict, is simply blindness. Carried to its logical conclusions, the struggle for black liberation *is* the struggle against imperialism; the struggle for a balanced environment *is* the struggle against commodity production; the struggle for women's liberation *is* the struggle for human freedom.

True, a great deal of the pursuit of this discontent can be diverted into established institutional channels for a time. But only for a time. The social crisis is too deep and world-historical for the established institutions to contain it. If the system failed to assimilate the black movement, the "love generation," and the student movement of the sixties, it was not for want of institutional flexibility and resources. Despite the Cassandra-like forebodings of the American "left," these movements essentially rejected what the established institutions had to offer. More precisely, their demands increased as each one was met. At the same time, the physical base of the movements expanded. Radiating out from a few isolated urban centers, black, hippie, and student radicalism percolated through the country, penetrating high schools as well as universities, suburbs as well as ghettoes, rural communities as well as cities.

To challenge the value of these movements because their recruits are often white middle-class youth begs the question. There is perhaps no better testimony to the instability of bourgeois society than the fact that many militant radicals tend to come from the relatively affluent strata. It is conveniently forgotten that the fifties had Cassandras of a different type—the "Orwell generation," which warned that bureaucratic society was engineering American youth into polished conformity with the establishment. According to the predictions of that time, bureaucratic society was to acquire its main support from succeeding generations of young people. The ebbing generation of the thirties, it was argued, would be the last repository of radical, humanistic values. As it turned out, the very reverse occurred. The generation of the thirties has become one of the most willfully reactionary sectors of society, while the young people of the sixties have be-come the most radical.

In this seeming paradox, the contradiction between scarcity and the potential for post-scarcity appears in the form of outright confrontation. A generation whose entire psyche has been shaped by scarcity—by the depression and insecurities of the thirties—confronts another whose psyche has been influenced by the potential for a post-scarcity society. White middle-class youth has the real privilege of rejecting false "privilege." In contrast to their depression-haunted parents, young people are disenchanted by a flatulent consumerism that pacifies but never satisfies. The generation gap is real. It reflects an objective gap that increasingly separates America today from its own social history, from a past that is becoming archaic. Although this past has yet to be interred, a generation is emerging that may well prove to be its gravediggers.

To criticize this generation for its "bourgeois roots" exhibits the wisdom of a dunce who doesn't know that his most serious remarks are evoking laughter. All who live in bourgeois society have "bourgeois roots," be they workers or students, young people or old, black people or white. How much of a bourgeois one becomes depends exclusively upon what one accepts from bourgeois society. If young people reject consumerism, the work ethic, hierarchy and authority, they are more "proletarian" than the proletariat—a bit of semantic nonsense that should encourage us to inter the threadbare elements of socialist ideology together with the archaic past from which they derive.

If this nonsense still commands any attention today, it is due to the anemic character of the revolutionary project in the United States. American revolutionaries have yet to find a voice that relates to American issues. First World problems are not Third World problems; the two, moreover, are not bridged by retreating to ideologies that deal with nineteenth-century problems. Insofar as American revolutionaries mechanically borrow their formulas and slogans from Asia and Latin America, they do the Third World a grave disservice. What the Third World needs is a revolution in America, not isolated sects that are incapable of affecting the course of events. To promote that revolution would be the highest act of internationalism and solidarity with oppressed people abroad; it would require an outlook and a movement that speak to the problems unique to the United States. We need a cohesive, revolutionary approach to American social problems. Anyone who is a revolutionary in the United States is *necessarily* an internationalist by virtue of America's world position, so I need make no apologies for the attention I give to this country.

The articles that make up this book must be seen as a unified whole. What essentially unifies them is the view that man's most visionary dreams of liberation have now become compelling necessities. All the articles are written from the perspective that hierarchical society, after many bloody millennia, has finally reached the culmination of its development. The problems of scarcity, from which emerged propertied forms, classes, the state and all the cultural paraphernalia of domination can now be resolved by a post-scarcity society. In reaching the point where scarcity can be eliminated, we find that a post-scarcity society is not merely desirable or possible, but absolutely necessary if society is to survive. The very development of the material preconditions for freedom makes the achievement of freedom a social necessity.

If humanity is to live in balance with nature, we must turn to ecology for the essential guidelines of how the future society should be organized. Again, we find that what is desirable is also necessary. Man's desire for unrepressed, spontaneous expression, for variety in experience and surroundings, and for an environment scaled to human dimensions must also be realized to achieve natural equilibrium. The ecological problems of the old society thus reveal the methods that will shape the new. The intuition that all of these processes are converging toward an entirely new way of life finds its most concrete confirmation in the youth culture. The rising generation, which has been largely spared the scarcity psychosis of its parents, anticipates the development that lies ahead. In the outlook and praxis of young people, which range from tribalism to a sweeping affirmation of sensuousness, one finds those cultural pre-figurations that point to a future utopia.

Though I devote most of my discussion to what is new in the current social development, I definitely do not mean to ignore what is old. Exploitation, racism, poverty, class struggle and imperialism are still with us—and in many respects have deepened their grip on society. These issues can never fade from revolutionary theory and praxis until they are resolved completely. There is little I can contribute to these issues, however, that has not been exhaustively discussed by others. What justifies my utopian emphasis is the nearly total lack of material on the potentialities of our time. If no effort is made to enlarge this meagerly explored area, even the traditional issues of the radical movement will appear to us in a false light—as traditional. This would distort our very contact with the familiar. Although the issues raised by exploitation are not supplanted by those of alienation, the development of the former is profoundly influenced by the development of the latter.

Let us turn to an example of what this means. The traditional workers' movement will never reappear. Despite rank and file revolts, "bread and butter" issues are often too well contained by bourgeois unionism to form the basis for the old socialist type of labor union. But workers may yet form radical organizations to fight for changes in the *quality* of their lives and work—ultimately for workers' management of production. Workers will not form radical organizations until they sense the same tension between what-is and what-could-be that many young people feel today. I believe they will have to undergo major changes in their values—and not merely those values that involve the factory, but those that involve their lives. Only when life issues dominate factory issues will factory issues be assimilated to life issues. Then the economic strike may one day become a social strike and culminate in a massive blow against bourgeois society.

That young people in working-class families have increasingly responded to the culture of their white middle-class peers is one of the most hopeful signs that the factory will not be impervious to revolutionary ideas. Once it has taken root, a cultural advance, like a technological advance, is ever more widely diffused—particularly among people whose minds have not been hardened by conditioning and age. The youth culture, with its freedom of the senses and spirit, has its own innate appeal. The spread of this culture to the high schools and elementary schools is one of the most subversive social phenomena in the world today.

The articles in this book are a careful elaboration of the ideas raised in the foregoing pages. They appeal for a new emphasis on the problems of freedom, the environment, sex roles and lifestyle, and they advance broad utopian alternatives to the present social order. These emphases, I am convinced, are absolutely indispensable to the development of the revolutionary project in America.

Most of the articles were written between 1965 and 1968, a mere few years ago by the calendar, but ages ago ideologically. The hippie movement was just getting underway in New York when "Ecology and Revolutionary Thought" was published, and the disastrous SDS convention of June 1969 had yet to occur when "Listen, Marxist!" was completed. Most of the articles were published in *Anarchos* magazine and as *Anarchos* pamphlets. A few were published in underground papers or republished in "New Left" collections. Except for some deletions and the inclusion of several paragraphs, most of my changes have been stylistic.

One article, "The Forms of Freedom," has been substantially rewritten to remove any misunderstanding about my views on workers' councils. That these forms will be necessary to take over and operate the economy in a post-revolutionary period is a view I've held for many years—with the proviso, of course, that the councils (I prefer the term "factory committees") are controlled completely by workers' assemblies. Originally, this article limited its discussion of workers' councils to a critique of their defects as policy-making bodies. In rewriting portions of "The Forms of Freedom" I have tried to distinguish the function of these councils as administrative organs from policy-making organs.

The dedication of this book to Josef Weber and Allan Hoffman is more than a sentimental gesture to two of my closest comrades. Josef Weber, a German revolutionary who died in 1958 at the age of fifty-eight, formulated more than twenty years ago the outlines of the utopian project developed in this book. Moreover, for me he was a living link with all that was vital and libertarian in the great intellectual tradition of German socialism in the pre-Leninist era. From Allan Hoffman, whose death in a truck accident this year at the age of twenty-eight was an irreparable loss to the commune movement in California, I acquired a broader sense of the totality sought by the counterculture and youth revolt.

I owe very much to my sisters and brothers in the *Anarchos* group for a continual cross-fertilization of ideas, as well as for the warmth of real human relationships. In a sense, what is of worth in this book draws from the insights of many people whom I knew on the Lower East Side in New York, at Alternate U, and in groups and collectives throughout the country.

To them—*Salud!*

Murray Bookchin
New York
August–October 1970

Introduction to the Second Edition

It would be easy to revise this book, to "update" it and give it greater contemporaneity since its publication by Ramparts Books fifteen years ago. Several publishers have asked me to do so since the book went out of print in the early eighties. But I have resisted, often unconsciously. There are works that should not be touched—and *Post-Scarcity Anarchism* is perhaps one of them. Whether deservedly or not, the book has entered into the literature of modem anarchism and voices in a reasonably coherent way some of the more inspired ideals of the sixties. To alter the book would be to violate a wondrous period of history itself—a period that produced a new, almost magical romance with life that I regard as imperishable if the human spirit is to come into its fulfillment.

It is also a book that was more influential than many ecological and radical theorists are likely to admit. I still hear its thoughts echoed in widely disparate places. That an ecological perspective had a rich radical content and would surface as an issue that socialist and anarchist theorists would be obliged to deal with was a very remote idea in the early sixties, however commonplace it has become today.

In any case, the book's sale ran into many thousands in North America and Europe. Some of its essays, particularly "Listen, Marxist!" (1969), were circulated in sizable numbers—not only in its original pamphlet form which I left unsigned, but in anthologies and as articles in the widely read "underground press" of the time. Much the same can be said for "Ecology and Revolutionary Thought," which I initially printed in my theoretical newsletter, *Comment,* in 1964 and republished a year later in the British monthly *Anarchy.*

The past fifteen years since the book's publication, however, have seen major changes in the radical "constituency" for which it was written. American radicalism has indeed made its "long march through the institutions," to use Rudi Dutschke's phrase, from the stormy student campuses of the sixties to the more serene faculty rooms of the eighties. Its buoyant populism has been abandoned for a restful Marxism. The journey, far from widening the horizon of the Marxist "professoriat," to use Theodore Draper's term, has turned it into a more "discriminating" body, a word I use in a highly partisan sense. Today almost anyone's book will make its way into the bibliographies of this professoriat if it is labeled "Marxist," irrespective of the hodge-podge of ideas the term is obliged to encompass. Use the word "anarchist," and the book is likely to be consigned to academic oblivion, even such historically important writers as a Peter Kropotkin or a Paul Goodman.

Which is not to say that I am convinced that these writers will disappear from the radical tradition: there are more long range factors that ultimately single out pioneering books and ideas from epigones who try to restate them in less original and more socially acceptable ways. What troubles me about epigonic writing is the way it obscures and hybridizes ideas. It is disconcerting, to say the least, to see attempts to meld an ecologism that is clearly libertarian in its view of nature with a Marxism that is structured around the domination of nature as a historic desideratum. Not only do such efforts violate the meaning of social ecology (as I choose to call my ideas) but also the thrust of Marx's own ideas. Just as I stress in my writings the fecundity, creativity, and complexity of nature as a potential "realm of freedom" so Marx's writings deal with nature as "stingy," as mere object for human exploitation, and as a grim "realm of necessity" that dominates "man" in his quest for a liberated world—a world liberated not only from human domination but the "domination" of humanity by nature.

Indeed, Marx's justification for the emergence of class society and the State, not to speak of his "class analysis," stems from an underlying imagery of the oppressed "savage" who must "wrestle" with an ungiving, intractable, natural world. The Victorian, largely *bourgeois,* origins of this imagery is an issue I have discussed in some detail in other books.* To wed this grim drama of social development to a libertarian conception of nature as fecund, creative, and a potential "realm of freedom" is not merely sloppy thinking; it is grossly obscurantist. One can always, to be sure, trot out a Gramsci or a Marcuse to paper over blatant contradictions that deserve respect and serious resolution. But to ignore them by prudently casting a veil of silence over works that seek to explore them with care is to divest ideas of their integrity and denature critical thinking as such.

What also troubles me is the moral condition of contemporary radicalism. There was a time, even as recently as the early thirties, when

* See particularly my essay "Marxism as Bourgeois Sociology" in *Toward an Ecological Society*), (Montréal: Black Rose Books, 1980), and my overall critique of Marxism in *The Ecology of Freedom* (Oakland: AK Press, 2005).

radicals of all kinds formed an ethical community, despite the many ideological differences that divided them. Whether as socialists, anarchists, syndicalists, or populists, they shared their views in free discourse, defended each other's rights, and even aided each other in publishing works that were ordinarily proscribed by the bourgeois press. Anarchists like Emma Goldman could find solace and help from Marxists like John Reed in times of difficulty, and anarchists like Sacco and Vanzetti rallied universal support from the Left, including Communists, despite their explicit criticisms of Soviet Russia.

These days are gone. The Left, today, is not only fragmented; it is closeted into dogmatic strongholds, and many of its members are notable not only for their lack of political influence but their professorial spitefulness. Polemic has lost its fire and honesty. It suffers from the sterility of the specialist's "journal": jargonized, stilted, pedantic, insidiously backbiting, and unrestrained in its capacity to plagiarize. Socialism has become an industry and its literary works are commodities. They are often vended by ambitious careerists who have long traded away their political ideals for their professional status. The "New Left" has aged badly. It lives in spiteful hatred of its own youth and in fear of a revival of student militancy, a revival that may jeopardize its academic positions and peer recognition.

In many cases, a strangely symbiotic relationship exists between the academic Right and its leftist counterparts: a few scholarly Marxists are not only a *sine qua non* for a sophisticated college curriculum, but departments, even control of academic journals and societies, are divided between Right and Left with an unspoken understanding that the stability of a university, even the effective control of the student body, depends upon a delicate balance of forces between the two and a "pluralism" that replaces intellectual stimuli by paralysis. I need hardly say that in this academic ecumene, anarchists are literally too gauche to have a place in the academic firmament and their literature must be closed out of reading lists and course adoptions. If there is a reasonable amount of peace in the academy today, it is due not only to the careerism of students in an economically precarious world, but the careerism of their "radical" professors in an academically tight market. The "professoriat" has become an interest in its own right and strategically tends to function more as a safety valve for student dissent than a stimulus—a fact which more intelligent conservatives appreciate only too well.

In rereading *Post-Scarcity Anarchism,* I find its sixties rebelliousness to be a healthy antidote to the prevailing mood of calculated disenchantment and reformism that is so prevalent within the "radical" movement today. The book spoke to a time when words like "revolution," "uprising," and even "bourgeoisie," were not seen as exotic terms. At the same time it was meant to be a careful correction of the revolutionary fervor that took possession of the young radicals I knew at the time: their earnest belief that revolution was imminent. (See pp xxi–xxii.*)* Already middle-aged in the sixties, with a long experience in the Left of the thirties behind me, I tried to warn my younger comrades that "there is no 'revolutionary situation' at this time in America..." Indeed, as I wrote, "There is no immediate prospect of a revolutionary challenge to the established order." Rather, there is "a greater susceptibility to radical ideas than at any time since the populist resurgence of seventy years ago... [but] still no reason to believe that the bulk of white America will accept, much less support, the idea of revolutionary change at the present time." These lines were published in the first issue of *Anarchos*, a magazine I launched in 1967 with the cooperation of a few friends in New York's Lower East Side.* What troubled me profoundly was the likelihood that revolutionary expectations among radical young people were outpacing reality—a fear that was more than amply justified, as the seventies were to show.

Yet the sixties had done wondrous things, many of which are sedimented into American life. Its linkage of the personal with the political, of aesthetic fantasy with social reality, of a nonhierarchical society with a classless one, of libertarian process with revolutionary ends—all, not to speak of its celebrated flood of experiments in communal living, sexual freedom, radical changes in dress, diet, educational techniques, and culture as such, were latently revolutionary and expressly utopian. The notion, so prevalent today, that this constellation of what was to be called a "counterculture" has been "co-opted" is grossly false. That business, ever on the lookout for new commercial opportunities, used bits and pieces of the counterculture to its profit is not evidence of its co-optation but rather of its fragmentation. One could say the same of the Paris Commune of 1871 because the Rothschilds offered to meet its monetary needs. To have co-opted the counterculture as a *whole,* even in the name of profit, would have planted a revolutionary way of experiencing reality in the very heart of the system.

* See Robert Keller (pseud.): "Revolution in America," *Anarchos*, No. 1, February, 1968, p. 3.

In any case, America could not accept these social and cultural changes overnight. To achieve them, even in part, would have required years of enlightenment. The "New Left" and the counterculture, initially so generous, populist, and anarchic in character, adopted a self-righteous and dogmatic stance as the years went by. The Vietnam War and the "cultural revolution" in China did these movements no service; as Barbara Garson has observed somewhere, it gave them a "bandwagon" to hitch on to, a phenomenon we are witnessing today in the case of Nicaragua. That the sixties opposed American imperialism is indubitably creditable and admirable, but certainly not its adoption of Vietnam and China as "models" of revolutionary wisdom and a new society. Disconnected from the American experience, the "New Left," became increasingly isolated, even more than the counterculture, which was already hemorrhaging from its own entanglement with drugs, musical impresarios, and self-anointed gurus. Intolerance replaced an understanding desire to educate the people; Marxist-Leninist dogma, more closely akin to Stalinism than Marxism, filtered through a political movement whose promising beginnings had been sidetracked into a form of cultural terrorism, as intolerant as the cultural conventions it professed to oppose.* Expectations for social change began to exceed the real possibility for achieving them so that failure, when it came, virtually demolished sizable movements that seemed to have limitless possibilities for growth. America's vicious reaction to the shootings at Kent State University—"the National Guard should have shot more!" was the characteristic reply of angry parents to their shocked children—the popularity of Nixon, and finally the onset of economic crises, placed a final seat on the closing of the sixties.

What stands out most sharply about this era was its innocence. The cultural upwelling that tried to enchant everyday life foundered on its inability to understand the historic trends that produced it. Everyday life, in effect, concealed the need to grasp the larger social context in which the "New Left" and the counterculture flourished. What was painfully lacking was the maturing, steadying effect of consciousness and a theoretical coherence of ideas which would have united the disparate threads of the

* Readers who still have a good knowledge of the period would do well to contrast the good-natured playfulness of the Dutch *Provos* with the repellent dogmatism of the French Situationists. The full measure of the degeneration that occurred between 1965 and 1968 can be understood by placing these two tendencies in juxtaposition to each other.

"Movement," as it came to be called, giving it meaning, a sense of direction, and ultimately the organizational structures that were needed to inter-link it and make it socially effective. Marxism, with its gospel of "class analysis" and economic determinism, functioned as an inertial drag on the "Movement," not as a clarifying light. For the "Movement" was nothing if it was not *transclass:* people united by age, a sense of community, ethnically, and, later, by gender—not by their status in the "relations of production." Lacking an adequate theoretical framework, indeed rooted in a typically American framework that eschewed ideas and the value of theory, the "Movement," beleaguered by growing uncertainties about its identity, became afraid of itself. It was seized by fear: fear of its direction, isolation, exploitation, lack of power, a loss of self-assurance that came from violated innocence, and its vulnerability to the sharks—commercial and lumpen—that began to encircle it. Finally it succumbed to the economic shocks that raised serious doubts about its material viability. The sudden scramble of young people from New York's Lower East Side after several highly publicized drug-related murders, the premature symbolic "burial of the hippie" in San Francisco's Haight-Ashbury district, and the stormy immolation of the Students for a Democratic Society at its Chicago convention in June 1969, essentially brought the era to an end.

The sixties will not recur—nor should it. What it addressed was a sense of disempowerment, alienation, displacement, and a need for existential meaning which a period, rich in the goodies that filled a vacuous life, could not supply. Above all, it sought an authentic and creative form of community. Not that these problems are unique to the sixties. They have existed in different forms and degrees since the end of the Second World War. The distinctive nature of the era lay in the fact that it saw the decay of a traditional society side-by-side with an unprecedented period of material abundance. The tension between the reality of social decay in a cultural sense and the prospect of social reconstruction in a material sense unavoidably produced unrest on the one hand and utopian visions on the other. Blacks provided the unrest in ghetto uprisings on a scale that had never been seen before, a product not only of their growing misery but also of their rising expectations. Compared to the ghetto explosions, the campus "revolts" were fairly tame affairs, but necessary ones. White youth, largely middle-class in background, provided the necessary sense of vision, such as it was or hoped to be.

But both were minorities within minorities. Black militants were barely accepted by their own people, except when a sense of shock was needed to give their more "responsible" leaders political clout. Leftist and countercultural youth were not really accepted by the majority students and the ordinary run of young people for whom they professed to speak, and, in the end, were more frightening, with their diet of dogmas and judgmental behavior, than inspiring. Sizable as both currents in the sixties became, they never acquired the lasting allegiance of their own kind. Nor did they try to earn it by painstaking education and patient forebearance.

A future movement for basic social change will not satisfy the needs of our time—its sense of disempowerment, alienation, displacement, meaning, and community—unless it pieces itself together *consciously*, bit by bit, with the aim of ideological clarity and theoretical coherence. Education, in my view, is the top "priority" for a radicalization of our time. To step rapidly out into another historic void will simply produce the same fear and sense of isolation that brought the sixties to an end. This education must speak clearly to the transclass phenomena—the re-emergence of "the People," as it were—with which the modem era started centuries ago, and it must deal with problems that are best defined as ethical, not simply economic.* Only by a supreme act of consciousness and ethical probity can this society be changed fundamentally. That it needs "objective forces" to promote that consciousness and ethics over and beyond educators is clear enough, but I hold more than ever that the *study* group, not only the "affinity group," is the indispensable form for this time—especially in view of the appalling intellectual and cultural degradation that marks our era.

As to the "objective forces" at work that may yet open a new period of social reconstruction, I have no reason whatever to diminish the enormous importance I attached to ecological problems thirty years ago. "Ecology and Revolutionary Thought" is one of the most prescient works to appear in radical theory. Its scope, projections, and anticipations, seen from 1964 onward, are as valid today as they were more than twenty years ago. That my identification of "revolutionary thought" with anarchism has precluded its extensive use by the Marxist professoriat is testimony to an inquisitorial dogmatism, indeed an ideological fanaticism, that

* See particularly my essay "Spontaneity and Organization" in *Toward an Ecological Society* (Montréal: Black Rose Books, 1980).

deserves the greatest contempt. Pilfered wholesale by many Marxists themselves, it stands as a lasting reproach to the myth that a radical "community" exists in the United States. The fact that ecological movements, at this writing, constitute the most serious source of social opposition in Germany is a reminder that the essay's prognoses justify the emphasis I give to it in this foreword.

So, too, is the importance of feminism—particularly ecofeminism—which has drawn a good deal of inspiration from the essay. Whether ecofeminism will go beyond the small-group syndrome that tends to marginalize it and bypass the liberal politics of the National Organization of Women (NOW) by becoming part of a larger, hopefully libertarian *Green* movement in the English-speaking world remains to be seen. The tendency of leftist feminists to withdraw into themselves is a problem that cannot be overlooked. It stands in flat contradiction to the justly universal claims of feminism in its more advanced forms to speak for "life on earth" against the assaults of patriarchalism, market competition, and a sensibility of domination and militarism.

The peace movement, another transclass "historic force," is faced with much the same problem of exclusivity and scope. The attempt to gauge its successes or failures by whether it can prevent the siting of nuclear missiles, bring the "superpowers" to the "negotiating table," or achieve appreciable arms reduction reveals a disturbing degree of naiveté. Its authentic and most on-going goal must ultimately be to oppose *militarism,* not only to advocate disarmament. This means that its basic orientation falls into the province of social ecology: to replace the hierarchical and domineering sensibility and social relations that link the domination of nature with the domination of human by human. No less than feminism, the peace movement must become part of a larger whole, a more encompassing coordination of the many separate threads, vital as each may be in its own right, into a well-focused and ultimately libertarian political movement.

Finally, the popular impulse toward community, which today stands in flat opposition to a homogenizing, atomizing, and privatizing urbanism—one that threatens to destroy both the city *and* the countryside—has moved to the forefront of the "forces" to which I have alluded. English socialism today is riddled by movements or tendencies that emphasize the locality rather than the nation-state, a new "local socialism" from which there is much to be learned. In any case, it is only on the local level—in the village, town, city, or neighborhood—that a new politics can be developed, one which brings together all of these "forces" as a form of ecological politics. Here, in municipalities, where people live out their lives in the most *immediate* and *personal* sense, we find the locus of real popular power. This public sphere provides the existential arena that makes for citizenship in an active sense. Social ecology brings all of these threads together in its opposition to hierarchy and domination as a critical theory and its emphasis on participation and differentiation as a reconstructive theory.

Elsewhere, I have drawn a sharp distinction between politics and statecraft.* Suffice it to say that politics, in my view, is the recovery of the Greek notion of a local public sphere—the municipality—in contrast to the statecraft of the nation-state which we have so mistakenly designated as "politics." We have yet to give enough attention to the city as a terrain for citizenship, self-empowerment, mutual aid, and a shared sense of *humanitas* that transcends the parochialism of tribal society and avoids the chauvinism of the nation-state. Yet the radical tradition is filled with revolutionary movements structured around the neighborhood or the city itself (the Parisian sections of 1793–94, the Paris Commune of 1871, and the town-meeting democracy of New England and the American Revolution, to cite only a few). We have yet to reclaim the democratic content of the great revolutions that liberal and Marxian historiography designate as "bourgeois"—an interpretation with which I emphatically disagree. This democratic content, I hold, has a distinctly libertarian core and speaks directly to existing libertarian traditions in America and possibly in Europe. Tragically, we have lost contact with our own radical traditions in Western society and, due in no small measure to Marxism-Leninism, have replaced them with ideologies and a vocabulary that is utterly alien to our own communities.

What I have tried to summarize are the issues and ideas that have come to the forefront of society since *Post-Scarcity Anarchism* was published. There was no environmental movement when I wrote "Ecology and Revolutionary Thought" (1964); no "appropriate technology" movement when I wrote "Toward a Liberatory Technology" (1965); no

* See my "Theses on Libertarian Municipalism" in *Our Generation*, Vol. 16, Nos. 3 & 4, my new introduction to *The Limits of the City* (Montreal: Black Rose Books, 1986), where the article is republished, and my book *Urbanization Without Cities* (San Francisco: Sierra Club Books, 1986).

communitarian movement of a political nature when I wrote "The Forms of Freedom" (1968). It should be kept in mind that proposals for using solar and wind energy, for example, had been abandoned by specialists in the field when my essay on technology was written, and no serious attention was given to community as a political phenomenon when I explored the need for liberatory institutions. For the traditional Left, these issues could have existed on the moon. Not only would it take a decade or more for Marxists to regard these issues as more than trivial but to desist from treating them as "petty bourgeois" at best or outright "reactionary" at worst.

For the most part, my ideas since writing *Post-Scarcity Anarchism* have expanded from the bases charted out in the book. There is very little I would want to discard since it was written. Rather, I have elaborated ideas that were dealt with in a fairly scanty fashion. Thus, I would want to develop "Forms of Freedom" to include my ideas on libertarian municipalism, deepen my criticism of Marxism in "Listen, Marxist!" and expand my discussion of technics and work in "Towards a Liberatory Technology." I would want to excise my use of Brecht's recipe for cynical socialism in the closing lines of the essay and temper the importance I gave the technological "preconditions" for freedom.

Do I hold that the abolition of "scarcity" is such a "precondition" in the *historic* sense emphasized by Marx? My acceptance of this view, largely an inheritance of Marxists who deeply influenced my thinking in the fifties, is not as unqualified as it would seem to be in a quick reading of the book. The original introduction, it should be noted, deals with scarcity more as a contemporary issue than a historical one. As I note: "Whether this long and tortuous development [around material scarcity] could have followed a different, more benign, course is now irrelevant, The development is now behind us" (p. iv). This equivocal statement was deliberately introduced fifteen years ago because I was doubtful about the concept of scarcity in a historical sense even as I seemed to argue for its role in many parts of the book. Viewed as a drama of history that our era has resolved technologically, I would have to say that such an interpretation is now unsatisfactory in my eyes, although the role of material deprivation in the past cannot be ignored. Yet I would still title this book *Post-Scarcity Anarchism* if I were to rewrite it. Capitalism is more of an economy than a society, as Karl Polanyi pointed out years ago. In dissolving most of the cultural, traditional, and ideological ties that kept needs under a measure of control, the market system has created a phenomenon that never existed in precapitalist or traditional society as a whole: a fetishization of needs, not only Marx's celebrated "fetishization of commodities." As I indicate in *The Ecology of Freedom:* "Needs, in effect, become a productive force, not a subjective force. They become blind in the same sense that the production of commodities becomes blind... To break the grip of the 'fetishization of needs,' to dispel it, is to recover the *freedom of choice,* a project that is tied to the freedom of the *self* to choose."* Post-scarcity is a "precondition" under *capitalism* for exorcising the hold of the economy over society, for creating a sufficiency in goods that permits the individual to choose what he or she *really* needs or wants, in short, for demystifying the economic by exploding it from within—by sheer abundance—as an all-presiding agent over the human condition. Put simply: under capitalism we must try to achieve a level of abundance that renders abundance meaningless and permits us to take possession of ourselves as free people, capable of choosing the lifeways that suit us.

By the same token, *Post-Scarcity Anarchism* does not fetishize technology. Quite to the contrary: the reader is warned early on in the book that "Technology and the resources of abundance furnish capitalism with the means of assimilating large sections of society to the established system of hierarchy and authority. They provide the system with the weaponry, the detecting devices and the propaganda media for the threat as well as the reality of massive repression. By their centralistic nature, the resources of abundance reinforce the monopolistic, centralistic and bureaucratic tendencies in the political apparatus. In short, they furnish the State with historically unprecedented means for manipulating and mobilizing the entire environment of life—and for perpetuating hierarchy, exploitation, and unfreedom.

Lest my emphasis on the liberatory potential of technology be mistaken as an argument for technocracy, the essay "Towards a Liberatory Technology" introduced themes that have taken on vastly greater significance over the years. The image that technology is now a matter of systematic design, not simply of inspired invention; the enormous range of uses to which "cybernated" devices lend themselves; the use of terms like

* Murray Bookchin: *The Ecology of Freedom* (Oakland: AK Press, 2005), pp. 68–69.

"miniaturization" to apply to technology as a whole; the notion that there is an ecological approach to technology that takes the form of *ensembles* of productive units, energized by solar and windpower units—all, taken together, are still pioneering concepts. They have yet to be fully assimilated by many environmentalists. The argument that we must recover local regional resources that were abandoned with the rise of a national division of labor is a pillar of the best bioregional thinking of the eighties. Finally, "The Forms of Freedom," written seventeen years ago, still constitutes the basis for my views on libertarian municipalism (including the assembly as the authentic basis for democracy) and for my criticism of syndicalism. There is much I hope to expand in this essay in a future book that will bear the same title. But there is little I would want to change in it.

Limitations of space do allow me to itemize point by point the ideas that are as relevant today as they were in the sixties. Apart from my qualifying remarks on scarcity and my use of words like "preconditions," *Post-Scarcity Anarchism* forms an indispensable introduction to views I have elaborated in later books and articles. Nor do I have any reason to eschew the word "anarchist." The libertarian tradition is as close to me as it was two decades ago and I freely align with it as a proponent, despite criticisms I have voiced of certain tendencies within it. Its persistence is a deserved one. And the many people in the ecology movement, not to speak of those on the Left who acknowledge their debt to this tradition, as well as those who use it without attribution, are living evidence of its value for later generations.

Changing shifts in the world economy and technology have made a number of items in the book somewhat dated. The United States is no longer the producer of "more than half of the world's goods," but rather a good deal less than a third. This relative decline, however, has not altered my view that it is the "keystone" in the imperial arch of world capitalism. Although its specific weight in production has diminished economically, its strategic position as a technological innovator and its military power is as great as ever. Nor can we judge the leading role a country can play by production figures at any given time, as the Axis powers discovered to their grief during the Second World War when a depression ridden America with some of the lowest production figures per capita in the world entered the war.

As to details: we can no longer speak of the need to increase electric-power production fivefold in the remaining years of the century. The estimates are now much smaller. Research on thermoelectric junctions has been supplanted by photoelectric junctions as of this writing. Electric cars, with their demands for electric power, might do more to increase pollution from power plants than to diminish it. My inclusion of nuclear fuels as part of a mosaic of energy sources was perhaps understandable two decades ago, especially since I had so-called "clean" thermonuclear sources in mind, but it now cuts across the entire grain of my thinking. The DDP-124 computer runs at 1.75 million cycles a second, not 1.75 "billion." Whether this was a typographical error, I do not know, but in any case it is wrong.*

I have been warned by a publisher that the student-worker movement that developed in France during May–June 1968 has all but been forgotten and my comments on it have little relevance. Here, I feel obliged to emphasize that the contemporaneity of an event is no guide to whether it should or should not be discussed. Not only has an entire generation described itself as the "people of '68," particularly in Europe, where the year and its events are regarded as the highpoint of the sixties; the '68 events themselves are too important in terms of the message they offered and the way they unfolded to be neglected. The failure of that great movement is no reason for forgetfulness but, to the contrary, reason for the most searching analyses. The two short pieces on "May–June," as it was called nearly twenty years ago, provide only part of such an analysis but one that is indispensable to a discussion of the way in which social movements develop in our era and the way in which they may unfold in the future.

The intellectual and political elaborations I have made since *Post-Scarcity Anarchism* was published are too complex to develop here. My criticisms of Marxism, which were anticipatory by any standards, have become more complex and fundamental since the publication of "Listen, Marxist!" Yet, on rereading this work, I find that it is as relevant today as it was when it first appeared at the crucial SDS convention of June 1969. The work is still being republished and its impact on potential converts to Marxism is still as powerful as it was many years ago. More elaborate

* I wish to thank Laurence Moore, of Ramparts Press, for singling out most of these errors in the book. Other observations, which Larry made, are interesting enough, but they are largely differences about our interpretation of social issues rather than mistakes of fact.

criticisms for which the essay lays the basis appear in *Toward an Ecological Society* and *The Ecology of Freedom.* My prediction in the pamphlet that soldiers could play a revolutionary role, not simply workers, was to acquire flesh-and-blood dimensions in Portugal, when rank-and-file troops proved to be more revolutionary than many socialists and their working-class followers. "Listen, Marxist!" it should be noted, was never seriously challenged by the Marxist press in the sixties and seventies. Despite its enormous distribution, it was carefully enveloped in a conspiracy of silence, which persists to this very day. Indeed, many of its ideas were simply appropriated by so-called "neo-Marxists" years after its publication and hybridized with elements of the Marxian canon.

Since the publication of *Post-Scarcity Anarchism* my development of social ecology has moved ahead by enormous strides and now includes works on nature philosophy, ecological ethics, criticisms of sociobiology and other reactionary forms of biologism, and a more ecological approach to natural evolution. My views on technology and social reconstruction, particularly ecological politics based on libertarian municipalism fill hundreds of pages in *Towards an Ecological Society, The Ecology of Freedom,* the Black Rose edition of *The Limits of the City,* and my latest book, *The Modern Crisis,* a common venture of Black Rose Books in Canada and New Society Publishers and the Institute for Social Ecology in the United States. This volume develops themes to which *The Limits of the City* forms an indispensable introduction. The two books complement each other and should be explored by readers who are interested in an ecological interpretation of politics and the recovery of genuine citizenship.

I have found "purity" nowhere in this world except in the mature music of Mozart and the moral probity of Fermin Salvochea, the Spanish anarchist "saint." Every idea advanced in this book is, in some sense, very "impure"—and, worse, has its antithesis in ideas and movements that are grossly wrong. Social ecology, a term that is already finding its way into the academic mainstream, is being cheapened by its antithesis in sociobiology, antihumanism, and outright ecofascism. Nature philosophy, such as I have advanced in my own writings, has its antithesis in an all-inclusive application of systems theory, reductionism as a mystique of a universal "Oneness," a myth of "interconnectedness" that loses sight of all distinctions or "mediations" (to use Hegel's term), and outright appeals to "blood-and-soil" chauvinism or dialectical materialism. An ecological ethics based on freedom has its antithesis in deterministic doctrines of "natural law," the "morality of the gene," social Darwinism, and the ethics of the "lifeboat" and "triage." Libertarian visions of community and politics have their antithesis in parliamentary politics, party organization, and electoral mobilization as distinguished from education. There is no magic strategy or pure dogma that provides us with principles or a practice that stands above the conflicts between right and wrong or good and evil—unless it is so far removed from the real world that it is insulated by distance and marginality from the taint of experience. I do not have to be reminded that social ecology can breed its opposite in utterly reactionary perversions of its truth. Or that it can be coopted in name and tarnished in spirit. Much of my life has been devoted to writing critical articles against those who pervert or infiltrate authentically ecological views with utterly alien notions that have been bred by explicit reactionaries as well as self-styled "radicals."

What the sixties should teach us, then, is that there is no substitute for consciousness. Truth will emerge only from insight,critical thinking, a reality principle that does not sacrifice principles to opportunistic gains, a moral probity that can resist descent into the surrender of ideals. Education remains on the order of the day—indeed, more so today than earlier because of the complexity of our problems and the massive drift toward intellectual vulgarity.

What the sixties should also teach us is that a counterculture is not enough—important as it is. What we need are the firm skeletal structures to support such a new culture—notably, *counterinstitutions.* This confronts us with the need to create a *political* movement that is libertarian and rescues the word "politics" from the ignominy of statecraft. Impure as they may be, there are still areas of life—notably, the municipalities—that can be reclaimed as a new political sphere by an active citizenry in popular assemblies, confederated, and ultimately developed into a counterpower with counterinstitutions that stand opposed to those of the nation-state. The eighties and sixties now face each other in direct confrontation—not as conflicting eras that raise opposing alternatives, but as complementary ones that, taken together, provide the opportunity for *fuller* alternatives than those which existed twenty years ago and today. Whether we can bring these complementary decades together, each of which has so much to give to the other, in a reconstructive politics that opens a new way to our present-day impasse will determine the future of this century and much of the one to come.

Murray Bookchin
September 1985

Introduction to the Third Edition

It is difficult to believe that some forty years have passed since I wrote "Ecology and Revolutionary Thought," one of the most influential works in this collection of 1960s essays. I tried to call the emerging consciousness of an environmental crisis "social ecology." The word *ecology* was meant to emphasize the need for Wholeness, or as Georg Lukács and the Frankfurt School would have called it, "Totality." *Social*, in turn, was meant to stand for "socialism," of the highly plastic kind that came into vogue during the interwar period, before Stalinism came to represent a cruel bureaucratic dogma. Properly nuanced and explored, the unconventional neo-socialism of Lukács and the pre-Hitler Eastern European academics imparted to the young Marx's language a new configuration—a sort of double helix, as I visualized it, in which one strand of the helix (the "legacy of freedom") interacted dialectically with the other (a developing "legacy of domination"), creating an ever-expanding spiral, hopefully to broaden and encompass freedom at the expense of domination.

This configuration, I believed, would lead to the expansion of freedom at the expense of domination. Dualism would not disappear; indeed, there would be a vital interaction between the two in which what was authoritarian in one legacy would yield the expansion of freedom. Formalistic as this conception of social development must now seem, I was wrestling, in effect, with a problem with which the Marxists of my generation had contended for decades: if historic development is marked by circularity (as Hegel seemed to say a century earlier) and every end is marked by a new, more advanced beginning, what level could a communism that would succeed the "end of history" reach? Or was Hegel's notion of circularity one of those philosophical myths that had to be supplanted by a notion of indefinite "progress" or, more dismally, by a gray liberalism of the kind suggested by Francis Fukuyama and his admirers?

My interest in the issue of the "end of history" was not metaphysical. When Fukuyama's book of that name appeared, the prospect of an end to humanity was not academic. Nuclear weapons, bioweapons, synthetic diseases, not to speak of climatic disruption on a vast scale and the actual extinction of thousands of species all portended the abiding reality of the end of life among advanced species, if not a vast die-off of ecologically sensitive species.

Accordingly, if history is marked by ascending spirals, the kind of society that would replace the modern capitalism was no longer a matter of dystopian speculation. Nothing, to be sure, exists indefinitely. Every society is obliged to consider the certainty of its ultimate demise. Long before nuclear weapons were produced, speculative writers turned their imagination to the disappearance of humanity—one thinks of Jack London's *The Scarlet Plague* or H. G. Wells's "The War of the Worlds." Judging by the tidal wave of fantasy that fills every conceivable form of electronic media today, we might assume that nearly every avenue of communication has been exploited to alert humanity of the likelihood of its self-extinction and every possible means for its extermination.

Ecology, in particular, has become the most realistic source of the new scenarios for supplanting the "invasions," "inventions," and endless variety of methods for achieving our species self-extermination. Indeed, not since the end of the medieval world has the human species devoted so much of its literature and art to depictions of how our species will bring itself to a spectacular end.

Earlier accounts of our demise were represented by artists who saw the human types around them in terms of physical attributes edging on genuine fantasy. They had a simian, and not quite truly human, appearance. Subtle changes seem to have expressed the drift of artistic sensibility toward humanization rather than animalization. In an age of mechanization—indeed, an Age of Steel—human life must cope with the requirements of giant factories, immensely destructive weapons, and murder on a mass scale. We are creating a radically new nature, a *second* nature, one that needs a mythic world of birdlike creatures to act as a counterweight to the harsh first nature from which we are emerging.

This fact alone has given ecology a centrality it never could have had several centuries ago. Ecology deals with the interface between first ("virginal") nature and humanity's second ("synthetic") nature. In the first place, more than purely environmental issues as chemicals in food, organic gardening, and solar and wind power, ecological issues deal with technology conceptualized not only as a means to an end but as a defining aspect of the end we hope to achieve by such methods.

Installing an array of solar engines, for example, will not resolve our energy problems unless they are integrated into an ecological Whole that is, in a sense, truly a part of a larger environmental horizon. Solar engines must be seen as a component of the Totality that includes moral, aesthetic, social, institutional, and creative factors, all sensitively interlaced with one another; in short, a technics that forms a unity with values and beauty. Technics, in short, seeks to raise and answer questions that by modern standards of beauty and truth are currently nontechnical, if not antitechnical. As Hegel or Schiller might have put it, they are part of the truth of the world, and are delicately and subtly interlaced with it. With its emphasis on unity in diversity, ecology—specifically social ecology—creates a tapestry of life that weaves all the elements of development into a Whole that is ever-expanding and all-encompassing, bringing together the many with the one along a *developing* horizon of phenomena, both subjectively and objectively and, like a fermenting brew, turning the Many into a One without violating the identity of each.

Wedded to socialism, social ecology opens a new ecological terrain that gives it the calling to create a second nature, bringing freedom into the realm of first primeval nature. It not only obliges ecology to play the role of arbiter in refashioning first nature; it sees in first nature the terrain for remaking the world institutionally as well as ethically, along rational political lines. Far from being a neutral domain of knowledge, it is highly partisan and committed to the authentic welfare of life. Here science becomes a politics: it is completely involved in the problems and hopes of the world. Ecology becomes a political movement and, most important, a means for changing the world, not passively observing it.

Finally, social ecology provides the compass for negotiating humanity's place in the natural world. It reveals the only dialectic that gives meaning to the natural world as a realm where mind can interpret first nature, employ it as a rational guide to an ever-developing wholeness, and use the Whole at every given stage as the means to make the parts meaningful in achieving self-awareness and creativity. In his virtually forgotten book, the great British archeologist of the 1920s and 1930s, V. Gordon Childe, not only wrote an account of the beginning of humanity's self-consciousness but also showed how this capacity for self-consciousness (unknown in any other life-form) took the concrete steps in fashioning a new second nature that reproduced not only old natural laws but also created new ones. In this great transcendental step (an *Aufhebung* equal only to the emergence of life itself) humanity became the principal medium for creating itself.

This was the most advanced form of political economy possible in the nineteenth and early twentieth centuries, and it was brilliantly critiqued, almost alone, by Karl Marx. Syndicalism was also the most comprehensive form of social theory that could have been devised at that time. Carried to its most simplified conclusion, syndicalism could easily be confused with anarchism, a form of unnuanced nihilism redolent of Artsybashev's 1907 novel *Sanin*, which totally confused thousands of young Russians in the aftermath of the 1905 Revolution.

There can be no society as such without institutions, systems of governance, and laws. The only issue in question is whether these structures and guidelines are authoritarian or libertarian, for they constitute the very forms of social existence. The state is an ensemble, not of institutions as such, but of authoritarian institutions (usually controlled by classes), which is where anarchism gets lost in a tangle of highly confused individualistic concepts.

Why, then, did I title this collection *Post-Scarcity Anarchism* and use that term in the essays within? I must acknowledge that my reasons were primarily propagandistic. The earliest essays in this book were published after I had become disillusioned with Marxist politics and was suffering from a exaggerated hostility to any form of directive radicalism. No less significantly, I was enamored of radical romanticism and myself suffered from a measure of confusion over the enormous differences between syndicalism and anarchism. In the 1970s, under the ubiquitous shadow of modern history, the Russian Revolution, I began to give zealous attention to the Spanish Civil War—and only then did I nuance my own views and realize how distant were the anarchists and the anarcho-syndicalists from each other. This recognition also made it possible for me to properly situate how much Karl Marx's writings could contribute to a new synthesis of socialist theory, one that could keep pace with changes that were going on over the past century.

Moreover, I was fortunate in developing a deeper insight into the changes that capitalism was undergoing and how they were producing new questions that required new answers. Of immense importance was the extent to which traditional Marxism's "breakdown theory" of capitalism was completely wrong. Capitalism, it was apparent to me, would not "decompose" because it had to limit economic growth; rather, it was faced with a permanent breakdown because it was expanding (indeed, coming into its own as a dominant economy) by ravaging the planet and simplifying complex ecosystems, reducing the earth's capacity to sustain advanced forms of life.

Today this thesis is not novel—it has been heard repeatedly. But when I first advanced it, it was regarded as a distraction from "pressing issues" like the class struggle and the coming "proletarian revolution"—concepts that tenaciously cling to socialist theory like hungry leeches, notwithstanding the fact that history has kept them on hold for a half-century.

Social ecology, it should be emphasized, is not anarchism any more than it is individualism. It is decidedly a new form of libertarian socialism: libertarian in its concept of an organic and "from-the-ground-up" mode of praxis; socialist in its belief that power must be conceived as confederal communities. As Gustav Lefrancais, a Parisian Communard of 1871, declared that he was "a communalist, not an anarchist, please." (See Kropotkin's *Memoirs of a Revolutionist,* Grove Press, page 393.)

Today Lefrancais might well have participated in regular municipal elections, as a libertarian municipalist. He might have called for the formation of popular municipal assemblies and tried to coordinate assemblies of municipalities into county-wide municipal confederations with diminishing authority, and into national confederations, each forming a dual power to supplant the parallel state institutions that, as components of the "legacy of domination," challenge their existence. A detailed account of a communalist political structure can be found in the closing chapter of my *From Urbanization to Cities.*

The oldest essay in this book, "Ecology and Revolutionary Thought," was published in 1964 in *Comment* and was revised for publication in *Post-Scarcity Anarchism* in 1971. In the early 1960s anarchism was a very scarce commodity in the United States and was preoccupied with refusals to vote with almost dogmatic fervor. I recall that it lived a fragile, almost senile existence in a small room in lower Manhattan; the majority of its members were pensioners, mostly foreign-born, and puzzled by the emerging 1960s "counterculture." When I emphasized to them the importance of technological development and the prospects it opened for a materially abundant socialist society, my "tried and tested fellow workers" (to use the language of the time) denounced me as a Marxist—but they might have denounced Diego Abad de Santillán, the Spanish FAI's principal theorist in the 1930s, for many of the same reasons.

I am pleased that, reprinted as it was repeatedly in anthologies and pamphlets, "Ecology and Revolutionary Thought" and "Listen, Marxist!" were read by many thousands and led to conversions from standard brands of Social Democracy and even Stalinism to anarchism. The reader should note that "Ecology and Revolutionary Thought" was filled with predictions that have never been acknowledged, notably, that the use of fossil fuels would produce "a growing blanket of carbon dioxide" and, "by intercepting heat radiated by the earth, [would] lead to more destructive storm patterns and, eventually, to melting of the polar ice caps, rising sea levels, and the inundation of vast land areas" (page 60). I warned of toxic wastes in water and on land and many of the ills that beset the planet today. These predictions were unheard of at the time and have never been duly accredited.

A year later "Toward a Liberatory Technology," my account of the social and technological alternatives to the sources of the "ecological crisis," as I called it then, was less widely read but was widely pilfered. The world was afflicted by the pop rubbish of "radical ecologists," exotic technicians and biologists like Buckminster Fuller, Barry Commoner, and the like, who in my view became celebrities more than serious social theorists. People who can on Monday applaud Paul Ehrlich, who flaunted neo-Malthusian opinions, then suddenly denounce the same neo-Malthusian views on Tuesday have hardly earned my admiration. But such is the way of the world, as my seventy years of active radicalism have taught me.

Murray Bookchin
August 20, 2004

PRECONDITIONS AND POSSIBILITIES

All the successful revolutions of the past have been particularistic revolutions of minority classes seeking to assert their specific interests over those of society as a whole. The great bourgeois revolutions of modern times offered an ideology of sweeping political reconstitution, but in reality they merely certified the social dominance of the bourgeoisie, giving formal political expression to the economic ascendancy of capital. The lofty notions of the "nation," the "free citizen," "of equality before the law," concealed the mundane reality of the centralized state, the atomized isolated man, the dominance of bourgeois interest. Despite their sweeping ideological claims, the particularistic revolutions replaced the rule of one class by another, one system of exploitation by another, one system of toil by another, and one system of psychological repression by another.

What is unique about our era is that the particularistic revolution has now been subsumed by the possibility of the generalized revolution—complete and totalistic. Bourgeois society, if it achieved nothing else, revolutionized the means of production on a scale unprecedented in history. This technological revolution, culminating in cybernation, has created the objective, quantitative basis for a world without class rule, exploitation, toil or material want. The means now exist for the development of the rounded man, the total man, freed of guilt and the workings of authoritarian modes of training, and given over to desire and the sensuous apprehension of the marvelous. It is now possible to conceive of man's future experience in terms of a coherent process in which the bifurcations of thought and activity, mind and sensuousness, discipline and spontaneity, individuality and community, man and nature, town and country, education and life, work and play are all resolved, harmonized, and organically wedded in a qualitatively new realm of freedom. Just as the particularized revolution produced a particularized, bifurcated society so the generalized revolution can produce an organically unified, many-sided community. The great wound opened by propertied society in the form of the "social question" can now be healed.

That freedom must be conceived of in human terms, not in animal terms—in terms of life, not of survival—is clear enough. Men do not remove their ties of bondage and become fully human merely by divesting themselves of social domination and obtaining freedom in its *abstract* form. They must also be free *concretely:* free from material want, from toil, from the burden of devoting the greater part of their time—indeed, the greater part of their lives—to the struggle with necessity. To have seen these material preconditions for human freedom, to have emphasized that freedom presupposes free time and the material abundance for abolishing free time as a social privilege, is the great contribution of Karl Marx to modern revolutionary theory.

By the same token, the *preconditions* for freedom must not be mistaken for the *conditions* of freedom. The *possibility* of liberation does not constitute its *reality.* Along with its positive aspects, technological advance has a distinctly negative, socially regressive side. If it is true that technological progress enlarges the historical potentiality for freedom, it is also true that the bourgeois control of technology reinforces the established organization of society and everyday life. Technology and the resources of abundance furnish capitalism with the means for assimilating large sections of society to the established system of hierarchy and authority. They provide the system with the weaponry, the detecting devices and the propaganda media for the threat as well as the reality of massive repression. By their centralistic nature, the resources of abundance reinforce the monopolistic, centralistic and bureaucratic tendencies in the political apparatus. In short, they furnish the state with historically unprecedented means for manipulating and mobilizing the entire environment of life—and for perpetuating hierarchy, exploitation and unfreedom.

It must be emphasized, however, that this manipulation and mobilization of the environment is extremely problematical and laden with crises. Far from leading to pacification (one can hardly speak, here, of harmonization), the attempt of bourgeois society to control and exploit its environment, natural as well as social, has devastating consequences. Volumes have been written on the pollution of the atmosphere and waterways, on the destruction of tree cover and soil, and on toxic materials in foods and liquids. Even more threatening in their final results are the pollution and destruction of the very ecology required for a complex organism like man. The concentration of radioactive wastes in living things is a menace to the health and genetic endowment of nearly all species. Worldwide contamination by pesticides that inhibit oxygen production in plankton or by the near-toxic level of lead from gasoline exhaust are examples of an enduring pollution that threatens the biological integrity of all advanced lifeforms—including man.

No less alarming is the fact that we must drastically revise our traditional notions of what constitutes an environmental pollutant. A few decades ago it would have been absurd to describe carbon dioxide and heat as pollutants in the customary sense of the term. Yet both may well rank among the most serious sources of future ecological imbalance and may pose major threats to the viability of the planet. As a result of industrial and domestic combustion activities, the quantity of carbon dioxide in the atmosphere has increased by roughly twenty-five percent in the past one hundred years, and may well double by the end of the century. The famous "greenhouse effect" which the increasing quantity of the gas is expected to produce has been widely discussed in the media; eventually, it is supposed, the gas will inhibit the dissipation of the world's heat into space, causing a rise in overall temperatures which will melt the polar ice caps and result in the inundation of vast coastal areas. Thermal pollution, the result mainly of warm water discharged by nuclear and conventional power plants, has had disastrous effects on the ecology of lakes, rivers and estuaries. Increases in water temperature not only damage the physiological and reproductive activities of the fish, they also promote the great blooms of algae that have become such formidable problems in waterways.

Ecologically, bourgeois exploitation and manipulation are undermining the very capacity of the earth to sustain advanced forms of life. The crisis is being heightened by massive increases in air and water pollution; by a mounting accumulation of nondegradable wastes, lead residues, pesticide residues and toxic additives in food; by the expansion of cities into vast urban belts; by increasing stresses due to congestion, noise and mass living; and by the wanton scarring of the earth as a result of mining operations, lumbering, and real estate speculation. As a result, the earth has been despoiled in a few decades on a scale that is unprecedented in the entire history of human habitation of the planet.

Socially, bourgeois exploitation and manipulation have brought everyday life to the most excruciating point of vacuity and boredom. As society has been converted into a factory and a marketplace, the very rationale of life has been reduced to production for its own sake—and consumption for its own sake.*

THE REDEMPTIVE DIALECTIC

Is there a redemptive dialectic that can guide the social development in the direction of an anarchic society where people will attain full control over their daily lives? Or does the social dialectic come to an end with capitalism, its possibilities sealed off by the use of a highly advanced technology for repressive and co-optative purposes?

We must learn here from the limits of Marxism, a project which, understandably in a period of material scarcity, anchored the social dialectic and the contradictions of capitalism in the economic realm. Marx, it has been emphasized, examined the *preconditions for* liberation, not the *conditions of* liberation. The Marxian critique is rooted in the past, in the era of material want and relatively limited technological development. Even its humanistic theory of alienation turns primarily on the issue of work and man's alienation from the product of his labor. Today, however, capitalism is a parasite on the future, a vampire that survives on the technology and resources of freedom. The industrial capitalism of Marx's time organized its commodity relations around a prevailing system of material scarcity; the state capitalism of our time organizes its commodity relations around a prevailing system of material abundance. A century ago, scarcity had to be endured; today, it has to be enforced—hence the importance of the state in the present era. It is not that modern capitalism has resolved its contradictions† and annulled the social dialectic, but rather that the social dialectic and the contradictions of capitalism have expanded from the economic to the hierarchical realms of society, from the abstract "historic" domain to the concrete minutiae of everyday experience, from the arena of survival to the arena of life.

The dialectic of bureaucratic state capitalism originates in the contradiction between the repressive character of commodity society and

* It is worth noting here that the emergence of the "consumer society" provides us with remarkable evidence of the difference between the industrial capitalism of Marx's time and state capitalism today. In Marx's view, capitalism as a system organized around "production for the sake of production" results in the economic immiseration of the proletariat. "Production for the sake of production" is paralleled today by "consumption for the sake of consumption," in which immiseration takes a spiritual rather than an economic form—it is starvation of life.

† The economic contradictions of capitalism have not disappeared, but the system can plan to such a degree that they no longer have the explosive characteristics they had in the past.

the enormous potential freedom opened by technological advance. This contradiction also opposes the exploitative organization of society to the natural world—a world that includes not only the natural environment, but also man's "nature"—his Eros-derived impulses. The contradiction between the exploitative organization of society and the natural environment is beyond co-optation: the atmosphere, the waterways, the soil and the ecology required for human survival are not redeemable by reforms, concessions, or modifications of strategic policy. There is no technology that can reproduce atmospheric oxygen in sufficient quantities to sustain life on this planet. There is no substitute for the hydrological systems of the earth. There is no technique for removing massive environmental pollution by radioactive isotopes, pesticides, lead and petroleum wastes. Nor is there the faintest evidence that bourgeois society will relent at any time in the foreseeable future in its disruption of vital ecological processes, its exploitation of natural resources, its use of the atmosphere and waterways as dumping areas for wastes, or in its cancerous mode of urbanization and land abuse.

Even more immediate is the contradiction between the exploitative organization of society and man's Eros-derived impulses—a contradiction that manifests itself as the banalization and impoverishment of experience in a bureaucratically manipulated, impersonal mass society. The Eros-derived impulses in man can be repressed and sublimated, but they can never be eliminated. They are renewed with every birth of a human being and with every generation of youth. It is not surprising today that the young, more than any economic class or stratum, articulate the life-impulses in humanity's nature—the urgings of desire, sensuousness, and the lure of the marvelous. Thus, the biological matrix, from which hierarchical society emerged ages ago, reappears at a new level with the era that marks the end of hierarchy, only now this matrix is saturated with social phenomena. Short of manipulating humanity's germ plasm, the life-impulses can be annulled only with the annihilation of man himself.

The contradictions within bureaucratic state capitalism permeate all the hierarchical forms developed and overdeveloped by bourgeois society. The hierarchical forms which nurtured propertied society for ages and promoted its development—the state, city, centralized economy, bureaucracy, patriarchal family, and marketplace—have reached their historic limits. They have exhausted their social functions as modes of stabilization. It is not a question of whether these hierarchical forms were ever "progressive" in the Marxian sense of the term. As Raoul Vaneigem has observed: "Perhaps it isn't enough to say that hierarchical power has preserved humanity for thousands of years as alcohol preserves a fetus, by arresting either growth or decay."[3] Today these forms constitute the target of all the revolutionary forces that are generated by modern capitalism, and whether one sees their outcome as nuclear catastrophe or ecological disaster *they now threaten the very survival of humanity.*

With the development of hierarchical forms into a threat to the very existence of humanity, the social dialectic, far from being annulled, acquires a new dimension. It poses the "social question" in an entirely new way. If man had to acquire the conditions of survival in order to live (as Marx emphasized), now he must acquire the conditions of life in order to survive. By this inversion of the relationship between survival and life, revolution acquires a new sense of urgency. No longer are we faced with Marx's famous choice of socialism or barbarism; we are confronted with the more drastic alternatives of anarchism or annihilation. The problems of necessity and survival have become congruent with the problems of freedom and life. They cease to require any theoretical mediation, "transitional" stages, or centralized organizations to bridge the gap between the existing and the possible. The possible, in fact, is all that can exist. Hence, the problems of "transition," which occupied the Marxists for nearly a century, are eliminated not only by the advance of technology, but by the social dialectic itself. The problems of social reconstruction have been reduced to practical tasks that can be solved spontaneously by self-liberatory acts of society.

Revolution, in fact, acquires not only a new sense of urgency, but a new sense of promise. In the hippies' tribalism, in the drop-out lifestyles and free sexuality of millions of youth, in the spontaneous affinity groups of the anarchists, we find forms of affirmation that follow from acts of negation. With the inversion of the "social question" there is also an inversion of the social dialectic; a "yea" emerges automatically and simultaneously with a "nay."

The solutions take their point of departure from the problems. When the time has arrived in history that the state, the city, bureaucracy, the centralized economy, the patriarchal family and the marketplace have reached their historic limits, what is posed is no longer a change in form but the absolute negation of *all* hierarchical forms *as such*. The absolute negation of the state is anarchism—a situation in which men liberate not only "history," but all the immediate circumstances of their everyday lives. The absolute negation of the city is community—a community in which the social environment is decentralized into rounded, ecologically balanced communes. The absolute negation of bureaucracy is immediate as distinguished from mediated relations—a situation in which representation is replaced by face-to-face relations in a general assembly of free individuals. The absolute negation of the centralized economy is regional ecotechnology—a situation in which the instruments of production are molded to the resources of an ecosystem. The absolute negation of the patriarchal family is liberated sexuality—in which all forms of sexual regulation are transcended by the spontaneous, untrammeled expression of eroticism among equals. The absolute negation of the marketplace is communism—in which collective abundance and cooperation transform labor into play and need into desire.

SPONTANEITY AND UTOPIA

It is not accidental that at a point in history when hierarchical power and manipulation have reached their most threatening proportions, the very concepts of hierarchy, power and manipulation are being brought into question. The challenge to these concepts comes from a rediscovery of the importance of spontaneity—a rediscovery nourished by ecology, by a heightened conception of self-development, and by a new understanding of the revolutionary process in society.

What ecology has shown is that balance in nature is achieved by organic variation and complexity, not by homogeneity and simplification. For example, the more varied the flora and fauna of an ecosystem, the more stable the population of a potential pest. The more environmental diversity is diminished, the greater will the population of a potential pest fluctuate, with the probability that it will get out of control. Left to itself, an ecosystem tends spontaneously toward organic differentiation, greater variety of flora and fauna, and diversity in the number of prey and predators. This does not mean that interference by man must be avoided. The need for a productive agriculture—itself a form of interference with nature—must always remain in the foreground of an ecological approach to food cultivation and forest management. No less important is the fact that man can often produce changes in an ecosystem that would vastly improve its ecological quality. But these efforts require insight and understanding, not the exercise of brute power and manipulation.

This concept of management, this new regard for the importance of spontaneity, has far-reaching applications for technology and community—indeed, for the social image of man in a liberated society. It challenges the capitalist ideal of agriculture as a factory operation, organized around immense, centrally controlled land-holdings, highly specialized forms of monoculture, the reduction of the terrain to a factory floor, the substitution of chemical for organic processes, the use of gang-labor, etc. If food cultivation is to be a mode of cooperation with nature rather than a contest between opponents, the agriculturist must become thoroughly familiar with the ecology of the land; he must acquire a new sensitivity to its needs and possibilities. This presupposes the reduction of agriculture to a human scale, the restoration of moderate-sized agricultural units, and the diversification of the agricultural situation; in short, it presupposes a decentralized, ecological system of food cultivation.

The same reasoning applies to pollution control. The development of giant factory complexes and the use of single or dual-energy sources are responsible for atmospheric pollution. Only by developing smaller industrial units and diversifying energy sources by the extensive use of clean power (solar, wind and water power) will it be possible to reduce industrial pollution. The means for this radical technological change are now at hand. Technologists have developed miniaturized substitutes for large-scale industrial operation—small versatile machines and sophisticated methods for converting solar, wind and water energy into power usable in industry and the home. These substitutes are often more productive and less wasteful than the large-scale facilities that exist today.*

The implications of small-scale agriculture and industry for a community are obvious: if humanity is to use the principles needed to manage an ecosystem, the basic communal unit of social life must itself become an ecosystem—an ecocommunity. It too must become diversified, balanced and well rounded. By no means is this concept of community motivated exclusively by the need for a lasting balance between man and the natural

* For a detailed discussion of this "miniaturized" technology see "Towards a Liberatory Technology."

world; it also accords with the utopian ideal of the rounded man, the individual whose sensibilities, range of experience and lifestyle are nourished by a wide range of stimuli, by a diversity of activities, and by a social scale that always remains within the comprehension of a single human being. Thus the means and conditions of survival become the means and conditions of life; need becomes desire and desire becomes need. The point is reached where the greatest social decomposition provides the source of the highest form of social integration, bringing the most pressing ecological necessities into a common focus with the highest utopian ideals.

If it is true, as Guy Debord observes, that "daily life is the measure of everything: of the fulfillment or rather the non-fulfillment of human relationships, of the use we make of our time,"[4] a question arises: Who are "we" whose daily lives are to be fulfilled? And how does the liberated self emerge that is capable of turning time into life, space into community, and human relationships into the marvelous?

The liberation of the self involves, above all, a social process. In a society that has shriveled the self into a commodity—into an object manufactured for exchange—there can be no fulfilled self. There can only be the beginnings of selfhood, the *emergence* of a self that seeks fulfillment—a self that is largely defined by the obstacles it must overcome to achieve realization. In a society whose belly is distended to the bursting point with revolution, whose chronic state is an unending series of labor pains, whose real condition is a mounting emergency, only one thought and act is relevant—giving birth. Any environment, private or social, that does not make this fact the center of human experience is a sham and diminishes whatever self remains to us after we have absorbed our daily poison of everyday life in bourgeois society.

It is plain that the goal of revolution today must be the liberation of daily life. Any revolution that fails to achieve this goal is counterrevolution. Above all, it is *we* who have to be liberated, *our* daily lives, with all their moments, hours and days, and not universals like "History" and "Society."* The self must always be *identifiable* in the revolution, not overwhelmed by it. The self must always be *perceivable* in the revolutionary process, not submerged by it. There is no word that is more sinister in the "revolutionary" vocabulary than "masses." Revolutionary liberation

* Despite its lip service to the dialectic, the traditional left has yet to take Hegel's "concrete universal" seriously and see it not merely as a philosophical concept but as a social program. This has been done only in Marx's early writings, in the writings of the great utopians (Fourier and William Morris) and, in our time, by the dropout youth.

must be a self-liberation that reaches social dimensions, not "mass liberation" or "class liberation" behind which lurks the rule of an elite, a hierarchy and a state. If a revolution fails to produce a new society by the self-activity and self-mobilization of revolutionaries, if it does not involve the forging of a self in the revolutionary process, the revolution will once again circumvent those whose lives are to be lived every day and leave daily life unaffected. Out of the revolution must emerge a self that takes full possession of daily life, not a daily life that once again takes full possession of the self. The most advanced form of class-consciousness thus becomes self-consciousness—the concretization in daily life of the great liberating universals.

If for this reason alone, the revolutionary movement is profoundly concerned with lifestyle. It must try to *live* the revolution in all its totality, not only participate in it. It must be deeply concerned with the way the revolutionist lives, his relations with the surrounding environment, and his degree of self-emancipation. In seeking to change society, the revolutionist cannot avoid changes in himself that demand the reconquest of his own being. Like the movement in which he participates, the revolutionist must try to reflect the conditions of the society he is trying to achieve—at least to the degree that this is possible today.

The treacheries and failures of the past half-century have made it axiomatic that there *can be no separation of the revolutionary process from the revolutionary goal.* A society whose fundamental aim is self-administration in all facets of life can be achieved only by self-activity. This implies a mode of administration that is always possessed by the self. The power of man over man can be destroyed only by the very process in which man acquires power over his own life and in which he not only "discovers" himself but, more meaningfully, in which he formulates his selfhood in all its social dimensions.

A libertarian society can be achieved only by a libertarian revolution. Freedom cannot be "delivered" to the individual as the "end-product" of a "revolution"; the assembly and community cannot be legislated or decreed into existence. A revolutionary group can seek, purposively and consciously, to promote the creation of these forms, but if assembly and community are not allowed to emerge organically, if their growth is not matured by the process of demassification, by self-activity and by self realization, they will remain nothing but forms, like the soviets in post revolutionary Russia. Assembly and community must arise within the revolutionary process; indeed, the revolutionary process must *be* the formation of assembly and community, and also the destruction of power, property, hierarchy and exploitation.

Revolution as self-activity is not unique to our time. It is the paramount feature of all the great revolutions in modern history. It marked the *journées* of the *sans-culottes* in 1792 and 1793, the famous "Five Days" of February 1917 in Petrograd, the uprising of the Barcelona proletariat in 1936, the early days of the Hungarian Revolution in 1956, and the May–June events in Paris in 1968. Nearly every revolutionary uprising in the history of our time has been initiated spontaneously by the self-activity of "masses"—often in flat defiance of the hesitant policies advanced by the revolutionary organizations. Every one of these revolutions has been marked by extraordinary individuation, by a joyousness and solidarity that turned everyday life into a festival. This surreal dimension of the revolutionary process, with its explosion of deep-seated libidinal forces, grins irascibly through the pages of history like the face of a satyr on shimmering water. It is not without reason that the Bolshevik commissars smashed the wine bottles in the Winter Palace on the night of November 7, 1917.

The puritanism and work ethic of the traditional left stem from one of the most powerful forces opposing revolution today—the capacity of the bourgeois environment to infiltrate the revolutionary framework. The origins of this power lie in the commodity nature of man under capitalism, a quality that is almost automatically transferred to the organized group—and which the group, in turn, reinforces in its members. As the late Josef Weber emphasized, all organized groups "have the tendency to render themselves autonomous, i.e., to alienate themselves from their original aim and to become an end in themselves in the hands of those administering them."[5] This phenomenon is as true of revolutionary organizations as it is of state and semi-state institutions, official parties and trade unions.

The problem of alienation can never be completely resolved apart from the revolutionary process itself, but it can be guarded against by an acute awareness that the problem exists, and partly solved by a voluntary but drastic remaking of the revolutionary and his group. This remaking can only begin when the revolutionary group recognizes that it is a catalyst in the revolutionary process, not a "vanguard." The revolutionary group must clearly see that its goal is not the seizure of power but the dissolution of power—indeed, it must see that the entire problem of power, of control from below and control from above, can be solved only if there is no above or below.

Above all, the revolutionary group must divest itself of the forms of power—statutes, hierarchies, property, prescribed opinions, fetishes, paraphernalia, official etiquette—and of the subtlest as well as the most obvious of bureaucratic and bourgeois traits that consciously and unconsciously reinforce authority and hierarchy. The group must remain open to public scrutiny not only in its formulated decisions but also in their very formulation. It must be coherent in the profound sense that its theory is its practice and its practice its theory. It must do away with all commodity relations in its day-to-day existence and constitute itself along the decentralizing organizational principles of the very society it seeks to achieve—community, assembly, spontaneity. It must, in Josef Weber's superb words, be "marked always by simplicity and clarity, always thousands of unprepared people can enter and direct it, always it remains *transparent* to and controlled by all."[6] Only then, when the revolutionary movement is congruent with the decentralized community it seeks to achieve, can it avoid becoming another elitist obstacle to the social development and dissolve into the revolution like surgical thread into a healing wound.

PROSPECT

The most important process going on in America today is the sweeping de-institutionalization of the bourgeois social structure. A basic, far-reaching disrespect and a profound disloyalty are developing toward the values, the forms, the aspirations and, above all, the institutions of the established order. On a scale unprecedented in American history, millions of people are shedding their commitment to the society in which they live. They no longer believe in its claims. They no longer respect its symbols. They no longer accept its goals, and, most significantly, they refuse almost intuitively to live by its institutional and social codes.

This growing refusal runs very deep. It extends from an opposition to war into a hatred of political manipulation in all its forms. Starting from a rejection of racism, it brings into question the very existence of hierarchical power as such. In its detestation of middle-class values and lifestyles it rapidly evolves into a rejection of the commodity system; from an irritation with environmental pollution, it passes into a rejection of the American city and modern urbanism. In short, it tends to transcend every particularistic critique of the society and to evolve into a generalized opposition to the bourgeois order on an ever-broadening scale.

In this respect, the period in which we live closely resembles the revolutionary Enlightenment that swept through France in the eighteenth century—a period that completely reworked French consciousness and prepared the conditions for the Great Revolution of 1789. Then as now, the old institutions were slowly pulverized by molecular action from below long before they were toppled by mass revolutionary action. This molecular movement creates an atmosphere of general lawlessness: a growing personal day-to-day disobedience, a tendency not to "go along" with the existing system, a seemingly "petty" but nevertheless critical attempt to circumvent restriction in every facet of daily life. The society, in effect, becomes disorderly, undisciplined, Dionysian—a condition that reveals itself most dramatically in an increasing rate of official crimes. A vast critique of the system develops—the actual Enlightenment itself, two centuries ago, and the sweeping critique that exists today—which seeps downward and accelerates the molecular movement at the base. Be it an angry gesture, a "riot" or a conscious change in lifestyle, an ever-increasing number of people—who have no more of a commitment to an organized revolutionary movement than they have to society itself—begin spontaneously to engage in their own defiant propaganda of the deed.

In its concrete details, the disintegrating social process is nourished by many sources. The process develops with all the unevenness, indeed with all the contradictions that mark every revolutionary trend. In eighteenth century France, radical ideology oscillated between a rigid scientism and a sloppy romanticism. Notions of freedom were anchored in a precise, logical ideal of self-control, and also a vague, instinctive norm of spontaneity. Rousseau stood at odds with d'Holbach, Diderot at odds with Voltaire, yet in retrospect we can see that one not only transcended but also presupposed the other in a *cumulative* development toward revolution.

The same uneven, contradictory and cumulative development exists today, and in many cases it follows a remarkably direct course. The "beat" movement created the most important breach in the solid, middle-class values of the 1950s, a breach that was widened enormously by the illegalities of pacifists, civil-rights workers, draft resisters and longhairs. Moreover, the merely reactive response of rebellious American youth has produced invaluable forms of libertarian and utopian affirmation—the right to make love without restriction, the goal of community, the disavowal of money and commodities, the belief in mutual aid, and a new respect for spontaneity. Easy as it is for revolutionaries to criticize certain pitfalls within this orientation of personal and social values, the fact remains that it has played a preparatory role of decisive importance in forming the present atmosphere of indiscipline, spontaneity, radicalism and freedom.

A second parallel between the revolutionary Enlightenment and our own period is the emergence of the crowd, the so-called "mob," as a major vehicle of social protest. The typical institutionalized forms of public dissatisfaction—in our own day, they are orderly elections, demonstration and mass meetings—tend to give way to direct action by crowds. This shift from predictable, highly organized protests within the institutionalized framework of the existing society to sporadic, spontaneous, near insurrectionary assaults from outside (and even against) socially acceptable forms reflects a profound change in popular psychology. The "rioter" has begun to break, however partially and intuitively, with those deep-seated norms of behavior which traditionally weld the "masses" to the established order. He actively sheds the internalized structure of authority, the long-cultivated body of conditioned reflexes, and the pattern of submission sustained by guilt that tie one to the system even more effectively than any fear of police violence and juridical reprisal. Contrary to the views of social psychologists, who see in these modes of direct action the submission of the individual to a terrifying collective entity called the "mob," the truth is that "riots" and crowd actions represent the first groupings of the mass toward individuation. The mass tends to become demassified in the sense that it begins to assert itself against the really massifying automatic responses produced by the bourgeois family, the school and the mass media. By the same token, crowd actions involve the rediscovery of the streets and the effort to liberate them. Ultimately, it is in the streets that power must be dissolved: for the streets, where daily life is endured, suffered and eroded, and where power is confronted and fought, must be turned into the domain where daily life is enjoyed, created and nourished. The rebellious crowd marked the beginning not only of a spontaneous transmutation of private into social revolt, but also of a return from the abstractions of social revolt to the issues of everyday life.

Finally, as in the Enlightenment, we are seeing the emergence of an immense and ever-growing stratum of *déclassés*, a body of lumpenized individuals drawn from every stratum of society. The chronically indebted and socially insecure middle classes of our period compare loosely with the chronically insolvent and flighty nobility of prerevolutionary France. A vast flotsam of educated people emerged then as now, living at loose ends, without fixed careers or established social roots. At the bottom of both structures we find a large number of chronic poor—vagabonds, drifters, people with part-time jobs or no jobs at all, threatening, unruly *sans-culottes*—surviving on public aid and on the garbage thrown off by society, the poor of the Parisian slums, the blacks of the American ghettoes.

But here all the parallels end. The French Enlightenment belongs to a period of revolutionary transition from feudalism to capitalism—both societies based on economic scarcity, class rule, exploitation, social hierarchy and state power. The day-to-day popular resistance which marked the eighteenth century and culminated in open revolution was soon disciplined by the newly emerging industrial order—as well as by naked force. The vast mass of *déclassés* and *sans-culottes* was largely absorbed into the factory system and tamed by industrial discipline. Formerly rootless intellectuals and footloose nobles found secure places in the economic, political, social and cultural hierarchy of the new bourgeois order. From a socially and culturally fluid condition, highly generalized in its structure and relations, society hardened again into rigid, particularized class and institutional forms—the classical Victorian era appeared not only in England but, to one degree or another, in all of Western Europe and America. Critique was consolidated into apologia, revolt into reform, *déclassés* into clearly defined classes and "mobs" into political constituencies. "Riots" became the well-behaved processionals we call "demonstrations," and spontaneous direct action turned into electoral rituals.

Our own era is also a transitional one, but with a profound and new difference. In the last of their great insurrections, the *sans-culottes* of the French Revolution rose under the fiery cry: "Bread and the Constitution of '93!" The black *sans-culottes* of the American ghettoes rise under the slogan: "Black is beautiful!" Between these two slogans lies a development of unprecedented importance. The *déclassés* of the eighteenth century were formed during a slow transition from an agricultural to an industrial era;

they were created out of a pause in the historical transition from one regime of toil to another. The demand for bread could have been heard at any time in the evolution of propertied society. The new *déclassés* of the twentieth century are being created as a result of the bankruptcy of all social forms based on toil. They are the end products of the process of propertied society itself and of the social problems of material survival. In the era when technological advances and cybernation have brought into question the exploitation of man by man, toil, and material want in any form whatever, the cry "Black is beautiful" or "Make love, not war" marks the transformation of the traditional demand for survival into a historically new demand for life.* What underpins every social conflict in the United States today is the demand for the realization of all human potentialities in a fully rounded, balanced, totalistic way of life. In short, the potentialities for revolution in America are now anchored in the potentialities of man himself.

What we are witnessing is the breakdown of a century and a half of embourgeoisement and a pulverization of all bourgeois institutions *at a point in history when the boldest concepts of utopia are realizable.* And there is nothing that the present bourgeois order can substitute for the destruction of its traditional institutions but bureaucratic manipulation and state capitalism. This process is unfolding most dramatically in the United States. Within a period of little more than two decades, we have seen the collapse of the "American Dream," or what amounts to the same thing, the steady destruction in the United States of the myth that material abundance, based on commodity relations between men, can conceal the inherent poverty of bourgeois life. Whether this process will culminate in revolution or in annihilation will depend in great part on the ability of revolutionists to extend social consciousness and defend the spontaneity of the revolutionary development from authoritarian ideologies, both of the "left" and of the right.

New York
Oct. 1967–Dec. 1968

* The above lines were written in 1966. Since then, we have seen the graffiti on the walls of Paris, during the May–June revolution: "All power to the imagination"; "I take my desires to be reality, because I believe in the reality of my desires"; "Never work"; "The more I make love, the more I want to make revolution"; "Life without dead times"; "The more you consume, the less you live"; "Culture is the inversion of life"; "One does not buy happiness, one steals it"; "Society is a carnivorous flower." These are not graffiti, they are a program for life and desire.

In almost every period since the Renaissance the development of revolutionary thought has been heavily influenced by a branch of science, often in conjunction with a school of philosophy.

Astronomy in the time of Copernicus and Galileo helped to change a sweeping movement of ideas from the medieval world, riddled by superstition, into one pervaded by a critical rationalism and openly naturalistic and humanistic in outlook. During the Enlightenment—the era that culminated in the French Revolution—this liberatory movement of ideas was reinforced by advances in mechanics and mathematics. The Victorian era was shaken to its very foundations by evolutionary theories in biology and anthropology, by Marx's contributions to political economy, and by Freudian psychology.

In our own time, we have seen the assimilation of these once- liberatory sciences by the established social order. Indeed, we have begun to regard science itself as an instrument of control over the thought processes and physical being of man. This distrust of science and of the scientific method is not without justification. "Many sensitive people, especially artists," observes Abraham Maslow, "are afraid that science besmirches and depresses, that it tears things apart rather than integrating them, thereby killing rather than creating."[7] What is perhaps equally important, modern science has lost its critical edge. Largely functional or instrumental in intent, the branches of science that once tore at the chains of man are now used to perpetuate and gild them. Even philosophy has yielded to instrumentalism and tends to be little more than a body of logical contrivances; it is the handmaiden of the computer rather than of the revolutionary.

There is one science, however, that may yet restore and even transcend the liberatory estate of the traditional sciences and philosophies. It passes rather loosely under the name "ecology"—a term coined by Haeckel a century ago to denote "the investigation of the total relations of the animal both to its inorganic and to its organic environment."[8] At first glance Haeckel's definition is innocuous enough; and ecology narrowly conceived of as one of the biological sciences, is often reduced to a variety of biometrics in which field workers focus on food chains and statistical studies of animal populations. There is an ecology of health that would hardly offend the sensibilities of the American Medical Association and a concept of social ecology that would conform to the most well-engineered notions of the New York City Planning Commission.

Broadly conceived of, however, ecology deals with the balance of nature. In as much as nature includes man, the science basically deals with the harmonization of nature and man. The explosive implications of an ecological approach arise not only because ecology is intrinsically a critical science—critical on a scale that the most radical systems of political economy have failed to attain—but also because it is an integrative and reconstructive science. This integrative, reconstructive aspect of ecology, carried through to all its implications, leads directly into anarchic areas of social thought. For, in the final analysis, it is impossible to achieve a harmonization of man and nature without creating a human community that lives in a lasting balance with its natural environment.

THE CRITICAL NATURE OF ECOLOGY

The critical edge of ecology, a unique feature of the science in a period of general scientific docility, derives from its subject matter—from its very domain. The issues with which ecology deals are imperishable in the sense that they cannot be ignored without bringing into question the survival of man and the survival of the planet itself. The critical edge of ecology is due not so much to the power of human reason—a power which science hallowed during its most revolutionary periods—but to a still higher power, the sovereignty of nature. It may be that man is manipulable, as the owners of the mass media argue, or that elements of nature are manipulable, as the engineers demonstrate, but ecology clearly shows that the *totality* of the natural world—nature viewed in all its aspects, cycles and interrelationships—cancels out all human pretensions to mastery over the planet. The great wastelands of the Mediterranean basin, once areas of a thriving agriculture or a rich natural flora, are historic evidence of nature's revenge against human parasitism.

No historic examples compare in weight and scope with the effects of man's despoliation—and nature's revenge—since the days of the Industrial Revolution, and especially since the end of the Second World War. Ancient examples of human parasitism were essentially local in scope; they were precisely *examples* of man's potential for destruction, and nothing more. Often, they were compensated by remarkable improvements in the natural ecology of a region, such as the European peasantry's superb reworking of the soil during centuries of cultivation and the achievements of Inca agriculturists in terracing the Andes Mountains during the pre-Columbian times.

Modern man's despoliation of the environment is global in scope, like his imperialisms. It is even extraterrestrial, as witness the disturbances of the Van Allen Belt a few years ago. Today human parasitism disrupts more than the atmosphere, climate, water resources, soil, flora and fauna of a region: it upsets virtually all the basic cycles of nature and threatens to undermine the stability of the environment on a worldwide scale.

As an example of the scope of modern man's disruptive role, it has been estimated that the burning of fossil fuels (coal and oil) adds 600 million tons of carbon dioxide to the air annually, about .03 percent of the total atmospheric mass—this, I may add, aside from an incalculable quantity of toxicants. Since the Industrial Revolution, the overall atmospheric mass of carbon dioxide has increased by 25 percent over earlier, more stable, levels. It can be argued on very sound theoretical grounds that this growing blanket of carbon dioxide, by intercepting heat radiated from the earth, will lead to more destructive storm patterns and eventually to melting of the polar ice caps, rising sea levels, and the inundation of vast land areas. Far removed as such a deluge may be, the changing proportion of carbon dioxide to other atmospheric gases is a warning about the impact man is having on the balance of nature.

A more immediate ecological issue is man's extensive pollution of the earth's waterways. What counts here is not the fact that man befouls a given stream, river or lake—a thing he has done for ages—but rather the magnitude water pollution has reached in the past two generations. Nearly all the surface waters of the United States are now polluted. Many American waterways are open cesspools that properly qualify as extensions of urban sewage systems. It is a euphemism to describe them as rivers or lakes. More significantly, large amounts of groundwater are sufficiently polluted to be undrinkable, and a number of local hepatitis epidemics have been traced to polluted wells in suburban areas. In contrast to surface-water pollution, the pollution of ground or subsurface water is immensely difficult to eliminate and tends to linger on for decades after the sources of pollution have been removed.

An article in a mass-circulation magazine appropriately describes the polluted waterways of the United States as "Our Dying Waters." This despairing, apocalyptic description of the water pollution problem in the

United States really applies to the world at large. The waters of the earth are literally dying. Massive pollution is destroying the rivers and lakes of Africa, Asia and Latin America, as well as the long-abused waterways of highly industrialized continents, as media of life. (I speak here not only of radioactive pollutants from nuclear bomb tests and power reactors, which apparently reach all the flora and fauna of the sea; the oil spills and the discharge of diesel oil have also become massive pollution problems, claiming marine life in enormous quantities every year.)

Accounts of this kind can be repeated for virtually every part of the biosphere. Pages could be written on the immense losses of productive soil that occur annually in almost every continent of the earth; on lethal air pollution episodes in major urban areas; on the worldwide distribution of toxic agents such as radioactive isotopes and lead; on the chemicalization of man's immediate environment—one might say his very dinner table—with pesticide residues and food additives. Pieced together like bits of a jigsaw puzzle, these affronts to the environment form a pattern of destruction that has no precedent in man's long history on earth.

Obviously, man could be described as a highly destructive parasite who threatens to destroy his host—the natural world—and eventually himself. In ecology, however, the word "parasite" is not an answer to a question, but raises a question itself. Ecologists know that a destructive parasitism of this kind usually reflects the disruption of an ecological situation; indeed, many species that seem highly destructive under one set of conditions are eminently useful under another set of conditions. What imparts a profoundly critical function to ecology is the question raised by man's destructive abilities: What is the disruption that has turned man into a destructive parasite? What produces a form of parasitism that results not only in vast natural imbalances but also threatens the existence of humanity itself?

Man has produced imbalances not only in nature, but, more fundamentally, in his relations with his fellow man and in the very structure of his society. The imbalances man has produced in the natural world are caused by the imbalances he has produced in the social world. A century ago it would have been possible to regard air pollution and water contamination as the result of the self-seeking activities of industrial barons and bureaucrats. Today, this moral explanation would be a gross oversimplification. It is doubtless true that most bourgeois enterprises are still guided by a public-be-damned attitude, as witness the reactions of power utilities, automobile concerns and steel corporations to pollution problems. But a more serious problem than the attitude of the owners is the size of the firms themselves—their enormous proportions, their location in a particular region, their density with respect to a community or waterway, their requirements for raw materials and water, and their role in the national division of labor.

What we are seeing today is a crisis in social ecology. Modern society, especially as we know it in the United States and Europe, is being organized around immense urban belts, a highly industrialized agriculture and, capping both, a swollen, bureaucratized, anonymous state apparatus. If we put all moral considerations aside for the moment and examine the physical structure of this society, what must necessarily impress us is the incredible logistical problems it is obliged to solve—problems of transportation, of density, of supply (of raw materials, manufactured commodities and foodstuffs), of economic and political organization, of industrial location, and so forth. The burden this type of urbanized and centralized society places on any continental area is enormous.

DIVERSITY AND SIMPLICITY

The problem runs even deeper. The notion that man must dominate nature emerges directly from the domination of man by man. The patriarchal family planted the seed of domination in the nuclear relations of humanity; the classical split in the ancient world between spirit and reality—indeed, between mind and labor—nourished it; the anti-naturalist bias of Christianity tended to its growth. But it was not until organic community relations, feudal or peasant in form, dissolved into market relationships that the planet itself was reduced to a resource for exploitation. This centuries-long tendency finds its most exacerbating development in modern capitalism. Owing to its inherently competitive nature, bourgeois society not only pits humans against each other, it also pits the mass of humanity against the natural world. Just as men are converted into commodities, so every aspect of nature is converted into a commodity, a resource to be manufactured and merchandised wantonly. The liberal euphemisms for the processes involved are "growth," "industrial society" and "urban blight." By whatever language they are described, the phenomena have their roots in the domination of man by man.

The phrase "consumer society" complements the description of the present social order as an "industrial society." Needs are tailored by the mass media to create a public demand for utterly useless commodities, each carefully engineered to deteriorate after a predetermined period of time. The plundering of the human spirit by the marketplace is paralleled by the plundering of the earth by capital. (The liberal identification is a metaphor that neutralizes the social thrust of the ecological crisis.)

Despite the current clamor about population growth, the strategic ratios in the ecological crisis are not the population growth rates of India but the production rates of the United States, a country that produces more than half of the world's goods. Here, too, liberal euphemisms like "affluence" conceal the critical thrust of a blunt word like "waste." With a ninth of its industrial capacity committed to war production, the U.S. is literally trampling upon the earth and shredding ecological links that are vital to human survival. If current industrial projections prove to be accurate, the remaining thirty years of the century will witness a fivefold increase in electric power production, based mostly on nuclear fuels and coal. The colossal burden in radioactive wastes and other effluents that this increase will place on the natural ecology of the earth hardly needs description.

In shorter perspective, the problem is no less disquieting. Within the next five years, lumber production may increase an overall twenty percent; the output of paper, five percent annually; folding boxes, three percent annually; plastics (which currently form one to two percent of municipal wastes), seven percent annually. Collectively, these industries account for the most serious pollutants in the environment. The utterly senseless nature of modern industrial activity is perhaps best illustrated by the decline in returnable (and reusable) beer bottles from 54 billion bottles in 1960 to 26 billion today. Their place has been taken over by "one-way" bottles (a rise from 8 to 21 billion in the same period) and cans (an increase from 38 to 53 billion). The "one-way" bottles and the cans, of course, pose tremendous problems in solid waste disposal.

The planet, conceived of as a lump of minerals, can support these mindless increases in the output of trash. The earth, conceived of as a complex web of life, certainly cannot. The only question is whether the earth can survive its looting long enough for man to replace the current destructive social system with a humanistic, ecologically oriented society.

Ecologists are often asked, rather tauntingly, to locate with scientific exactness the ecological breaking point of nature—the point at which the natural world will cave in on man. This is equivalent to asking a psychiatrist for the precise moment when a neurotic will become a nonfunctional psychotic. No such answer is ever likely to be available. But the ecologist can supply a strategic insight into the directions man seems to be following as a result of his split with the natural world.

From the standpoint of ecology, man is dangerously over-simplifying his environment. The modern city represents a regressive encroachment of the synthetic on the natural, of the inorganic (concrete, metals, and glass) on the organic, of crude, elemental stimuli on variegated, wide-ranging ones. The vast urban belts now developing in industrialized areas of the world are not only grossly offensive to the eye and the ear, they are chronically smog-ridden, noisy, and virtually immobilized by congestion.

The process of simplifying man's environment and rendering it increasingly elemental and crude has a cultural as well as a physical dimension. The need to manipulate immense urban populations—to transport, feed, employ, educate and somehow entertain millions of densely concentrated people—leads to a crucial decline in civic and social standards. A mass concept of human relations—totalitarian, centralistic and regimented in orientation—tends to dominate the more individuated concepts of the past. Bureaucratic techniques of social management tend to replace humanistic approaches. All that is spontaneous, creative and individuated is circumscribed by the standardized, the regulated and the massified. The space of the individual is steadily narrowed by restrictions imposed upon him by a faceless, impersonal social apparatus. Any recognition of unique personal qualities is increasingly surrendered to the manipulation of the lowest common denominator of the mass. A quantitative statistical approach, a beehive manner of dealing with man, tends to triumph over the precious individualized and qualitative approach which places the strongest emphasis on personal uniqueness, free expression and cultural complexity.

The same regressive simplification of the environment occurs in modern agriculture.* The manipulated people in modern cities must be fed

* For insight into this problem the reader may consult *The Ecology of Invasions* by Charles S. Elton (Wiley; New York, 1958), *Soil and Civilisation* by Edward Hyams (Thames and Hudson; London, 1952), *Our Synthetic Environment* by Murray Bookchin [pseud. Lewis Herber] (Knopf; New York, 1962), and, *Silent Spring* by Rachel Carson (Houghton Mifflin; Boston, 1962). The last should be read not as a diatribe against pesticides but as plea for ecological diversification.

and to feed them involves an extension of industrial farming. Food plants must be cultivated in a manner that allows for a high degree of mechanization—not to reduce human toil but to increase productivity and efficiency, to maximize investments, and to exploit the biosphere. Accordingly, the terrain must be reduced to a flat plain—to a factory floor, if you will—and natural variations in topography must be diminished as much as possible. Plant growth must be closely regulated to meet the tight schedules of food-processing factories. Plowing, soil fertilization, sowing and harvesting must be handled on a mass scale, often in total disregard of the natural ecology of an area. Large areas of the land must be used to cultivate a single crop—a form of plantation agriculture that not only lends itself to mechanization but also to pest infestation. A single crop is the ideal environment for the proliferation of pest species. Finally, chemical agents must be used lavishly to deal with the problems created by insects, weeds, and plant diseases, to regulate crop production, and to maximize soil exploitation. The real symbol of modern agriculture is not the sickle (or, for that matter, the tractor), but the airplane. The modern food cultivator is represented not by the peasant, the yeoman, or even the agronomist—men who could be expected to have an intimate relationship with the unique qualities of the land on which they grow crops—but the pilot or chemist, for whom soil is a mere resource, an inorganic raw material.

The simplification process is carried still further by an exaggerated regional (indeed, national) division of labor. Immense areas of the planet are increasingly reserved for specific industrial tasks or reduced to depots for raw materials. Others are turned into centers of urban population, largely occupied with commerce and trade. Cities and regions (in fact, countries and continents) are specifically identified with special products—Pittsburgh, Cleveland and Youngstown with steel, New York with finance, Bolivia with tin, Arabia with oil, Europe and the U.S. with industrial goods, and the rest of the world with raw materials of one kind or another. The complex ecosystems which make up the regions of a continent are submerged by an organization of entire nations into economically rationalized entities, each a way station in a vast industrial belt-system, global in its dimensions. It is only a matter of time before the most attractive areas of the countryside succumb to the concrete mixer, just as most of the Eastern seashore areas of the United States have already succumbed to subdivisions and bungalows. What will remain in the way of natural beauty will be debased by trailer lots, canvas slums, "scenic" highways, motels, food stalls, and the oil slicks of motor boats.

The point is that man is undoing the work of organic evolution. By creating vast urban agglomerations of concrete, metal and glass, by overriding and undermining the complex, subtly organized ecosystems that constitute local differences in the natural world—in short, by replacing a highly complex, organic environment with a simplified, inorganic one—man is disassembling the biotic pyramid that supported humanity for countless millennia. In the course of replacing the complex ecological relationships, on which all advanced living things depend, for more elementary relationships, man is steadily restoring the biosphere to a stage which will be able to support only simpler forms of life. If this great reversal of the evolutionary process continues, it is by no means fanciful to suppose that the preconditions for higher forms of life will be irreparably destroyed and the earth will become incapable of supporting man himself.

Ecology derives its critical edge not only from the fact that it alone, among all the sciences, presents this awesome message to humanity, but also because it presents this message in a new social dimension. From an ecological viewpoint, the reversal of organic evolution is the result of appalling contradictions between town and country, state and community, industry and husbandry, mass manufacture and craftsmanship, centralism and regionalism, the bureaucratic scale and the human scale.

THE RECONSTRUCTIVE NATURE OF ECOLOGY

Until recently, attempts to resolve the contradictions created by urbanization, centralization, bureaucratic growth and statification were viewed as a vain counterdrift to "progress"—a counterdrift that could be dismissed as chimerical and reactionary. The anarchist was regarded as a forlorn visionary, a social outcast, filled with nostalgia for the peasant village or the medieval commune. His yearnings for a decentralized society and for a humanistic community at one with nature and the needs of the individual—the spontaneous individual, unfettered by authority—were viewed as the reactions of a romantic, of a declassed craftsman or an intellectual "misfit." His protest against centralization and statification seemed all the less persuasive because it was supported primarily by ethical considerations—by utopian, ostensibly "unrealistic," notions of what man could be, not by what he was. In response to this protest, opponents of anarchist thought—liberals, rightists and authoritarian "leftists"—argued that they were the voices of historic reality, that their statist and centralist notions were rooted in the objective, practical world.

Time is not very kind to the conflict of ideas. Whatever may have been the validity of libertarian and non-libertarian views a few years ago, historical development has rendered virtually all objections to anarchist thought meaningless today. The modern city and state, the massive coal-steel technology of the Industrial Revolution, the later, more rationalized, systems of mass production and assembly-line systems of labor organization, the centralized nation, the state and its bureaucratic apparatus—all have reached their limits. Whatever progressive or liberatory role they may have possessed, they have now become entirely regressive and oppressive. They are regressive not only because they erode the human spirit and drain the community of all its cohesiveness, solidarity and ethico-cultural standards; they are regressive from an objective standpoint, from an ecological standpoint. For they undermine not only the human spirit and the human community but also the viability of the planet and all living things on it.

It cannot be emphasized too strongly that the anarchist concepts of a balanced community, a face-to-face democracy, a humanistic technology and a decentralized society—these rich libertarian concepts—are not only desirable, they are also necessary. They belong not only to the great visions of man's future, they now constitute the preconditions for human survival. The process of social development has carried them out of the ethical, subjective dimension into a practical, objective dimension. What was once regarded as impractical and visionary has become eminently practical. And what was once regarded as practical and objective has become eminently impractical and irrelevant in terms of man's development towards a fuller, unfettered existence. If we conceive of demands for community, face-to-face democracy, a humanistic liberatory technology and decentralization merely as reactions to the prevailing state of affairs—a vigorous "nay" to the "yea" of what exists today—a compelling, objective case can now be made for the practicality of an anarchist society.

A rejection of the prevailing state of affairs accounts, I think, for the explosive growth of intuitive anarchism among young people today. Their love of nature is a reaction against the highly synthetic qualities of our urban environment and its shabby products. Their informality of dress and manners is a reaction against the formalized, standardized nature of modern institutionalized living. Their predisposition for direct action is a reaction against the bureaucratization and centralization of society. Their tendency to drop out, to avoid toil and the rat race, reflects a growing anger towards the mindless industrial routine bred by modern mass manufacture in the factory, the office or the university. Their intense individualism is, in its own elemental way, a *de facto* decentralization of social life—a personal withdrawal from mass society.

What is most significant about ecology is its ability to convert this often nihilistic rejection of the status quo into an emphatic affirmation of life—indeed, into a reconstructive credo for a humanistic society. The essence of ecology's reconstructive message can be summed up in the word "diversity." From an ecological viewpoint, balance and harmony in nature, in society and, by inference, in behavior, are achieved not by mechanical standardization but by its opposite, organic differentiation. This message can be understood clearly only by examining its practical meaning.

Let us consider the ecological principle of diversity—what Charles Elton calls the "conservation of variety"—as it applies to biology, specifically to agriculture. A number of studies—Lotka's and Volterra's mathematical models, Bause's experiments with protozoa and mites in controlled environments, and extensive field research—clearly demonstrate that fluctuations in animal and plant populations, ranging from mild to pest like proportions, depend heavily upon the number of species in an ecosystem and on the degree of variety in the environment. The greater the variety of prey and predators, the more stable the population; the more diversified the environment in terms of flora and fauna, the less likely there is to be ecological instability. Stability is a function of variety and diversity: if the environment is simplified and the variety of animal and plant species is reduced, fluctuations in population become marked and tend to get out of control. They tend to reach pest proportions.

In the case of pest control, many ecologists now conclude that we can avoid the repetitive use of toxic chemicals such as insecticides and herbicides by allowing for a greater interplay between living things. We must leave more room for natural spontaneity, for the diverse biological forces that make up an ecological situation. "European entomologists now speak of managing the entire plant-insect community," observes Robert L.

Rudd. "It is called manipulation of the biocenose.* The biocenetic environment is varied, complex and dynamic. Although numbers of individuals will constantly change, no one species will normally reach pest proportions. The special conditions which allow high populations of a single species in a complex ecosystem are rare events. Management of the biocenose or ecosystem should become our goal, challenging as it is."[9]

The "manipulation" of the biocenose in a meaningful way, however, presupposes a far-reaching decentralization of agriculture. Wherever feasible, industrial agriculture must give way to soil and agricultural husbandry; the factory floor must yield to gardening and horticulture. I do not wish to imply that we must surrender the gains acquired by large-scale agriculture and mechanization. What I do contend, however, is that the land must be cultivated as though it were, a garden; its flora must be diversified and carefully tended, balanced by fauna and tree shelter appropriate to the region. Decentralization is important, moreover, for the development of the agriculturist as well as for the development of agriculture. Food cultivation, practiced in a truly ecological sense, presupposes that the agriculturist is familiar with all the features and subtleties of the terrain on which the crops are grown. He must have a thorough knowledge of the physiography of the land, its variegated soils—crop land, forest land, pasture land—its mineral and organic content and its micro-climate, and he must be engaged in a continuing study of the effects produced by new flora and fauna. He must develop his sensitivity to the land's possibilities and needs while he becomes an organic part of the agricultural situation. We can hardly hope to achieve this high degree of sensitivity and integration in the food cultivator without reducing agriculture to a human scale, without bringing agriculture within the scope of the individual. To meet the demands of an ecological approach to food cultivation, agriculture must be re-scaled from huge industrial farms to moderate-sized units.

The same reasoning applies to a rational development of energy resources. The Industrial Revolution increased the *quantity* of energy used by man. Although it is certainly true that pre-industrial societies relied primarily on animal power and human muscles, complex energy patterns

* Rudd's use of the word "manipulation" is likely to create the erroneous impression that an ecological situation can be described by simple mechanical terms. Lest this impression arise, I would like to emphasize that our knowledge of an ecological situation and the practical use of this knowledge are matters of insight rather than power. Charles Elton states the case for the management of an ecological situation when he writes: "The world's future has to be managed, but this management would not be like a game of chess... [but] more like steering a boat."

developed in many regions of Europe, involving a subtle integration of resources such as wind and water power, and a variety of fuels (wood, peat, coal, vegetable starches and animal fats).

The Industrial Revolution overwhelmed and largely destroyed these regional energy patterns, replacing them first by a single energy system (coal) and later by a dual system (coal and petroleum). Regions disappeared as models of integrated energy patterns—indeed, the very concept of *integration through diversity* was obliterated. As I indicated earlier, many regions became predominantly mining areas, devoted to the extraction of a single resource, while others were turned into immense industrial areas, often devoted to the production of a few commodities. We need not review the role this breakdown in true regionalism has played in producing air and water pollution, the damage it has inflicted on large areas of the countryside, and the prospect we face in the depletion of our precious hydrocarbon fuels.

We can, of course, turn to nuclear fuels, but it is chilling to think of the lethal radioactive wastes that would require disposal if power reactors were our sole energy source. Eventually, an energy system based on radioactive materials would lead to the widespread contamination of the environment—at first in a subtle form, but later on a massive and palpably destructive scale. Or we could apply ecological principles to the solution of our energy problems. We could try to re-establish earlier regional energy patterns, using a combined system of energy provided by wind, water and solar power. We would be aided by devices more sophisticated than any known in the past.

Solar devices, wind turbines and hydroelectric resources, taken singly, do not provide a solution for our energy problems and the ecological disruption created by conventional fuels. Pieced together as a mosaic, as an organic energy pattern developed from the potentialities of a region, they could amply meet the needs of a decentralized society. In sunny latitudes, we could rely more heavily on solar energy than on combustible fuels. In areas marked by atmospheric turbulence, we could rely more heavily on wind devices; and in suitable coastal areas or inland regions with a good network of rivers, the greater part of our energy would come from hydroelectric installations. In all cases, we would use a *mosaic* of non-combustible, combustible, and nuclear fuels. The point I wish to make is that by diversifying our use of energy resources, by organizing them into an ecologically balanced pattern, we could combine wind, solar and water power in a given region to meet the industrial and domestic needs of a given community with only a minimal use of harmful fuels. And, eventually, we might sophisticate our non-combustion energy devices to a point where all harmful sources of energy could be eliminated.

As in the case of agriculture, however, the application of ecological principles to energy resources presupposes a far reaching decentralization of society and a truly regional concept of social organization. To maintain a large city requires immense quantities of coal and petroleum. By contrast, solar, wind and tidal energy reach us mainly in small packets; except for spectacular tidal dams, the new devices seldom provide more than a few thousand kilowatt-hours of electricity. It is difficult to believe that we will ever be able to design solar collectors that can furnish us with the immense blocks of electric power produced by a giant steam plant; it is equally difficult to conceive of a battery of wind turbines that will provide us with enough electricity to illuminate Manhattan Island. If homes and factories are heavily concentrated, devices for using clean sources of energy will probably remain mere playthings; but if urban communities are reduced in size and widely dispersed over the land, there is no reason why these devices cannot be combined to provide us with all the amenities of an industrialized civilization. To use solar, wind and tidal power effectively, the megalopolis must be decentralized. A new type of community, carefully tailored to the characteristics and resources of a region, must replace the sprawling urban belts that are emerging today.

To be sure, an objective case for decentralization does not end with a discussion of agriculture and the problems created by combustible energy resources. The validity of the decentralist case can be demonstrated for nearly all the "logistical" problems of our time. Let me cite an example from the problematical area of transportation. A great deal has been written about the harmful effects of gasoline driven motor vehicles—their wastefulness, their role in urban air pollution, the noise they contribute to the city environment, the enormous death toll they claim annually in the large cities of the world and on highways. In a highly urbanized civilization it would be useless to replace these noxious vehicles by clean, efficient, virtually noiseless, and certainly safer, battery-powered vehicles. The best of our electric cars must be recharged about every hundred miles—a feature which limits their usefulness for transportation in large cities. In a small, decentralized community, however, it would be feasible to use these electric vehicles for urban or regional transportation and establish monorail networks for long-distance transportation.

It is fairly well known that gasoline-powered vehicles contribute enormously to urban air pollution, and there is a strong sentiment to "engineer" the more noxious features of the automobile into oblivion. Our age characteristically tries to solve all its irrationalities with a gimmick—afterburners for toxic gasoline fumes, antibiotics for ill health, tranquilizers for psychic disturbances. But the problem of urban air pollution is too intractable for gimmicks; perhaps it is more intractable than we care to believe. Basically, air pollution is caused by high population densities—by an excessive concentration of people in a small area. Millions of people, densely concentrated in a large city, necessarily produce serious *local* air pollution merely by their day-to-day activities. They must burn fuels for domestic and industrial reasons; they must construct or tear down buildings (the aerial debris produced by these activities is a major source of urban air pollution); they must dispose of immense quantities of rubbish; they must travel on roads with rubber tires (the particles produced by the erosion of tires and roadway materials add significantly to air pollution). Whatever pollution-control devices we add to automobiles and power plants, the improvements these devices will produce in the quality of urban air will be more than canceled out by future megalopolitan growth.

There is more to anarchism than decentralized communities. If I have examined this possibility in some detail, it has been to demonstrate that an anarchist society, far from being a remote ideal, has become a precondition for the practice of ecological principles. To sum up the critical message of ecology: if we diminish variety in the natural world, we debase its unity and wholeness; we destroy the forces making for natural harmony and for a lasting equilibrium; and, what is even more significant, we introduce an absolute retrogression in the development of the natural world which may eventually render the environment unfit for advanced forms of life. To sum up the reconstructive message of ecology: if we wish to advance the unity and stability of the natural world, if we wish to harmonize it, we must conserve and promote variety. To be sure, mere variety for its own sake is a vacuous goal. In nature, variety emerges spontaneously. The capacities of a new species are tested by the rigors of climate, by its ability to deal with predators and by its capacity to establish and enlarge its niche. *Yet the species that succeeds in enlarging its niche in the environment also enlarges the ecological situation as a whole.* To borrow E. A. Gutkind's phrase, it "expands the environment,"[10] both for itself and for the species with which it enters into a balanced relationship.

How do these concepts apply to social theory? To many readers, I suppose, it should suffice to say that, inasmuch as man is part of nature, an expanding natural environment enlarges the basis for social development. But the answer to the question goes much deeper than many ecologists and libertarians suspect. Again, allow me to return to the ecological principle of wholeness and balance as a product of diversity. Keeping this principle in mind, the first step towards an answer is provided by a passage in Herbert Read's "The Philosophy of Anarchism." In presenting his "measure of progress," Read observes: "Progress is measured by the degree of differentiation within a society. If the individual is a unit in a corporate mass, his life will be limited, dull, and mechanical. If the individual is a unit on his own, with space and potentiality for separate action, then he may be more subject to accident or chance, but at least he can expand and express himself. He can develop—develop in the only real meaning of the word—develop in consciousness of strength, vitality, and joy."

Read's thought, unfortunately, is not fully developed, but it provides an interesting point of departure. What first strikes us is that both the ecologist and the anarchist place a strong emphasis on spontaneity. The ecologist, insofar as he is more than a technician, tends to reject the notion of "power over nature." He speaks, instead, of "steering" his way through an ecological situation, of *managing* rather than *recreating* an ecosystem. The anarchist, in turn, speaks in terms of social spontaneity, of releasing the potentialities of society and humanity, of giving free and unfettered rein to the creativity of people. Both, in their own way, regard authority as inhibitory, as a weight limiting the creative potential of a natural and social situation. Their object is not to *rule* a domain, but to *release* it. They regard insight, reason and knowledge as means for fulfilling the potentialities of a situation, as facilitating the working out of the logic of a situation, not as replacing its potentialities with preconceived notions or distorting their development with dogmas.

Turning to Read's words, what strikes us is that both the ecologist and the anarchist view differentiation as a measure of progress. The ecologist uses the term "biotic pyramid" in speaking of biological advances; the anarchist, the word "individuation" to denote social advances. If we go beyond Read we will observe that, to both the ecologist and the anarchist, an ever-increasing unity is achieved by growing differentiation. *An expanding whole is created by the diversification and enrichment of its parts.*

Just as the ecologist seeks to expand the range of an ecosystem and promote a free interplay between species, so the anarchist seeks to expand the range of social experience and remove all fetters to its development. Anarchism is not only a stateless society but also a harmonized society which exposes man to the stimuli provided by both agrarian and urban life, to physical activity and mental activity, to unrepressed sensuality and self-directed spirituality, to communal solidarity and individual development, to regional uniqueness and worldwide brotherhood, to spontaneity and self-discipline, to the elimination of toil and the promotion of craftsmanship. In our schizoid society, these goals are regarded as mutually exclusive, indeed as sharply opposed. They appear as dualities because of the very logistics of present-day society—the separation of town and country, the specialization of labor, the atomization of man—and it would be preposterous to believe that these dualities could be resolved without a general idea of the *physical* structure of an anarchist society. We can gain some idea of what such a society would be like by reading William Morris's *News from Nowhere* and the writings of Peter Kropotkin. But these works provide us with mere glimpses. They do not take into account the post-World War II developments of technology and the contributions made by the development of ecology. This is not the place to embark on "utopian writing," but certain guidelines can be presented even in a general discussion. And in presenting these guidelines, I am eager to emphasize not only the more obvious ecological premises that support them, but also the humanistic ones.

An anarchist society should be a decentralized society, not only to establish a lasting basis for the harmonization of man and nature, *but also to add new dimensions to the harmonization of man and man.* The Greeks, we are often reminded, would have been horrified by a city whose size and population precluded a face-to-face, often familiar, relationship between citizens. There is plainly a need to reduce the dimensions of the human community—partly to solve our pollution and transportation problems, partly also to create *real* communities. In a sense, we must *humanize* humanity. Electronic devices such as telephones, telegraphs, radios and television receivers should be used as little as possible to mediate the relations between people. In making collective decisions—the ancient Athenian ecclesia was, in some ways, a model for making social decisions—all members of the community should have an opportunity to acquire in full the measure of anyone who addresses the assembly. They should be in a position to absorb his attitudes, study his expressions, and weigh his motives as well as his ideas in a direct personal encounter and through face-to-face discussion.

Our small communities should be economically balanced and well rounded, partly so that they can make full use of local raw materials and energy resources, partly also to enlarge the agricultural and industrial stimuli to which individuals are exposed. The member of a community who has a predilection for engineering, for instance, should be encouraged to steep his hands in humus; the man of ideas should be encouraged to employ his musculature; the "inborn" farmer should gain a familiarity with the workings of a rolling mill. To separate the engineer from the soil, the thinker from the spade, and the farmer from the industrial plant promotes a degree of vocational overspecialization that leads to a dangerous measure of social control by specialists. What is equally important, professional and vocational specialization prevents society from achieving a vital goal: the humanization of nature by the technician and the naturalization of society by the biologist.

I submit that an anarchist community would approximate a clearly definable ecosystem; it would be diversified, balanced and harmonious. It is arguable whether such an ecosystem would acquire the configuration of an urban entity with a distinct center, such as we find in the Greek *polis* or the medieval commune, or whether, as Gutkind proposes, society would consist of widely dispersed communities without a distinct center. In any case, the ecological scale for any of these communities would be determined by the smallest ecosystem capable of supporting a population of moderate size.

A relatively self-sufficient community, visibly dependent on its environment for the means of life, would gain a new respect for the organic interrelationships that sustain it. In the long run, the attempt to approximate self-sufficiency would, I think, prove more efficient than the exaggerated national division of labor that prevails today. Although there would doubtless be many duplications of small industrial facilities from community to community, the familiarity of each group with its local environment and its ecological roots would make for a more intelligent and more loving use of its environment. I submit that, far from producing provincialism, relative self-sufficiency would create a new matrix for individual and communal development—a oneness with the surroundings that would vitalize the community.

The rotation of civic, vocational and professional responsibilities would stimulate the senses in the being of the individual, creating and rounding out new dimensions in self-development. In a complete society we could hope to create complete men; in a rounded society, rounded men. In the Western world, the Athenians, for all their shortcomings and limitations, were the first to give us a notion of this completeness. "The *polis* was made for the amateur," H.D.F. Kitto tells us. "Its ideal was that every citizen (more or less, according as the *polis* was democratic or oligarchic) should play his part in all of its many activities—an ideal that is recognizably descended from the generous Homeric conception of *arete* as an all-round excellence and an all-round activity. It implies a respect for the wholeness or the oneness of life, and a consequent dislike of specialization. It implies a contempt for efficiency—or rather a much higher ideal of efficiency; and efficiency which exists not in one department of life, but in life itself."[11] An anarchist society, although it would surely aspire to more, could hardly hope to achieve less than this state of mind.

If the ecological community is ever achieved in practice, social life will yield a sensitive development of human and natural diversity, falling together into a well balanced, harmonious whole. Ranging from community through region to entire continents, we will see a colorful differentiation of human groups and ecosystems, each developing its unique potentialities and exposing members of the community to a wide spectrum of economic, cultural and behavioral stimuli. Falling within our purview will be an exciting, often dramatic, variety of communal forms—here marked by architectural and industrial adaptations to semi-arid ecosystems, there to grasslands, elsewhere by adaptation to forested areas. We will witness a creative interplay between individual and group, community and environment, humanity and nature. The cast of mind that today organizes differences among humans and other life forms along hierarchical lines, defining the external in terms of its "superiority" or "inferiority," will give way to an outlook that deals with diversity in an ecological manner.

Differences among people will be respected, indeed fostered, as elements that enrich the unity of experience and phenomena. The traditional relationship which pits subject against object will be altered qualitatively; the "external," the "different," the "other" will be conceived of as individual parts of a whole all the richer because of its complexity. This sense of unity will reflect the harmonization of interests between individuals and between society and nature. Freed from an oppressive routine, from paralyzing repressions and insecurities, from the burdens of toil and false needs, from the trammels of authority and irrational compulsion, individuals will finally, for the first time in history, be in a position to realize their potentialities as members of the human community and the natural world.

New York
February 1965

Not since the days of the Industrial Revolution have popular attitudes toward technology fluctuated as sharply as in the past few decades. During most of the twenties, and even well into the thirties, public opinion generally welcomed technological innovation and identified man's welfare with the industrial advances of the time. This was a period when Soviet apologists could justify Stalin's most brutal methods and worst crimes merely by describing him as the "industrializer" of modern Russia. It was also a period when the most effective critique of capitalist society could rest on the brute facts of economic and technological stagnation in the United States and Western Europe. To many people there seemed to be a direct, one-to-one relationship between technological advances and social progress; a fetishism of the word "industrialization" excused the most abusive of economic plans and programs.

Today, we would regard these attitudes as naive. Except perhaps for the technicians and scientists who design the "hardware," the feeling of most people toward technological innovation could be described as schizoid, divided into a gnawing fear of nuclear extinction on the one hand, and a yearning for material abundance, leisure and security on the other. Technology, too, seems to be at odds with itself. The bomb is pitted against the power reactor, the intercontinental missile against the communications satellite. The same technological discipline tends to appear both as a foe and a friend of humanity, and even traditionally human-oriented sciences, such as medicine, occupy an ambivalent position—as witness the promise of advances in chemotherapy and the threat created by research in biological warfare.

It is not surprising to find that the tension between promise and threat is increasingly being resolved in favor of threat by a blanket rejection of technology. To an ever-growing extent, technology is viewed as a demon, imbued with a sinister life of its own, that is likely to mechanize man if it fails to exterminate him. The deep pessimism this view produces is often as simplistic as the optimism that prevailed in earlier decades. There is a very real danger that we will lose our perspective toward technology, that we will neglect its liberatory tendencies, and, worse, submit fatalistically to its use for destructive ends. If we are not to be paralyzed by this new form of social fatalism, a balance must be struck.

The purpose of this article is to explore three questions. What is the liberatory potential of modern technology, both materially and spiritually?

What tendencies, if any, are reshaping the machine for use in an organic, human oriented society? And finally, how can the new technology and resources be used in an ecological manner—that is, to promote the balance of nature, the full development of natural regions, and the creation of organic, humanistic communities?

The emphasis in the above remarks should be placed on the word "potential." I make no claim that technology is necessarily liberatory or consistently beneficial to man's development. But I surely do not believe that man is destined to be enslaved by technology and technological modes of thought (as Juenger and Elul imply in their books on the subject*). On the contrary, I shall try to show that an organic mode of life deprived of its technological component would be as nonfunctional as a man deprived of his skeleton. Technology must be viewed as the basic structural support of a society; it is literally the framework of an economy and of many social institutions.

TECHNOLOGY AND FREEDOM

The year 1848 stands out as a turning point in the history of modern revolutions. This was the year when Marxism made its debut as a distinct ideology in the pages of the *Communist Manifesto,* and when the proletariat, represented by the Parisian workers, made its debut as a distinct political force on the barricades of June. It could also be said that 1848, a year close to the halfway mark of the nineteenth century, represents the culmination of the traditional steam-powered technology initiated by the Newcomen engine a century and a half earlier.

What strikes us about the convergence of these ideological, political and technological milestones is the extent to which the *Communist Manifesto* and the June barricades were in advance of their time. In the 1840s, the Industrial Revolution centered around three areas of the economy: textile production, ironmaking and transportation. The invention of Arkwright's spinning machine, Watt's steam engine and Cartwright's power loom had finally brought the factory system to the textile industry; meanwhile, a number of striking innovations in iron-making technology

* Both Juenger and Elul believe that the debasement of man by the machine is intrinsic to the development of technology, and their works conclude on a grim note of resignation. This viewpoint reflects the social fatalism I have in mind—especially as expressed by Elul, whose ideas are more symptomatic of the contemporary human condition. See Friedrich George Juenger, *The Failure of Technology* (Regnery; Chicago, 1956) and Jacques Elul, *The Technological Society* (Knopf; New York, 1968).

assured the supply of high-quality, inexpensive metals needed to sustain factory and railway expansion. But these innovations, important as they were, were not accompanied by commensurate changes in other areas of industrial technology. For one thing, few steam engines were rated at more than fifteen horsepower, and the best blast furnaces provided little more than a hundred tons of iron a week—a fraction of the thousands of tons produced daily by modern furnaces. More important, the remaining areas of the economy were not yet significantly affected by technological innovation. Mining techniques, for example, had changed little since the days of the Renaissance. The miner still worked the ore face with a hand pick and a crowbar, and drainage pumps, ventilation systems and hauling techniques were not greatly improved over the descriptions we find in Agricola's classic on mining written three centuries earlier. Agriculture was only emerging from its centuries-old sleep. Although a great deal of land had been cleared for food cultivation, soil studies were still a novelty. So heavy, in fact, was the weight of tradition and conservatism that most harvesting was still done by hand, despite the fact that a mechanical reaper had been perfected as early as 1822. Buildings, despite their massiveness and ornateness, were erected primarily by sheer muscle power; the hand crane and windlass still occupied the mechanical center of the construction site. Steel was a relatively rare metal: as late as 1850 it was priced at $250 a ton and, until the discovery of the Bessemer converter, steel-making techniques had stagnated for centuries. Finally, although precision tools had made great forward strides, it is worth noting that Charles Babbage's efforts to build a sophisticated mechanical computer were thwarted by the inadequate machining techniques of the time.

I have reviewed these technological developments because both their promise and their limitations exercised a profound influence on nineteenth century revolutionary thought. The innovations in textile and iron-making technology provided a new sense of promise, indeed a new stimulus, to socialist and utopian thought. It seemed to the revolutionary theorist that for the first time in history he could anchor his dream of a liberatory society in the visible prospect of material abundance and increased leisure for the mass of humanity. Socialism, the theorists argued, could be based on self-interest rather than on man's dubious nobility of mind and spirit. Technological innovation had transmuted the socialist ideal from a vague humanitarian hope into a practical program.

The newly acquired practicality compelled many socialist theorists, particularly Marx and Engels, to grapple with the technological limitations of their time. They were faced with a strategic issue: in all previous revolutions, technology had not yet developed to a level where men could be freed from material want, toil and the struggle over the necessities of life. However glowing and lofty were the revolutionary ideals of the past, the vast majority of the people, burdened by material want, had to leave the stage of history after the revolution, return to work, and deliver the management of society to a new leisured class of exploiters. Indeed, any attempt to equalize the wealth of society at a low level of technological development would not have eliminated want, but would have merely made it into a general feature of society as a whole, thereby recreating all the conditions for a new struggle over the material things of life, for new forms of property, and eventually for a new system of class domination. A development of the productive forces is the "absolutely necessary practical premise [of communism]," wrote Marx and Engels in 1846, "because without it *want* is generalized, and with want the struggle for necessities and all the old filthy business would necessarily be reproduced."[12]

Virtually all the utopias, theories and revolutionary programs of the early nineteenth century were faced with problems of necessity—of how to allocate labor and material goods at a relatively low level of technological development. These problems permeated revolutionary thought in a way comparable only to the impact of original sin on Christian theology. The fact that men would have to devote a substantial portion of their time to toil, for which they would get scant returns, formed a major premise of all socialist ideology—authoritarian and libertarian, utopian and scientific, Marxist and anarchist. Implicit in the Marxist notion of a planned economy was the fact, incontestably clear in Marx's day, that socialism would still be burdened by relatively scarce resources. Men would have to plan—in effect, to restrict—the distribution of goods and would have to rationalize—in effect, to intensify—the use of labor. Toil, under socialism, would be a duty, a responsibility which every able-bodied individual would have to undertake. Even Proudhon advanced this dour view when he wrote: "Yes, life is a struggle. But this struggle is not between man and man—it is between man and Nature; and it is each one's duty to share it."[13] This austere, almost biblical, emphasis on struggle and duty reflects the harsh quality of socialist thought during the Industrial Revolution.

The problem of dealing with want and work—an age-old problem perpetuated by the early Industrial Revolution—produced the great divergence in revolutionary ideas between socialism and anarchism. Freedom would still be circumscribed by necessity in the event of a revolution. How was this world of necessity to be "administered"? How could the allocation of goods and duties be decided? Marx left this decision to a state power, a transitional "proletarian" state power, to be sure, but nevertheless a coercive body, established above society. According to Marx, the state would "wither away" as technology developed and enlarged the domain of freedom, granting humanity material plenty and the leisure to control its affairs directly. This strange calculus, in which necessity and freedom were mediated by the state, differed very little politically from the common run of bourgeois democratic radical opinion in the last century. The anarchist hope for the abolition of the state, on the other hand, rested largely on a belief in the viability of man's social instincts. Bakunin, for example, thought custom would compel any individuals with antisocial proclivities to abide by collectivist values and needs without obliging society to use coercion. Kropotkin, who exercised more influence among anarchists in this area of speculation, invoked man's propensity for mutual aid—essentially a social instinct—as the guarantor of solidarity in an anarchist community (a concept which he derived from his study of animal and social evolution).

The fact remains, however, that in both cases—the Marxist and the anarchist—the answer to the problem of want and work was shot through with ambiguity. The realm of necessity was brutally present; it could not be conjured away by mere theory and speculation. The Marxists could hope to administer necessity by means of a state, and the anarchists, to deal with it through free communities, but given the limited technological development of the last century, in the last analysis both schools depended on an act of faith to cope with the problem of want and work. Anarchists could argue against the Marxists that any transitional state, however revolutionary its rhetoric and democratic its structure, would be self-perpetuating; it would tend to become an end in itself and to preserve the very material and social conditions it had been created to remove. For such a state to "wither away" (that is, promote its own dissolution) would require its leaders and bureaucracy to be people of superhuman moral qualities. The Marxists, in turn, could invoke history to show that custom and mutualistic propensities were never effective barriers to the pressures of material need, or to the onslaught of property, or to the development of exploitation and class domination. Accordingly, they dismissed anarchism as an ethical doctrine which revived the mystique of the natural man and his inborn social virtues.

The problem of want and work—of the realm of necessity—was never satisfactorily resolved by either body of doctrine in the last century. It is to the lasting credit of anarchism that it uncompromisingly retained its high ideal of freedom—the ideal of spontaneous organization, community, and the abolition of all authority—although this ideal remained only a vision of man's future, of the time when technology would eliminate the realm of necessity entirely. Marxism increasingly compromised its ideal of freedom, painfully qualifying it with transitional stages and political expediencies, until today it is an ideology of naked power, pragmatic efficiency and social centralization almost indistinguishable from the ideologies of modern state capitalism.*

In retrospect, it is astonishing to consider how long the problem of want and work cast its shadow over revolutionary theory. In a span of only nine decades—the years between 1850 and 1940—Western society created, passed through and evolved beyond two major epochs of technological history—the paleotechnic age of coal and steel, and the neotechnic age of electric power, synthetic chemicals, electricity and internal combustion engines. Ironically, both ages of technology seemed to enhance the importance of toil in society. As the number of industrial workers increased in proportion to other social classes, labor—more precisely, toil†—acquired an increasingly high status in revolutionary thought. During this period, the propaganda of the socialists often sounded like a paean to toil; not only was toil "ennobling," but the workers were extolled as the only useful individuals in the social fabric. They were endowed with a supposedly superior instinctive ability that made them the arbiters of philosophy, art, and social organization. This puritanical work ethic of the left did not diminish with the passage of time and in fact acquired a certain urgency in the 1930s. Mass unemployment made the job and the social organization of labor the central themes of socialist propaganda in the 1930s. Instead of

* It is my own belief that the development of the "workers' state" in Russia thoroughly supports the anarchist critique of Marxist statism. Indeed, modern Marxists would do well to consult Marx's own discussion of commodity fetishism in *Capital* to understand how everything (including the state) tends to become an end in itself under conditions of commodity exchange.

† The distinction between pleasurable work and onerous toil should always be kept in mind.

focusing their message on the emancipation of man from toil, socialists tended to depict socialism as a beehive of industrial activity, humming with work for all. The Communists pointed to Russia as a land where every able bodied individual was employed and where labor was continually in demand. Surprising as it may seem today, little more than a generation ago socialism was equated with a work-oriented society and liberty with the material security provided by full employment. The world of necessity had subtly invaded and corrupted the ideal of freedom.

That the socialist notions of the last generation now seem to be anachronisms is not due to any superior insights that prevail today. The last three decades, particularly the years of the late 1950s, mark a turning point in technological development, a technological revolution that negates all the values, political schemes and social perspectives held by mankind throughout all previous recorded history. After thousands of years of torturous development, the countries of the Western world (and potentially all countries) are confronted by the possibility of a materially abundant, almost workless era in which most of the means of life can be provided by machines. As we shall see, a new technology has developed that could largely replace the realm of necessity by the realm of freedom. So obvious is this fact to millions of people in the United States and Europe that it no longer requires elaborate explanations or theoretical exegesis. This technological revolution and the prospects it holds for society as a whole form the premises of radically new lifestyles among today's young people, a generation that is rapidly divesting itself of the values and the age-old work-oriented traditions of its elders. Even recent demands for a guaranteed annual income sound like faint echoes of the new reality that currently permeates the thinking of the young. Owing to the development of a cybernetic technology, the notion of a toil-less mode of life has become an article of faith to an ever-increasing number of young people.

In fact, the real issue we face today is not whether this new technology can provide us with the means of life in a toil-less society, but whether it can help to *humanize* society, whether it can contribute to the creation of entirely new relationships between man and man. The demand for a guaranteed annual income is still anchored in the *quantitative* promise of technology—in the possibility of satisfying material needs without toil. This quantitative approach is already lagging behind technological developments that carry a new *qualitative* promise—the promise of decentralized, communitarian lifestyles, or what I prefer to call ecological forms of human association.*

I am asking a question that is quite different from what is ordinarily posed with respect to modern technology. Is this technology staking out a new dimension in human freedom, in the liberation of man? Can it not only liberate man from want and work, but also lead him to a free, harmonious, balanced human community—an ecocommunity that would promote the unrestricted development of his potentialities? Finally, can it carry man beyond the realm of freedom into the realm of life and desire?

THE POTENTIALITIES OF MODERN TECHNOLOGY

Let me try to answer these questions by pointing to a new feature of modern technology. For the first time in history, technology has reached an open end. The potential for technological development, for providing machines as substitutes for labor is virtually unlimited. Technology has finally passed from the realm of *invention* to that of *design*—in other words, from fortuitous discoveries to systematic innovations.

The meaning of this qualitative advance has been stated in a rather freewheeling way by Vannevar Bush, the former director of the Office of Scientific Research and Development:

> Suppose, fifty years ago, that someone had proposed making a device which would cause an automobile to follow a white line down the middle of the road, automatically and even if the driver fell asleep... He would have been laughed at, and his idea would have been called preposterous. So it would have been then. But suppose someone called for such a device today, and was willing to pay for it, leaving aside the question of whether it would actually be of any genuine use whatever. Any number of concerns would stand ready to contract and build it. No real invention would be required. There are thousands of young men in the country to whom the design of such a

* An exclusively quantitative approach to the new technology, I may add, is not only economically archaic, but morally regressive. This approach partakes of the old principle of justice, as distinguished from the new principle of freedom. Historically, justice is derived from the world of material necessity and toil; it implies relatively scarce resources which are apportioned by a moral principle which is either "just" or "unjust." Justice, even "equal" justice, is a concept of limitation, involving the denial of goods and the sacrifice of time and energy to production. Once we transcend the concept of justice—indeed, once we pass from the quantitative to the qualitative potentialities of modern technology—we enter the unexplored domain of freedom, based on spontaneous organization and full access to the means of life.

> device would be a pleasure. They would simply take off the shelf some photocells, thermionic tubes, servomechanisms, relays and, if urged, they would build what they call a breadboard model, and it would work. The point is that the presence of a host of versatile, cheap, reliable gadgets, and the presence of men who understand fully all their queer ways, has rendered the building of automatic devices almost straightforward and routine. It is no longer a question of whether they can be built, it is rather a question of whether they are worth building.[14]

Bush focuses here on the two most important features of the new, so-called "second," industrial revolution, namely the enormous potentialities of modern technology and the cost-oriented, nonhuman limitations that are imposed upon it. I shall not belabor the fact that the cost factor—the profit motive, to state it bluntly—inhibits the use of technological innovations. It is fairly well established that in many areas of the economy it is cheaper to use labor than machines.* Instead, I would like to review several developments which have brought us to an open end in technology and deal with a number of practical applications that have profoundly affected the role of labor in industry and agriculture.

Perhaps the most obvious development leading to the new technology has been the increasing interpenetration of scientific abstraction, mathematics and analytic methods with the concrete, pragmatic and rather mundane tasks of industry. This order of relationships is relatively new. Traditionally, speculation, generalization and rational activity were sharply divorced from technology. This chasm reflected the sharp split between the leisured and working classes in ancient and medieval society. If one leaves aside the inspired works of a few rare men, applied science did not come into its own until the Renaissance, and it only began to flourish in the eighteenth and nineteenth centuries.

The men who personify the application of science to technological innovation are not the inventive tinkerers like Edison, but the systematic investigators with catholic interests like Faraday, who add simultaneously to man's knowledge of scientific principles and to engineering. In our own day this synthesis, once embodied by the work of a single, inspired genius, is the work of anonymous teams. Although these teams have obvious

* For example, in cotton plantations in the Deep South, in automobile assembly plants, and in the garment industry.

advantages, they often have all the traits of bureaucratic agencies—which leads to a mediocre, unimaginative treatment of problems.

Less obvious is the impact produced by industrial growth. This impact is not always technological; it is more than the substitution of machines for human labor. One of the most effective means of increasing output, in fact, has been the continual reorganization of the labor process, extending and sophisticating the division of labor. Ironically, the steady breakdown of tasks to ever more inhuman dimensions—to an intolerably minute, fragmented series of operations and to a cruel simplification of the work process—suggests the machine that will recombine all the separate tasks of many workers into a single mechanized operation. Historically, it would be difficult to understand how mechanized mass manufacture emerged, how the machine increasingly displaced labor, without tracing the development of the work process from craftsmanship, where an independent, highly skilled worker engages in many diverse operations, through the purgatory of the factory, where these diverse tasks are parceled out among a multitude of unskilled or semiskilled employees, to the highly mechanized mill, where the tasks of many are largely taken over by machines manipulated by a few operatives, and finally to the automated and cybernated plant, where operatives are replaced by supervisory technicians and highly skilled maintenance men.

Looking further into the matter, we find still another new development: the machine has evolved from an extension of human muscles into an extension of the human nervous system. In the past, both tools and machines enhanced man's muscular power over raw materials and natural forces. The mechanical devices and engines developed during the eighteenth and nineteenth centuries did not replace human muscles but rather enlarged their effectiveness. Although the machines increased output enormously, the worker's muscles and brain were still required to operate them, even for fairly routine tasks. The calculus of technological advance could be formulated in strict terms of labor productivity: one man, using a given machine, produced as many commodities as five, ten, fifty, or a hundred before the machine was employed. Nasmyth's steam hammer, exhibited in 1851, could shape iron beams with only a few blows, an effort that would have required many manhours of labor without the machine. But the hammer required the muscles and judgment of half a dozen able-bodied men to pull, hold and remove the casting. In time, much of this work was diminished by the invention of handling devices, but the labor and judgment involved in operating the machines formed an indispensable part of the productive process.

The development of fully automatic machines for complex mass-manufacturing operations requires the successful application of at least three technological principles: such machines must have a built-in ability to correct their own errors; they must have sensory devices for replacing the visual, auditory and tactile senses of the worker; and, finally, they must have devices that substitute for the worker's judgment, skill and memory. The effective use of these three principles presupposes that we have also developed the technological means (the effectors, if you will) for applying the sensory, control and mind-like devices in everyday industrial operation; further, effective use presupposes that we can adapt existing machines or develop new ones for handling, shaping, assembling, packaging and transporting semi-finished and finished products.

The use of automatic, self-correcting control devices in industrial operations is not new. James Watt's flyball governor, invented in 1788, provides an early mechanical example of how steam engines were self-regulated. The governor, which is attached by metal arms to the engine valve, consists of two freely mounted metal balls supported by a thin, rotating rod. If the engine begins to operate too rapidly, the increased rotation of the rod impels the balls outward by centrifugal force, closing the valve; conversely, if the valve does not admit sufficient steam to operate the engine at the desired rate, the balls collapse inward, opening the valve further. A similar principle is involved in the operation of thermostatically controlled heating equipment. The thermostat, manually preset by a dial to a desired temperature level, automatically starts up heating equipment when the temperature falls and turns off the equipment when the temperature rises.

Both control devices illustrate what is now called the "feedback principle." In modern electronic equipment, the deviation of a machine from a desired level of operation produces electrical signals which are then used by the control device to correct the deviation or error. The electrical signals induced by the error are amplified and fed back by the control system to other devices which adjust the machine. A control system in which a departure from the norm is actually used to adjust a machine is called a *closed* system. This may be contrasted with an *open* system—a manually operated wall switch or the arms that automatically rotate an electrical fan—in which the control operates without regard to the function of the device. Thus, if the wall switch is flicked, electric lights go on or off whether it is night or day; similarly the electric fan will rotate at the same speed whether a room is warm or cool. The fan may be automatic in the popular sense of the term, but it is not self-regulating like the flyball governor and the thermostat.

An important step toward developing self-regulating control mechanisms was the discovery of sensory devices. Today these include thermocouples, photoelectric cells, X-ray machines, television cameras and radar transmitters. Used together or singly they provide machines with an amazing degree of autonomy. Even without computers, these sensory devices make it possible for workers to engage in extremely hazardous operations by remote control. They can also be used to turn many traditional open systems into closed ones, thereby expanding the scope of automatic operations. For example, an electric light controlled by a clock represents a fairly simple open system; its effectiveness depends entirely upon mechanical factors. Regulated by a photoelectric cell that turns it off when daylight approaches, the light responds to daily variations in sunrise and sunset. Its operation is now meshed with its function.

With the advent of the computer we enter an entirely new dimension of industrial control systems. The computer is capable of performing all the routine tasks that ordinarily burdened the mind of the worker a generation or so ago. Basically, the modern digital computer is an electronic calculator capable of performing arithmetical operations enormously faster than the human brain.* This element of speed is a crucial factor: the enormous rapidity of computer operations—a quantitative superiority of computer over human calculations—has profound qualitative significance. By virtue of its speed, the computer can perform highly sophisticated mathematical and logical operations. Supported by memory units that store millions of bits of information, and using binary arithmetic (the substitution of the digits 0 and 1 for the digits 0 through 9), a properly programmed digital computer can perform operations that approximate many highly developed logical activities of the mind. It is arguable whether computer "intelligence" is, or ever will be, creative or innovative (although every few years bring sweeping changes in computer technology), but there is no

* There are two broad classes of computers in use today: analogue and digital computers. The analogue computer has a fairly limited use in industrial operations. My discussion on computers in this article will deal entirely with digital computers.

doubt that the digital computer is capable of taking over all the onerous and distinctly uncreative mental tasks of man in industry, science, engineering, information retrieval and transportation. Modern man, in effect, has produced an electronic "mind" for coordinating, building and evaluating most of his routine industrial operations. Properly used within the sphere of competence for which they are designed, computers are faster and more efficient than man himself.

What is the concrete significance of this new industrial revolution? What are its immediate and foreseeable implications for work? Let us trace the impact of the new technology on the work process by examining its application to the manufacture of automobile engines at the Ford plant in Cleveland. This single instance of technological sophistication will help us assess the liberatory potential of the new technology in all manufacturing industries.

Until the advent of cybernation in the automobile industry, the Ford plant required about three hundred workers, using a large variety of tools and machines, to turn an engine block into an engine. The process from foundry casting to a fully machined engine took many manhours to perform. With the development of what we commonly call an "automated" machine system, the time required to transform the casting into an engine was reduced to less than fifteen minutes. Aside from a few monitors to watch the automatic control panels, the original three-hundred-man labor force was eliminated. Later a computer was added to the machining system, turning it into a truly closed, cybernated system. The computer regulates the entire machining process, operating on an electronic pulse that cycles at a rate of three-tenths of a millionth of a second.

But even this system is obsolete. "The next generation of computing machines operates a thousand times as fast—at a pulse rate of one in every three-tenths of a billionth of a second," observes Alice Mary Hilton. "Speeds of millionths and billionths of a second are not really intelligible to our finite minds. But we can certainly understand that the advance has been a thousand-fold within a year or two. A thousand times as much information can be handled or the same amount of information can be handled a thousand times as fast. A job that takes more than sixteen hours can be done in one minute! And without any human intervention! Such a system does not control merely an assembly line but a complete manufacturing and industrial process!"[15]

There is no reason why the basic technological principles involved in cybernating the manufacture of automobile engines cannot be applied to virtually every area of mass manufacture—from the metallurgical industry to the food processing industry, from the electronics industry to the toy-making industry, from the manufacture of prefabricated bridges to the manufacture of prefabricated houses. Many phases of steel production, tool-and-die making, electronic equipment manufacture and industrial chemical production are now partly or largely automated. What tends to delay the advance of complete automation to every phase of modern industry is the enormous cost involved in replacing existing industrial facilities by new, more sophisticated ones and also the innate conservatism of many major corporations. Finally, as I mentioned before, it is still cheaper to use labor instead of machines in many industries.

To be sure, every industry has its own particular problems, and the application of a toil-less technology to a specific plant would doubtless reveal a multitude of kinks that would require painstaking solutions. In many industries it would be necessary to alter the shape of the product and the layout of the plants so that the manufacturing process would lend itself to automated techniques. But to argue from these problems that the application of a fully automated technology to a specific industry is impossible would be as preposterous as to have argued eighty years ago that flight was impossible because the propeller of an experimental airplane did not revolve fast enough or the frame was too fragile to withstand buffeting by the wind. There is practically no industry that cannot be fully automated if we are willing to redesign the product, the plant, the manufacturing procedures and the handling methods. In fact, any difficulty in describing how, where or when a given industry will be automated arises not from the unique problems we can expect to encounter but rather from the enormous leaps that occur every few years in modern technology. Almost every account of applied automation today must be regarded as provisional: as soon as one describes a partially automated industry, technological advances make the description obsolete.

There is one area of the economy, however, in which any form of technological advance is worth describing—the area of work that is most brutalizing and degrading for man. If it is true that the moral level of a society can be gauged by the way it treats women, its sensitivity to human suffering can be gauged by the working conditions it provides for people in raw materials industries, particularly in mines and quarries. In the ancient world, mining was often a form of penal servitude, reserved primarily for the most hardened criminals, the most intractable slaves, and the most hated prisoners of war. The mine is the day-to-day actualization of man's image of hell; it is a deadening, dismal, inorganic world that demands pure mindless toil.

> Field and forest and stream and ocean are the environment of life: the mine is the environment alone of ores, minerals, metals [writes Lewis Mumford]... In hacking and digging the contents of the earth, the miner has no eye for the forms of things. What he sees is sheer matter and until he gets to his vein it is only an obstacle which he breaks through stubbornly and sends up to the surface. If the miner sees shapes on the walls of his cavern, as the candle flickers, they are only the monstrous distortions of his pick or his arm: shapes of fear. Day has been abolished and the rhythm of nature broken: continuous day-and-night production first came into existence here. The miner must work by artificial light even though the sun be shining outside; still further down in the seams, he must work by artificial ventilation, too: a triumph of the 'manufactured environment.'[16]

The abolition of mining as a sphere of human activity would symbolize, in its own way, the triumph of a liberatory technology. That we can point to this achievement already, even in a single case at this writing, presages the freedom from toil implicit in the technology of our time. The first major step in this direction was the continuous miner, a giant cutting machine with nine-foot blades that slices up eight tons of coal a minute from the coal face. It was this machine, together with mobile loading machines, power drills and roof bolting, that reduced mine employment in areas like West Virginia to about a third of the 1948 levels, at the same time nearly doubling individual output. The coal mine still required miners to place and operate the machines. The most recent technological advances, however, replace the operators by radar sensing devices and eliminate the miner completely.

By adding sensing devices to automatic machinery we could easily remove the worker not only from the large, productive mines needed by the economy, but also from forms of agricultural activity patterned on modern industry. Although the wisdom of industrializing and mechanizing agriculture is highly questionable (I shall return to this subject at a later point), the fact remains that if society so chooses, it can automate large areas of industrial agriculture, ranging from cotton picking to rice harvesting. We could operate almost any machine, from a giant shovel in an open-strip mine to a grain harvester in the Great Plains, either by cybernated sensing devices or by remote control with television cameras. The effort needed to operate these devices and machines at a safe distance, in comfortable quarters, would be minimal, assuming that a human operator were required at all.

It is easy to foresee a time, by no means remote, when a rationally organized economy could automatically manufacture small "packaged" factories without human labor; parts could be produced with so little effort that most maintenance tasks would be reduced to the simple act of removing a defective unit from a machine and replacing it by another—a job no more difficult than pulling out and putting in a tray. Machines would make and repair most of the machines required to maintain such a highly industrialized economy. Such a technology, oriented entirely toward human needs and freed from all consideration of profit and loss, would eliminate the pain of want and toil—the penalty, inflicted in the form of denial, suffering and inhumanity, exacted by a society based on scarcity and labor.

The possibilities created by a cybernated technology would no longer be limited merely to the satisfaction of man's material needs. We would be free to ask how the machine, the factory and the mine could be used to foster human solidarity and to create a balanced relationship with nature and a truly organic ecocommunity. Would our new technology be based on the same national division of labor that exists today? The current type of industrial organization—an extension, in effect, of the industrial forms created by the Industrial Revolution—fosters industrial centralization (although a system of workers' management based on the individual factory and local community would go far toward eliminating this feature).

Or does the new technology lend itself to a system of small-scale production, based on a regional economy and structured physically on a human scale? This type of industrial organization places *all* economic decisions in the hands of the local community. To the degree that material production is decentralized and localized, the primacy of the community is asserted over national institutions—assuming that any such national institutions develop to a significant extent. In these circumstances, the popular assembly of the local community, convened in a face-to-face democracy, takes over the *full* management of social life. The question is whether a future society will be organized around technology or whether technology is now sufficiently malleable so that it can be organized around society. To answer this question, we must further examine certain features of the new technology.

THE NEW TECHNOLOGY AND THE HUMAN SCALE

In 1945, J. Presper Eckert, Jr. and John W. Mauchly of the University of Pennsylvania unveiled ENIAC, the first digital computer to be designed entirely along electronic principles. Commissioned for use in solving ballistic problems, ENIAC required nearly three years of work to design and build. The computer was enormous. It weighed more than thirty tons, contained 18,800 vacuum tubes with half a million connections (these connections took Eckert and Mauchly two and a half years to solder), a vast network of resistors, and miles of wiring. The computer required a large air-conditioning unit to cool its electronic components. It often broke down or behaved erratically, requiring time-consuming repairs and maintenance. Yet by all previous standards of computer development, ENIAC was an electronic marvel. It could perform five thousand computations a second, generating electrical pulse signals that cycled at 100,000 a second. None of the mechanical or electro-mechanical computers in use at the time could approach this rate of computational speed.

Some twenty years later, the Computer Control Company of Framingham, Massachusetts, offered the DDP-124 for public sale. The DDP-124 is a small, compact computer that closely resembles a bedside AM-radio receiver. The entire ensemble, together with a typewriter and memory unit, occupies a typical office desk. The DDP-124 performs over 285,000 computations a second. It has a true stored-program memory that can be expanded to retain nearly 33,000 words (the "memory" of ENIAC, based on preset plug wires, lacked anything like the flexibility of present-day computers); its pulses cycle at 1.75 billion per second. The DDP-124 does not require any air-conditioning unit; it is completely reliable, and it creates very few maintenance problems. It can be built at a minute fraction of the cost required to construct ENIAC.

The difference between ENIAC and DDP-124 is one of degree rather than kind. Leaving aside their memory units, both digital computers operate according to the same electronic principles. ENIAC, however, was composed primarily of traditional electronic components (vacuum tubes, resistors, etc.) and thousands of feet of wire; the DDP-124 on the other hand, relies primarily on microcircuits. These microcircuits are very small electronic units that pack the equivalent of ENIAC's key electronic components into squares a mere fraction of an inch in size.

Paralleling the miniaturization of computer components is the remarkable sophistication of traditional forms of technology. Ever smaller machines are beginning to replace large ones. For example, a fascinating breakthrough has been achieved in reducing the size of continuous hot-strip steel rolling mills. This kind of mill is one of the largest and costliest facilities in modern industry. It may be regarded as a single machine, nearly a half mile in length, capable of reducing a ten-ton slab of steel about six inches thick and fifty inches wide to a thin strip of sheet metal a tenth or a twelfth of an inch thick. This installation alone, including heating furnaces, coilers, long roller tables, scalebreaker stands and buildings, may cost tens of millions of dollars and occupy fifty acres or more. It produces three hundred tons of steel sheet an hour. To be used efficiently, such a continuous hot-strip mill must be operated together with large batteries of coke ovens, open-hearth furnaces, blooming mills, etc. These facilities, in conjunction with hot and cold rolling mills, may cover several square miles. Such a steel complex is geared to a national division of labor, to highly concentrated sources of raw materials (generally located at a great distance from the complex), and to large national and international markets. Even if it is totally automated, its operating and management needs far transcend the capabilities of a small, decentralized community. The type of administration it requires tends to foster centralized social forms.

Fortunately, we now have a number of alternatives—more efficient alternatives in many respects—to the modern steel complex. We can replace blast furnaces and openhearth furnaces by a variety of electric furnaces which are generally quite small and produce excellent pig iron and steel; they can operate not only with coke but also with anthracite coal, charcoal, and even lignite. Or we can choose the HyL process, a batch process in which natural gas is used to turn high-grade ores or concentrates into sponge iron. Or we can turn to the Wiberg process, which involves the use of charcoal, carbon monoxide and hydrogen. In any case, we can reduce the need for coke ovens, blast furnaces, open hearth furnaces, and possibly even solid reducing agents.

One of the most important steps towards scaling a steel complex to community dimensions is the development of the planetary mill by T. Sendzimir. The planetary mill reduces the typical continuous hot-strip mill to a single planetary stand and a light finishing stand. Hot steel slabs, two and a quarter inches thick, pass through two small pairs of heated feed rolls and a set of work rolls mounted in two circular cages which also contain two backup rolls. By operating the cages and backup rolls at different rotational speeds, the work rolls are made to turn in two directions. This gives the steel slab a terrific mauling and reduces it to a thickness of only one-tenth of an inch. Sendzimir's planetary mill is a stroke of engineering genius; the small work rolls, turning on the two circular cages, replace the need for the four huge roughing stands and six finishing stands in a continuous hot-strip mill.

The rolling of hot steel slabs by the Sendzimir process requires a much smaller operational area than a continuous hot-strip mill. With continuous casting, moreover, we can produce steel slabs without the need for large, costly slabbing mills. A future steel complex based on electric furnaces, continuous casting, a planetary mill and a small continuous cold-reducing mill would require a fraction of the acreage occupied by a conventional installation. It would be fully capable of meeting the steel needs of several moderate-sized communities with low quantities of fuel.

The complex I have described is not designed to meet the needs of a national market, on the contrary, it is suited only for meeting the steel requirements of small or moderate-sized communities and industrially undeveloped countries. Most electric furnaces for pig-iron production produce about a hundred to two hundred and fifty tons a day, while large blast furnaces produce three thousand tons daily. A planetary mill can roll only a hundred tons of steel strip an hour, roughly a third of the output of a continuous hot-strip mill. Yet the very scale of our hypothetical steel complex constitutes one of its most attractive features. Also, the steel produced by our complex is more durable, so the community's rate of replenishing its steel products would be appreciably reduced. Since the smaller complex requires ore, fuel and reducing agents in relatively small quantities, many communities could rely on local resources for their raw materials, thereby conserving the more concentrated resources of centrally located sources of supply, strengthening the independence of the community itself vis-à-vis the traditional centralized economy, and reducing the expense of transportation. What would at first glance seem to be a costly, inefficient duplication of effort that could be avoided by building a few centralized steel complexes would prove, in the long run, to be more efficient as well as socially more desirable.

The new technology has produced not only miniaturized electronic components and smaller production facilities but also highly versatile, multi-purpose machines. For more than a century, the trend in machine design moved increasingly toward technological specialization and single purpose devices, underpinning the intensive division of labor required by the new factory system. Industrial operations were subordinated entirely to the product. In time, this narrow pragmatic approach has "led industry far from the rational line of development in production machinery," observe Eric W. Leaver and John J. Brown. "It has led to increasingly uneconomic specialization... Specialization of machines in terms of end product requires that the machine be thrown away when the product is no longer needed. Yet the work the production machine does can be reduced to a set of basic functions—forming, holding, cutting, and so on—and these functions, if correctly analyzed, can be packaged and applied to operate on a part as needed."[17]

Ideally, a drilling machine of the kind envisioned by Leaver and Brown would be able to produce a hole small enough to hold a thin wire or large enough to admit a pipe. Machines with this operational range were once regarded as economically prohibitive. By the mid-1950s, however, a number of such machines were actually designed and put to use. In 1954, for example, a horizontal boring mill was built in Switzerland for the Ford Motor Company's River Rouge Plant at Dearborn, Michigan. This boring mill would qualify beautifully as a Leaver and Brown machine. Equipped with five optical microscope-type illuminated control gauges, the mill drills holes smaller than a needle's eye or larger than a man's fist. The holes are accurate to a ten-thousandth of an inch.

The importance of machines with this kind of operational range can hardly be overestimated. They make it possible to produce a large variety of products in a single plant. A small or moderate-sized community using multipurpose machines could satisfy many of its limited industrial needs without being burdened with underused industrial facilities. There would be less loss in scrapping tools and less need for single-purpose plants. The community's economy would be more compact and versatile, more rounded and self-contained, than anything we find in the communities of industrially advanced countries. The effort that goes into retooling machines for new products would be enormously reduced. Retooling would generally consist of changes in dimensioning rather than in design. Finally, multipurpose machines with a wide operational range are relatively easy to automate. The changes required to use these machines in a cybernated industrial facility would generally be in circuitry and programming rather than in machine form and structure.

Single purpose machines, of course, would continue to exist, and they would still be used for the mass manufacture of a large variety of goods. At present many highly automatic, single-purpose machines could be employed with very little modification by decentralized communities. Bottling and canning machines, for example, are compact, automatic and highly rationalized installations. We could expect to see smaller automatic textile, chemical processing and food processing machines. A major shift from conventional automobiles, buses and trucks to electric vehicles would undoubtedly lead to industrial facilities much smaller in size than existing automobile plants. Many of the remaining centralized facilities could be effectively decentralized simply by making them as small as possible and sharing their use among several communities.

I do not claim that all of man's economic activities can be completely decentralized, but the majority can surely be scaled to human and communitarian dimensions. This much is certain: we can shift the center of economic power from national to local scale and from centralized bureaucratic forms to local, popular assemblies. This shift would be a revolutionary change of vast proportions, for it would create powerful economic foundations for the sovereignty and autonomy of the local community.

THE ECOLOGICAL USE OF TECHNOLOGY

I have tried, thus far, to deal with the possibility of eliminating toil, material insecurity, and centralized economic control—issues which, if "utopian," are at least tangible. In the present section I would like to deal with a problem that may seem highly subjective but which is nonetheless of compelling importance—the need to make man's dependence upon the natural world a visible and living part of his culture.

Actually, this problem is peculiar only to a highly urbanized and industrialized society. In nearly all pre-industrial cultures, man's relationship to his natural environment was well defined, viable, and sanctified by the full weight of tradition. Changes in season, variations in rainfall, the life cycles of the plants and animals on which humans depended for food and clothing, the distinctive features of the area occupied by the community—all were familiar and comprehensible, and evoked in men a sense of religious awe, of oneness with nature, and, more pragmatically, a sense of respectful dependence. Looking back to the earliest civilizations of the Western world, we rarely find evidence of a system of social tyranny so overbearing and ruthless that it ignored this relationship. Barbarian invasions and, more insidiously, the development of commercial civilizations may have destroyed the reverential attitude of agrarian cultures toward nature, but the normal development of agricultural systems, however exploitative they were of men, rarely led to the destruction of the soil and terrain. During the most oppressive periods in the history of ancient Egypt and Mesopotamia, the ruling classes kept the irrigation dikes in good repair and tried to promote rational methods of food cultivation. Even the ancient Greeks, heirs to a thin, mountainous forest soil that suffered heavily from erosion, shrewdly reclaimed much of their arable land by turning to orchardry and viticulture. It was not until commercial agricultural systems and highly urbanized societies developed that the natural environment was unsparingly exploited. Some of the worst cases of soil destruction in the ancient world were provided by the giant, slave-worked commercial farms of North Africa and the Italian peninsula.

In our own time, the development of technology and the growth of cities has brought man's alienation from nature to the breaking point. Western man finds himself confined to a largely synthetic urban environment, far removed physically from the land, and his relationship to the natural world is mediated entirely by machines. He lacks familiarity with how most of his goods are produced, and his foods bear only the faintest resemblance to the animals and plants from which they were derived. Boxed into a sanitized urban milieu (almost institutional in form and appearance), modern man is denied even a spectator's role in the agricultural and industrial systems that satisfy his material needs. He is a pure consumer, an insensate receptacle. It would be unfair, perhaps, to say that he is disrespectful toward the natural environment; the fact is, he scarcely knows what ecology means or what his environment requires to remain in balance.

The balance between man and nature must be restored. I have tried to show elsewhere that unless we establish some kind of equilibrium between man and the natural world, the viability of the human species will be placed in grave jeopardy.* Here I shall try to show how the new technology can be used ecologically to reawaken man's sense of dependence upon the environment; I shall try to show how, by reintroducing the natural world into the human experience, we can contribute to the achievement of human wholeness.

The classical utopians fully realized that the first step towards wholeness must be to remove the contradiction between town and country. "It is impossible," wrote Fourier nearly a century and a half ago, "to organize a regular and well balanced association without bringing into play the labors of the field, or at least gardens, orchards, flocks and herds, poultry yards, and a great variety of species, animal and vegetable." Shocked by the social effects of the Industrial Revolution, Fourier added: "They are ignorant of this principle in England, where they experiment with artisans, with manufacturing labor alone, which cannot by itself suffice to sustain social union."[18]

To argue that the modern urban dweller should once again enjoy "the labors of the field" might well seem like gallows humor. A restoration of peasant agriculture prevalent in Fourier's day is neither possible nor desirable. Charles Gide was surely correct when he observed that agricultural labor "is not necessarily more attractive than industrial labor; to till the earth has always been regarded… as the type of painful toil, of toil which is done with the sweat of one's brow."[19] Fourier does not answer this objection by suggesting that his phalansteries will mainly cultivate fruits and vegetables instead of grains. If our vision were to extend no further than prevailing techniques of land management, the only alternative to peasant agriculture would seem to be a highly specialized and centralized form of farming, its techniques paralleling the methods used in present-day industry. Far from achieving a balance between town and country,

* See "Ecology and Revolutionary Thought."

we would be faced with a synthetic environment that had totally assimilated the natural world.

If we grant that the land and the community must be reintegrated physically, that the community must exist in an agricultural matrix which renders man's dependence upon nature explicit, the problem we face is how to achieve this transformation without imposing "painful toil" on the community. How, in short, can husbandry, ecological forms of food cultivation and farming on a human scale be practiced without sacrificing mechanization?

Some of the most promising technological advances in agriculture made since World War II are as suitable for small-scale, ecological forms of land management as they are for the immense, industrial-type commercial units that have become prevalent over the past few decades. Let us consider an example. The augermatic feeding of livestock illustrates a cardinal principle of rational farm mechanization—the deployment of conventional machines and devices in a way that virtually eliminates arduous farm labor. By linking a battery of silos with augers, different nutrients can be mixed and transported to feed pens merely by pushing some buttons and pulling a few switches. A job that may have required the labor of five or six men working half a day with pitchforks and buckets can now be performed by one man in a few minutes. This type of mechanization is intrinsically neutral: it can be used to feed immense herds or just a few hundred head of cattle; the silos may contain natural feed or synthetic, hormonized nutrients; the feeder can be employed on relatively small farms with mixed livestock or on large beef-raising ranches, or on dairy farms of all sizes. In short, augermatic feeding can be placed in the service of the most abusive kind of commercial exploitation or of the most sensitive applications of ecological principles.

This holds true for most of the farm machines that have been designed (in many cases simply redesigned to achieve greater versatility) in recent years. The modern tractor, for example, is a work of superb mechanical ingenuity. Garden-type models can be used with extraordinary flexibility for a large variety of tasks; they are light and extremely manageable, and they can follow the contour of the most exacting terrain without damaging the land. Large tractors, especially those used in hot climates, are likely to have air-conditioned cabs; in addition to pulling equipment, they may have attachments for digging postholes, for doing the work of forklift trucks, or even for providing power units for grain elevators. Plows have been developed to meet every contingency in tillage. Advanced models are even regulated hydraulically to rise and fall with the lay of the land. Mechanical planters are available for virtually every kind of crop. "Minimum tillage" is achieved by planters which apply seed, fertilizer and pesticides (of course!) simultaneously, a technique that telescopes several different operations into a single one and reduces the soil compaction often produced by the recurrent use of heavy machines.

The variety of mechanical harvesters has reached dazzling proportions. Harvesters have been developed for many different kinds of orchards, berries, vines, vegetables and field crops. Barns, feed pens and storage units have been totally revolutionized by augers, conveyor belts, air tight silos, automatic manure removers, climate-control devices, etc. Crops are mechanically shelled, washed, counted, preserved by freezing or canning, packaged and crated. The construction of concrete-lined irrigation ditches has become a simple mechanical operation that can be performed by one or two excavating machines. Terrain with poor drainage or subsoil can be improved by earthmoving equipment and by tillage devices that penetrate beyond the true soil.

Although a great deal of agricultural research is devoted to the development of harmful chemical agents and nutritionally dubious crops, there have been extraordinary advances in the genetic improvement of food plants. Many new grain and vegetable varieties are resistant to insect predators, plant diseases, and cold weather. In many cases, these varieties are a definite improvement over natural ancestral types and they have been used to open large areas of intractable land to food cultivation.

Let us pause at this point to envision how our free community might be integrated with its natural environment. We suppose the community to have been established after a careful study has been made of its natural ecology—its air and water resources, its climate, its geological formations, its raw materials, its soils, and its natural flora and fauna. Land management by the community is guided entirely by ecological principles, so that an equilibrium is maintained between the environment and its human inhabitants. Industrially rounded, the community forms a distinct unit within a natural matrix; it is socially and aesthetically in balance with the area it occupies.

Agriculture is highly mechanized in the community, but as mixed as possible with respect to crops, livestock and timber. Variety of flora and fauna is promoted as a means of controlling pest infestations and enhancing scenic beauty. Large-scale farming is practiced only where it does not conflict with the ecology of the region. Owing to the generally mixed character of food cultivation, agriculture is pursued by small farming units, each demarcated from the others by tree belts, shrubs, pastures and meadows. In rolling, hilly or mountainous country, land with sharp gradients is covered by timber to prevent erosion and conserve water. The soil on each acre is studied carefully and committed only to those crops for which it is most suited. Every effort is made to blend town and country without sacrificing the distinctive contribution that each has to offer to the human experience. The ecological region forms the living social, cultural and biotic boundaries of the community or of the several communities that share its resources. Each community contains many vegetable and flower gardens, attractive arbors, park land, even streams and ponds which support fish and aquatic birds. The countryside, from which food and raw materials are acquired, not only constitutes the immediate environs of the community, accessible to all by foot, but also invades the community. Although town and country retain their identity and the uniqueness of each is highly prized and fostered, nature appears everywhere in the town, and the town seems to have caressed and left a gentle, human imprint on nature.

I believe that a free community will regard agriculture as husbandry, an activity as expressive and enjoyable as crafts. Relieved of toil by agricultural machines, communitarians will approach food cultivation with the same playful and creative attitude that men so often bring to gardening. Agriculture will become a living part of human society, a source of pleasant physical activity and, by virtue of its ecological demands, an intellectual, scientific and artistic challenge. Communitarians will blend with the world of life around them as organically as the community blends with its region. They will regain the sense of oneness with nature that existed in humans from primordial times. Nature and the organic modes of thought it always fosters will become an integral part of human culture; it will reappear with a fresh spirit in man's paintings, literature, philosophy, dances, architecture, domestic furnishings, and in his very gestures and day-to-day activities. Culture and the human psyche will be thoroughly suffused by a new animism. The region will never be exploited, but it will be used as fully as possible. Every attempt will be made by the community to satisfy its requirements locally—to use the region's energy resources, minerals, timber, soil, water, animals and plants as rationally and humanistically as possible and without violating ecological principles. In this connection, we can foresee that the community will employ new techniques that are still being developed today, many of which lend themselves superbly to a regionally based economy. I refer here to methods for extracting trace and diluted resources from the earth, water and air; to solar, wind, hydroelectric and geothermal energy; to the use of heat pumps, vegetable fuels, solar ponds, thermoelectric converters and, eventually, controlled thermonuclear reactions.

There is a kind of industrial archeology that reveals in many areas the evidence of a once-burgeoning economic activity long abandoned by our predecessors. In the Hudson Valley, the Rhine Valley, the Appalachians and the Pyrenees, we find the relics of mines and once highly developed metallurgical crafts, the fragmentary remains of local industries, and the outlines of long-deserted farms—all vestiges of flourishing communities based on local raw materials and resources. These communities declined because the products they once furnished were elbowed out by large-scale, national industries based on mass production techniques and concentrated sources of raw materials. The old resources are often still available for use by each locality; "valueless" in a highly urbanized society, they are eminently suitable for use by decentralized communities and they await the application of industrial techniques that are adapted for small-scale quality production. If we were to take a careful inventory of the resources available in many depopulated regions of the world, the possibility that communities could satisfy many of their material needs locally is likely to be much greater than we suspect.

Technology, by its continual development, tends to expand local possibilities. As an example, let us consider how seemingly inferior and highly intractable resources are made available by technological advances. Throughout the late nineteenth and early twentieth centuries, the Mesabi range in Minnesota provided the American steel industry with extremely rich ores, an advantage which promoted the rapid expansion of the domestic metal industry. As these reserves declined, the country was faced with the problem of mining taconite, a low-grade ore that is about forty percent iron. Conventional mining methods are virtually impossible; it takes a chum drill an hour to bite through only one foot of taconite. Recently, however, the mining of taconite became feasible; a jet-flame drill was developed which cuts through the ore at the rate of twenty to thirty feet an hour. After holes are burned by the flame, the ore is blasted and processed for the steel industry by newly perfected grinding, separating and agglomerating operations.

Soon it may be possible to extract highly diffused or diluted materials from the earth, from a wide variety of gaseous waste products, and from the sea. Some of our most valuable metals are actually fairly common, but they exist in highly diffused or trace amounts. Hardly a patch of soil or a common rock exists that does not contain traces of gold, larger quantities of uranium, and even larger amounts of other industrially useful elements such as magnesium, zinc, copper and sulfur. About five percent of the earth's crust is made of iron. How can we extract these resources? The problem has been solved, in principle at least, by the analytical techniques chemists use to detect these elements. As the chemist Jacob Rosin argues, if an element can be detected in the laboratory, there is reason to hope that it can be extracted on a sufficiently large scale to be used by industry.

For more than half a century, most of the world's commercial nitrogen has been extracted from the atmosphere. Magnesium, chlorine, bromine and caustic soda are acquired from sea water and sulfur from calcium sulfate and industrial wastes. Large amounts of industrially useful hydrogen could be collected as a byproduct of the electrolysis of brine, but normally it is burned or released in the air by chlorine-producing plants. Carbon could be rescued in enormous quantities from smoke and used economically (carbon is comparatively rare in nature) but is dissipated together with other gaseous compounds in the atmosphere.

The problem industrial chemist's face in extracting valuable elements and compounds from the sea and ordinary rock is the cost of the energy needed. Two methods exist—ion exchange and chromatography—and, if further perfected for industrial uses, they could be used to select or separate the desired substances from solutions, but the amount of energy needed to use these methods would be very costly in terms of real wealth. Unless there is an unexpected breakthrough in extractive techniques, there is little likelihood that conventional sources of energy—fossil fuels like coal and oil—will be used to solve the problem.

It is not that we lack energy *per se,* but we are just beginning to learn how to use sources that are available in almost limitless quantity. The gross radiant energy striking the Earth's surface from the sun is estimated to be more than three thousand times the annual energy consumption of mankind today. Although a portion of this energy is converted into wind or used for photosynthesis by vegetation, a staggering quantity is available for other uses. The problem is how to collect it to satisfy a portion of our energy needs. If solar energy could be collected for house heating, for example, twenty to thirty percent of the conventional energy resources we normally employ could be redirected to other purposes. If we could collect solar energy for all or most of our cooking, water heating, smelting and power production, we would have relatively little need for fossil fuels. Solar devices have been designed for nearly all of these functions. We can heat houses, cook food, boil water, melt metals and produce electricity with devices that use the sun's energy exclusively, but we can't do it efficiently in every latitude of the earth, and we are still confronted with a number of technical problems that can be solved only by crash research programs.

At this writing, quite a few houses have been built that are effectively heated by solar energy. In the United States, the best known of these are the MIT experimental buildings in Massachusetts, the Lof house in Denver, and the Thomason homes in Washington, D.C. Thomason, whose fuel cost for a solar-heated house barely reaches $5 a year, seems to have developed one of the most practical systems at hand. Solar heat in a Thomason home is collected from the roof and transferred by circulating water to a storage tank in the basement. (The water, incidentally, can also be used for cooling the house and as an emergency supply for fire and drinking.) The system is simple and fairly cheap. Located in Washington near the fortieth parallel of latitude, the Thomason houses stand at the edge of the "solar belt"—the latitudes from zero to forty degrees north and south. This belt is the geographic area where the sun's rays can be used most effectively for domestic and industrial energy. With efficient solar heating, Thomason requires a miniscule amount of supplemental conventional fuel to heat his Washington homes.

Two approaches to solar house-heating are possible in cooler areas: heating systems could be more elaborate, which would reduce the consumption of conventional fuel to levels approximating those of the Thomason homes; or simple conventional fuel systems could be used to satisfy anywhere from ten to fifty percent of the heating needs. As Hans Thirring observes (with an eye toward cost and effort):

> The decisive advantage of solar heating lies in the fact that no running costs arise, except the electricity bill for driving the fans, which is very small. Thus the one single investment for the installation pays once and for all the heating costs for the life-time of the house. In addition, the system works automatically without smoke, soot, and fume production, and saves all trouble in stoking, refueling, cleaning, repair and other work. Adding solar heat to the energy system of a country helps to increase the wealth of the nation, and if all houses in areas with favorable conditions were equipped with solar heating systems, fuel saving worth millions of pounds yearly could be achieved. The work of Telkes, Hottel, Lof, Bliss, and other scientists who are paving the way for solar heating is real pioneer work, the full significance of which will emerge more clearly in the future.[20]

The most widespread applications of solar energy devices are in cooking and water heating. Many thousands of solar stoves are used in underdeveloped countries, in Japan, and in the warm latitudes of the United States. A solar stove is simply an umbrella-like reflector equipped with a grill that can broil meat or boil a quart of water within fifteen minutes in bright sunlight. Such a stove is safe, portable and clean; it requires no fuel or matches, nor does it produce any annoying smoke. A portable solar oven delivers temperatures as high as four hundred fifty degrees and is even more compact and easier to handle than a solar stove. Solar water-heaters are used widely in private homes, apartment buildings, laundries and swimming pools. Some twenty-five thousand of these units are employed in Florida and they are gradually coming into vogue in California.

Some of the most impressive advances in the use of solar energy have occurred in industry, although the majority of these applications are marginal at best and largely experimental in nature. The simplest is the solar furnace. The collector is usually a single large parabolic mirror, or, more likely, a huge array of many parabolic mirrors mounted in a large housing. A heliostat—a smaller, horizontally mounted mirror that follows the movement of the sun—reflects the rays into the collector. Several hundred of these furnaces are currently in use. One of the largest, Dr. Felix

Trombe's Mont Louis furnace, develops seventy-five kilowatts of electric power and is used primarily in high temperature research. Since the sun's rays do not contain any impurities, the furnace will melt a hundred pounds of metal without the contamination produced by conventional techniques. A solar furnace built by the U.S. Quartermaster Corps at Nattick, Massachusetts, develops five thousand degrees Centigrade—a temperature high enough to melt steel I-beams.

Solar furnaces have many limitations, but these are not insurmountable. The efficiency of the furnaces can be appreciably reduced by haze, fog, clouds and atmospheric dust, and also by heavy wind loadings which deflect equipment and interfere with the accurate focusing of the sun's rays. Attempts are being made to resolve some of these problems by sliding roofs, covering material for the mirrors, and firm, protective housings. On the other hand, solar furnaces are clean, they are efficient when they are in good working order, and they produce extremely high grade metals which none of the conventional furnaces currently in use can match.

Equally promising as an area of research are current attempts to convert solar energy into electricity. Theoretically, an area roughly a square yard in size placed perpendicular to the sun's rays receives energy equivalent to one kilowatt. "Considering that in the arid zones of the world many millions of square meters of desert land are free for power production," observes Thirring, "we find that by utilizing only one percent of the available ground for solar plants a capacity could be reached far higher than the present installed capacity of all fuel-operated and hydroelectric power plants in the world."[21] In practice, work along the lines suggested by Thirring has been inhibited by cost considerations, by market factors (there is no large demand for electricity in those underdeveloped, hot areas of the world where the project is most feasible) and by essentially the conservatism of designers in the power field. Research emphasis has been placed on the development of solar batteries—a result largely of work on the "space program."

Solar batteries are based on the thermoelectric effect. If strips of antimony and bismuth are joined in a loop, for example, a temperature differential made, say, by producing heat in one junction, yields electric power. Research on solar batteries over the past decade or so resulted in devices that have a power-converting efficiency as high as fifteen percent, and twenty to twenty-five percent is quite attainable in the not too distant future.* Grouped in large panels, solar batteries have been used to power electric cars, small boats, telephone lines, radios, phonographs, clocks, sewing machines and other appliances. Eventually, the cost of producing solar batteries is expected to diminish to a point where they will provide electric power for homes and even small industrial facilities.

Finally, the sun's energy can be used in still another way—by collecting heat in a body of water. For some time now, engineers have been studying ways of acquiring electric power from the temperature differences produced by the sun's heat in the sea. Theoretically, a solar pond occupying a square kilometer could yield thirty million kilowatt-hours of electricity annually—enough to match the output of a sizeable power station operating more than twelve hours every day of the year. The power, as Henry Tabor observes, can be acquired without any fuel costs, "merely by the pond lying in the sun."[22] Heat can be extracted from the bottom of the pond by passing the hot water over a heat exchanger and then returning the water to the pond. In warm latitudes, ten thousand square miles committed to this method of power production would provide enough electricity to satisfy the needs of four hundred million people!

The ocean's tides are still another untapped resource to which we could turn for electric power. We could trap the ocean's waters at high tide in a natural basin—say a bay or the mouth of a river—and release them through turbines at low tide. A number of places exist where the tides are high enough to produce electric power in large quantities. The French have already built an immense tidal-power installation near the mouth of the Rance River at St. Malo with an expected net yield of 544 million kilowatt-hours annually. They also plan to build another dam in the bay of Mont-Saint-Michel. In England, highly suitable conditions for a tidal dam exist above the confluence of the Severn and Wye rivers. A dam here could provide the electric power produced by a million tons of coal annually. A superb location for producing tide-generated electricity exists at Passamaquoddy Bay on the border between Maine and New Brunswick, and good locales exist on the Mezen Gulf, a Russian coastal area in the Arctic. Argentina has plans for building a tidal dam across the estuary of the Deseado River near Puerto Desire on the Atlantic coast. Many other coastal areas could be used to generate electricity from tidal power, but except for France no country has started work on this resource.

* The efficiency of the gasoline engine is rated at around eleven percent, to cite a comparison.

We could use temperature differences in the sea or in the earth to generate electric power in sizeable quantities. A temperature differential as high as seventeen degrees Centigrade is not uncommon in the surface layers of tropical waters; along coastal areas of Siberia, winter differences of thirty degrees exist between water below the ice crust and the air. The interior of the earth becomes progressively warmer as we descend, providing selective temperature differentials with respect to the surface. Heat pumps could be used to avail ourselves of these differentials for industrial purposes or to heat homes. The heat pump works like a mechanical refrigerator: a circulating refrigerant draws off heat from a medium, dissipates it, and returns to repeat the process. During winter months, the pumps, circulating a refrigerant in a shallow well, could be used to absorb subsurface heat and release it in a house. In the summer the process could be reversed: heat withdrawn from the house could be dissipated in the earth. The pumps do not require costly chimneys, they do not pollute the atmosphere, and they eliminate the nuisance of stoking furnaces and carrying out ashes. If we could acquire electricity or direct heat from solar energy, wind power or temperature differentials, the heating system of a home or factory would be completely self-sustaining; it would not drain valuable hydrocarbon resources or require external sources of supply.

Winds could also be used to provide electric power in many areas of the world. About one-fortieth of the solar energy reaching the earth's surface is converted into wind. Although much of this goes into making the jet stream, a great deal of wind energy is available a few hundred feet above the ground. A UN report, using monetary terms to gauge the feasibility of wind power, finds that efficient wind plants in many areas could produce electricity at an overall cost of five mills per kilowatt-hour, a figure that approximates the price of commercially generated electric power. Several wind generators have already been used with success. The famous 1,250 kilowatt generator at Grandpa's Knob near Rutland, Vermont, successfully fed alternating current into the lines of the Central Vermont Public Service Co. until a parts shortage during World War II made it difficult to keep the installation in good repair. Since then, larger, more efficient generators have been designed. P. H. Thomas, working for the Federal Power Commission, has designed a 7,500 kilowatt windmill that would provide electricity at a capital investment of $68 per kilowatt.

Eugene Ayres notes that if the construction costs of Thomas's windmill were double the amount estimated by its designer, "wind turbines would seem nevertheless to compare favorably with hydroelectric installations which cost around $300 per kilowatt."[23] An enormous potential for generating electricity by means of wind power exists in many regions of the world. In England, for example, where a careful three-year survey was made of possible wind-power sites, it was found that the newer wind turbines could generate several million kilowatts, saving from two to four million tons of coal annually.

There should be no illusions about the extraction of trace minerals from rocks, about solar and wind power, or about the use of heat pumps. Except perhaps for tidal power and the extraction of raw materials from the sea, these sources cannot supply man with the bulky quantities of raw materials and the large blocks of energy needed to sustain densely concentrated populations and highly centralized industries. Solar devices, wind turbines, and heat pumps will produce relatively small quantities of power. Used locally and in conjunction with each other, they could probably meet all the power needs of small communities, but we cannot foresee a time when they will be able to furnish the electricity currently used by cities the size of New York, London or Paris.

Limitation of scope, however, could represent a profound advantage from an ecological point of view. The sun, the wind and the earth are experiential realities to which men have responded sensuously and reverently from time immemorial. Out of these primal elements man developed his sense of dependence on—and respect for—the natural environment, a dependence that kept his destructive activities in check. The Industrial Revolution and the urbanized world that followed obscured nature's role in human experience—hiding the sun with a pall of smoke, blocking the winds with massive buildings, desecrating the earth with sprawling cities. Man's dependence on the natural world became invisible; it became theoretical and intellectual in character, the subject matter of textbooks, monographs and lectures. True, this theoretical dependence supplied us with insights (partial ones at best) into the natural world, but its onesidedness robbed us of all sensuous dependence on and all visible contact and unity with nature. In losing these, we lost a part of ourselves as feeling beings. We became alienated from nature. Our technology and environment became totally inanimate, totally synthetic—a purely inorganic physical milieu that promoted the deanimization of man and his thought.

To bring the sun, the wind, the earth, indeed the world of life, back into technology, into the means of human survival, would be a revolutionary renewal of man's ties to nature. To restore this dependence in a way that evoked a sense of regional uniqueness in each community—a sense not only of generalized dependence but of dependence on a specific region with distinct qualities of its own—would give this renewal a truly ecological character. A real ecological system would emerge, a delicately interlaced pattern of local resources, honored by continual study and artful modification. With the growth of a true sense of regionalism every resource would find its place in a natural, stable balance, an organic unity of social, technological and natural elements. Art would assimilate technology by becoming social art, the art of the community as a whole. The free community would be able to rescale the tempo of life, the work patterns of man, its own architecture and its systems of transportation and communication to human dimensions. The electric car, quiet, slow-moving and clean, would become the preferred mode of urban transportation, replacing the noisy, filthy, highspeed automobile. Monorails would link community to community, reducing the number of highways that scar the countryside. Crafts would regain their honored position as supplements to mass manufacture; they would become a form of domestic, day-to-day artistry. A high standard of excellence, I believe, would replace the strictly quantitative criteria of production that prevail today; a respect for the durability of goods and the conservation of raw materials would replace the shabby, huckster-oriented criteria that result in built-in obsolescence and an insensate consumer society. The community would become a beautifully molded arena of life, a vitalizing source of culture and a deeply personal, ever-nourishing source of human solidarity.

TECHNOLOGY FOR LIFE

In a future revolution, the most pressing task of technology will be to produce a surfeit of goods with a minimum of toil. The immediate purpose of this task will be to open the social arena permanently to the revolutionary people, *to keep the revolution in permanence.* Thus far every social revolution has foundered because the peal of the tocsin could not be heard over the din of the workshop. Dreams of freedom and plenty were polluted by the mundane, workaday responsibility of producing the means of survival. Looking back at the brute facts of history, we find that as long as revolution meant continual sacrifice and denial for the people, the reins of power fell into the hands of the political "professionals," the mediocrities of Thermidor. How well the liberal Girondins of the French Convention understood this reality can be judged by their effort to reduce the revolutionary fervor of the Parisian popular assemblies—the great sections of 1793—by decreeing that the meetings should close "at ten in the evening," or, as Carlyle tells us, "before the working people come…" from their jobs.[24] The decree proved ineffective, but it was well aimed. Essentially, the tragedy of past revolutions has been that, sooner or later, their doors closed, "at ten in the evening." *The most critical function of modern technology must be to keep the doors of the revolution open forever!*

Nearly a half century ago, while Social-Democratic and Communist theoreticians babbled about a society with "work for all," the Dadaists, those magnificent madmen, demanded unemployment for everybody. The decades have detracted nothing from the significance of this demand, and they have added to its content. From the moment toil is reduced to the barest possible minimum or disappears entirely, the problems of survival pass into the problems of life, and technology itself passes from being the servant of man's immediate needs to being the partner of his creativity.

Let us look at this matter closely. Much has been written about technology as an "extension of man." The phrase is misleading if it is meant to apply to technology as a whole. It has validity primarily for the traditional handicraft shop and, perhaps, for the early stages of machine development. The craftsman dominates his tool; his labor, artistic inclinations, and personality are the sovereign factors in the productive process. Labor is not merely an expenditure of energy; it is also the personalized work of a man whose activities are sensuously directed toward preparing his product, fashioning it, and finally decorating it for human use. The craftsman guides the tool, not the tool the craftsman. Whatever alienation may exist between the craftsman and his product is immediately overcome, as Friedrich Wilhelmsen emphasized, "by an artistic judgment—a judgment bearing on a thing to be made."[25] The tool amplifies the powers of the craftsman as a *human;* it amplifies his power to exercise his artistry and impart his identity as a creative being to raw materials.

The development of the machine tends to rupture the intimate relationship between man and the means of production. It assimilates the worker to preset industrial tasks, tasks over which he exercises no control. The machine now appears as an alien force—apart from and yet wedded to the production of the means of survival. Although initially an "extension of man," technology is transformed into a force above man, orchestrating his life according to a score contrived by an industrial bureaucracy; not *men*, I repeat, but a *bureaucracy*, a *social machine*. With the arrival of mass production as the predominant mode of production, man became an extension of the machine, and not only of mechanical devices in the productive process but also of social devices in the social process. When he becomes an extension of a machine, man ceases to exist for his own sake. Society is ruled by the harsh maxim: "production for the sake of production." The decline from craftsman to worker, from an active to an increasingly passive personality, is completed by man *qua* consumer—an economic entity whose tastes, values, thoughts and sensibilities are engineered by bureaucratic "teams" in "think tanks." Man, standardized by machines, is reduced to a machine.

Man-the-machine is the bureaucratic ideal.* It is an ideal that is continually defied by the rebirth of life, by the reappearance of the young, and by the contradictions that unsettle the bureaucracy. Every generation has to be assimilated again, and each time with explosive resistance. The bureaucracy, in turn, never lives up to its own technical ideal. Congested with mediocrities, it errs continually. Its judgment lags behind new situations; insensate, it suffers from social inertia and is always buffeted by chance. Any crack that opens in the social machine is widened by the forces of life.

How can we heal the fracture that separates living men from dead machines without sacrificing either men or machines? How can we transform a technology for survival into a technology for life? To answer any of these questions with Olympian assurance would be idiotic. The future liberated men will choose from a large variety of mutually exclusive or combinable work styles, all of which will be based on unforeseeable

* The "ideal man" of the police bureaucracy is a being whose innermost thoughts can be invaded by lie detectors, electronic listening devices, and "truth" drugs. The "ideal man" of the political bureaucracy is a being whose innermost life can be shaped by mutagenic chemicals and socially assimilated by the mass media. The "ideal man" of the industrial bureaucracy is a being whose innermost life can be invaded by subliminal and predictively reliable advertising. The "ideal man" of the military bureaucracy is a being whose innermost life can be invaded by regimentation for genocide.

technological innovations. Or these humans of the future may simply choose to step over the body of technology. They may submerge the cybernated machine in a technological underworld, divorcing it entirely from social life, the community and creativity. All but hidden from society, the machines would work for man. Free communities would stand at the end of a cybernated assembly line with baskets to cart the goods home. Industry, like the autonomic nervous system, would work on its own, subject to the repairs that our own bodies require in occasional bouts of illness. The fracture separating man from machine would not be healed. It would simply be ignored.

Ignoring technology, of course, is no solution. Man would be closing off a vital human experience—the stimulus of productive activity, the stimulus of the machine. Technology can play a vital role in forming the personality of man. Every art, as Lewis Mumford has argued, has its technical side, requiring the self-mobilization of spontaneity into expressed order and providing contact with the objective world during the most ecstatic moments of experience.

A liberated society, I believe, will not want to negate technology precisely because it is liberated and can strike a balance. It may well want to assimilate the machine to artistic craftsmanship. By this I mean the machine will remove the toil from the productive process, leaving its artistic completion to man. The machine, in effect, will participate in human creativity. There is no reason why automatic, cybernated machinery cannot be used so that the finishing of products, especially those destined for personal use, is left to the community. The machine can absorb the toil involved in mining, smelting, transporting and shaping raw materials, leaving the final stages of artistry and craftsmanship to the individual. Most of the stones that make up a medieval cathedral were carefully squared and standardized to facilitate their laying and bonding—a thankless, repetitive and boring task that can now be done rapidly and effortlessly by modern machines. Once the stone blocks were set in place, the craftsmen made their appearance; toil was replaced by creative human work. In a liberated community the combination of industrial machines and the craftsman's tools could reach a degree of sophistication and of creative interdependence unparalleled in any period in human history. William Morris's vision of a return to craftsmanship would be freed of its nostalgic nuances. We could truly speak of a qualitatively new advance in technics—a technology for life.

Having acquired a vitalizing respect for the natural environment and its resources, the free decentralized community would give a new interpretation to the word "need." Marx's "realm of necessity," instead of expanding indefinitely, would tend to contract; needs would be humanized and scaled by a higher valuation of life and creativity. Quality and artistry would supplant the current emphasis on quantity and standardization; durability would replace the current emphasis on expendability; an economy of cherished things, sanctified by a sense of tradition and by a sense of wonder for the personality and artistry of dead generations, would replace the mindless seasonal restyling of commodities; innovations would be made with a sensitivity for the natural inclinations of man as distinguished from the engineered pollution of taste by the mass media. Conservation would replace waste in all things. Freed of bureaucratic manipulation, men would rediscover the beauty of a simpler, uncluttered material life. Clothing, diet, furnishings and homes would become more artistic, more personalized and more Spartan. Man would recover a sense of the things that are *for* man, as against the things that have been imposed upon man. The repulsive ritual of bargaining and hoarding would be replaced by the sensitive acts of making and giving. Things would cease to be the crutches for an impoverished ego and the mediators between aborted personalities; they would become the products of rounded, creative individuals and the gifts of integrated, developing selves.

A technology for life could play the vital role of integrating one community with another. Resealed to a revival of crafts and a new conception of material needs, technology could also function as the sinews of confederation. A national division of labor and industrial centralization are dangerous because technology begins to transcend the human scale; it becomes increasingly incomprehensible and lends itself to bureaucratic manipulation. To the extent that a shift away from community control occurs in real material terms (technologically and economically), centralized institutions acquire real power over the lives of men and threaten to become sources of coercion. A technology for life must be *based* on the community; it must be tailored to the community and the regional level. On this level, however, the sharing of factories and resources could actually promote solidarity between community groups; it could serve to confederate them on the basis not only of common spiritual and cultural interests but also of common material needs. Depending upon the resources and uniqueness of regions, a rational, humanistic balance could be struck between autarky, industrial confederation, and a national division of labor.

Is society so "complex" that an advanced industrial civilization stands in contradiction to a decentralized technology for life? My answer to this question is a categorical *no*. Much of the social "complexity" of our time originates in the paperwork, administration, manipulation and constant wastefulness of capitalist enterprise. The petty bourgeois stands in awe of the bourgeois filing system—the rows of cabinets filled with invoices, accounting books, insurance records, tax forms and the inevitable dossiers. He is spellbound by the "expertise" of industrial managers, engineers, stylemongers, financial manipulators, and the architects of market consent. He is totally mystified by the state—the police, courts, jails, federal offices, secretariats, the whole stinking, sick body of coercion, control and domination. Modern society is incredibly complex, complex even beyond human comprehension, if we grant its premises—property, "production for the sake of production," competition, capital accumulation, exploitation, finance, centralization, coercion, bureaucracy and the domination of man by man. Linked to every one of these premises are the institutions that actualize it—offices, millions of "personnel" forms, immense tons of paper, desks, typewriters, telephones, and, of course, rows upon rows of filing cabinets. As in Kafka's novels, these things are real but strangely dreamlike, indefinable shadows on the social landscape. The economy has a greater reality to it and is easily mastered by the mind and senses, but it too is highly intricate—if we grant that buttons must be styled in a thousand different forms, textiles varied endlessly in kind and pattern to create the illusion of innovation and novelty, bathrooms filled to overflowing with a dazzling variety of pharmaceuticals and lotions, and kitchens cluttered with an endless number of imbecile appliances. If we single out of this odious garbage one or two goods of high quality in the more useful categories and if we eliminate the money economy, the state power, the credit system, the paperwork and the police work required to hold society in an enforced state of want, insecurity and domination, society would not only become reasonably human but also fairly simple.

I do not wish to belittle the fact that behind a single yard of high quality electric wiring lies a copper mine, the machinery needed to operate it, a plant for producing insulating material, a copper smelting and shaping complex, a transportation system for distributing the wiring—and behind each of these complexes other mines, plants, machine shops and so forth. Copper mines, certainly of a kind that can be exploited by existing machinery, are not to be found everywhere, although enough copper and other useful metals can be recovered as scrap from the debris of our present society to provide future generations with all they need. But let us grant that copper will fall within the sizeable category of material that can be furnished only by a nationwide system of distribution. In what sense need there be a division of labor in the current sense of the term? There need be none at all. First, copper can be distributed, together with other goods, among free, autonomous communities, be they those that mine it or those that require it. This distribution system need not require the mediation of centralized bureaucratic institutions. Second, and perhaps more significant, a community that lives in a region with ample copper resources would not be a mere mining community. Copper mining would be one of the many economic activities in which it was engaged—a part of a larger, rounded, organic economic arena. The same would hold for communities whose climate was most suitable for growing specialized foods or whose resources were rare and uniquely valuable to society as a whole. Every community would approximate local or regional autarky. It would seek to achieve wholeness, because wholeness produces complete, rounded men who live in symbiotic relationship with their environment. Even if a substantial portion of the economy fell within the sphere of a national division of labor, the overall economic weight of society would still rest with the community. If there is no distortion of communities, there will be no sacrifice of any portion of humanity to the interests of humanity as a whole.

A basic sense of decency, sympathy and mutual aid lies at the core of human behavior. Even in this lousy bourgeois society we do not find it unusual that adults will rescue children from danger although the act may imperil their lives; we do not find it strange that miners, for example, will risk death to save their fellow workers in cave-ins or that soldiers will crawl under heavy fire to carry a wounded comrade to safety. What tends to shock us are those occasions when aid is refused—when the cries of a girl who has been stabbed and is being murdered are ignored in a middle-class neighborhood.

Yet there is nothing in this society that would seem to warrant a molecule of solidarity. What solidarity we do find exists despite the society, against all its realities, as an unending struggle between the innate decency of man and the innate indecency of society. Can we imagine how men would behave if this decency could find full release, if society earned the respect, even the love, of the individual? We are still the offspring of a violent, blood-soaked, ignoble history—the end products of man's domination of man. We may never end this condition of domination. The future may bring us and our shoddy civilization down in a Wagnerian *Gütterddämmerung.* How idiotic it would all be! But we may also end the domination of man by man. We may finally succeed in breaking the chain to the past and gain a humanistic, anarchist society. Would it not be the height of absurdity, indeed of impudence, to gauge the behavior of future generations by the very criteria we despise in our own time? Free men will not be greedy, one liberated community will not try to dominate another because it has a potential monopoly of copper, computer "experts" will not try to enslave grease monkeys, and sentimental novels about pining, tubercular virgins will not be written. We can ask only one thing of the free men and women of the future: to forgive us that it took so long and that it was such a hard pull. Like Brecht, we can ask that they try not to think of us too harshly, that they give us their sympathy and understand that we lived in the depths of a social hell.

But then, they will surely know what to think without our telling them.

New York
May 1965

Freedom has its forms. However personalized, individuated or dadaesque may be the attack upon prevailing institutions, a liberatory revolution always poses the question of what social forms will replace existing ones. At one point or another, a revolutionary people must deal with how it will manage the land and the factories from which it acquires the means of life. It must deal with the manner in which it will arrive at decisions that affect the community as a whole. Thus if revolutionary thought is to be taken at all seriously it must speak directly to the problems and forms of social management. It must open to public discussion the problems that are involved in a creative development of liberatory social forms. Although there is no theory of liberation that can replace experience, there is sufficient historical experience, and a sufficient theoretical formulation of the issues involved, to indicate what social forms are consistent with the fullest realization of personal and social freedom.

What social forms will replace existing ones depends on what relations free people decide to establish between themselves. Every personal relationship has a social dimension; every social relationship has a deeply personal side to it. Ordinarily, these two aspects and their relationship to each other are mystified and difficult to see clearly. The institutions created by hierarchical society, especially the state institutions, produce the illusion that social relations exist in a universe of their own, in specialized political or bureaucratic compartments. In reality, there exists no strictly "impersonal" political or social dimension; all the social institutions of the past and present depend on the relations between people in daily life, especially in those aspects of daily life which are necessary for survival—the production and distribution of the means of life, the rearing of the young, the maintenance and reproduction of life. The liberation of man—not in some vague "historical," moral, or philosophical sense, but in the intimate details of day-to-day life—is a profoundly social act and raises the problem of social forms as modes of relations between individuals.

The relationship between the social and the individual requires special emphasis in our own time, for never before have personal relations become so impersonal and never before have social relations become so asocial. Bourgeois society has brought all relations between people to the highest point of abstraction by divesting them of their *human* content and dealing with them as *objects*. The object—the commodity—takes on roles that formerly belonged to the community; exchange relationships (actualized in most cases as money relationships) supplant nearly all other modes of human relationships. In this respect, the bourgeois commodity system becomes the historical culmination of all societies, precapitalist as well as capitalist, in which human relationships are *mediated* rather than direct or face-to-face.

THE MEDIATION OF SOCIAL RELATIONS

To place this development in clearer perspective, let us briefly look back in time and establish what the mediation of social relations has come to mean.

The earliest social "specialists" who interposed themselves between people—the priests and tribal chiefs who permanently mediated their relations—established the *formal* conditions for hierarchy and exploitation. These formal conditions were consolidated and deepened by technological advances—advances which provided only enough material surplus for the few to live at the expense of the many. The tribal assembly, in which all members of the community had decided and directly managed their common affairs, dissolved into chieftainship, and the community dissolved into social classes.

Despite the increasing investiture of social control in a handful of men and even one man, the fact remains that men in precapitalist societies mediated the relations of other people—council supplanting assembly, and chieftainship supplanted council. In bourgeois society, on the other hand, the mediation of social relations by men is replaced by the mediation of social relations by *things*, by commodities. Having brought social mediation to the highest point of impersonality, commodity society turns attention to mediation as such; it brings into question *all* forms of social organization based on indirect representation, on the management of public affairs by the few, on the distinctive existence of concepts and practices such as "election," "legislation," "administration."

The most striking evidence of this social refocusing are the demands voiced almost intuitively by increasing numbers of American youth for tribalism and community. These demands are "regressive" only in the sense that they go back *temporally* to pre-hierarchical forms of freedom. They are profoundly progressive in the sense that they go back *structurally* to *non*-hierarchical forms of freedom.

By contrast, the traditional revolutionary demand for *council* forms of organization (what Hannah Arendt describes as "the revolutionary heritage") does not break completely with the terrain of hierarchical society. *Workers'* councils originate as *class* councils. Unless one assumes that workers are driven by their interests *as workers* to revolutionary measures against hierarchical society (an assumption I flatly deny), then these councils can be used just as much to perpetuate class society as to destroy it.* We shall see, in fact, that the council form contains many structural limitations which favor the development of hierarchy. For the present, it suffices to say that most advocates of workers' councils tend to conceive of people primarily as economic entities, either as workers or nonworkers. This conception leaves the onesidedness of the self completely intact. Man is viewed as a bifurcated being, the product of a social development that divides man from man and each man from himself.

Nor is this one-sided view completely corrected by demands for workers' management of production and the shortening of the work week, for these demands leave the *nature* of the work process and the *quality* of the worker's free time completely untouched. If workers' councils and workers' management of production do not transform the work into a joyful activity, free time into a marvelous experience, and the workplace into a community, then they remain merely formal structures, in fact, *class* structures. They perpetuate the limitations of the proletariat as a product of bourgeois social conditions. Indeed, no movement that raises the demand for workers' councils can be regarded as revolutionary unless it tries to promote sweeping transformations in the environment of the work place.

Finally, council organizations are forms of mediated relationships rather than face-to-face relationships. Unless these mediated relationships are limited by direct relationships, leaving policy decisions to the latter and mere administration to the former, the councils tend to become focuses of power. Indeed, unless the councils are finally assimilated by a popular assembly, and factories are integrated into new types of community, both the councils and the factories perpetuate the alienation between man and man and between man and work. Fundamentally, the degree of freedom in a society can be gauged by the kind of relationships that unite the people in it. If these relationships are open, unalienated and creative,

* For a discussion on the myth of the working class see "Listen, Marxist!"

the society will be free. If structures exist that inhibit open relationships, either by coercion or mediation, then freedom will not exist, whether there is workers' management of production or not. For *all* the workers will manage will be production—the preconditions of life, not the conditions of life. No mode of social organization can be isolated from the social conditions it is organizing. Both councils and assemblies have furthered the interests of hierarchical society as well as those of revolution. To assume that the forms of freedom can be treated merely as forms would be as absurd as to assume that legal concepts can be treated merely as questions of jurisprudence. The form and content of freedom, like law and society, are mutually determined. By the same token, there are forms of organization that promote and forms that vitiate the goal of freedom, and social conditions favor sometimes the one and sometimes the other. To one degree or another, these forms either alter the individual who uses them or inhibit his further development.

This article does not dispute the need for workers' councils—more properly, *factory committees*—as a revolutionary means of appropriating the bourgeois economy. On the contrary, experience has shown repeatedly that the factory committee is vitally important as an initial form of economic administration. But no revolution can settle for councils and committees as its final, or even its exemplary, mode of social organization, any more than "workers' management of production" can be regarded as a final mode of economic administration. Neither of these two relationships is *broad* enough to revolutionize work, free time, needs, and the structure of society as a whole. In this article I take the revolutionary aspect of the council and committee forms for granted; my purpose is to examine the conservative traits in them which vitiate the revolutionary project.

It has always been fashionable to look for models of social institutions in the so-called "proletarian" revolutions of the past hundred years. The Paris Commune of 1871, the Russian soviets of 1905 and 1917, the Spanish revolutionary syndicates of the 1930s, and the Hungarian councils of 1956 have all been raked over for examples of future social organization. What, it is worth asking, do these models of organization have in common? The answer is, very little, other than their limitations as mediated forms. Spain, as we shall see, provides a welcome exception: the others were either too short-lived or simply too distorted to supply us with more than the material for myths.

The Paris Commune may be revered for many different reasons—for its intoxicating sense of libidinal release, for its radical populism, for its deeply revolutionary impact on the oppressed, or for its defiant heroism in defeat. But the Commune itself, viewed as a *structural* entity, was little more than a popular municipal council. More democratic and plebeian than other such bodies, the council was nevertheless structured along parliamentary lines. It was elected by "citizens," grouped according to geographic constituencies. In combining legislation with administration, the Commune was hardly more advanced than the municipal bodies in the U.S. today.

Fortunately, revolutionary Paris largely ignored the Commune after it was installed. The insurrection, the actual management of the city's affairs, and finally the fighting against the Versaillese, were undertaken mainly by the popular clubs, the neighborhood vigilance committees, and the battalions of the National Guard. Had the Paris Commune (the Municipal Council) survived, it is extremely doubtful that it could have avoided conflict with these loosely formed street and militia formations. Indeed, by the end of April, some six weeks after the insurrection, the Commune constituted an "all-powerful" Committee of Public Safety, a body redolent with memories of the Jacobin dictatorship and the Terror, which suppressed not only the right in the Great Revolution of a century earlier, but also the left. In any case, history left the Commune a mere three weeks of life, two of which were consumed in the death throes of barricade fighting against Thiers and the Versaillese.

It does not malign the Paris Commune to divest it of "historical" burdens it never actually carried. The Commune was a festival of the streets, its partisans primarily handicraftsmen, itinerant intellectuals, the social debris of a precapitalist era, and lumpens. To regard these strata as "proletarian" is to caricature the word to the point of absurdity. The industrial proletariat constituted a minority of the Communards.*

The Commune was the last great rebellion of the French *sans-culottes*, a class that lingered on in Paris for a century after the Great Revolution.

* If we are to regard the bulk of the Communards as "proletarians," or describe any social stratum as "proletarian" (as the French Situationists do) simply because it has no control over the conditions of its life, we might just as well call slaves, serfs, peasants and large sections of the middle class "proletarians." To create such sweeping antitheses between "proletarian" and bourgeois, however, eliminates all the determinations that characterize these classes as specific, historically limited strata. This giddy approach to social analysis divests the industrial proletariat and the bourgeoisie of all the historically unique features which Marx believed he had discovered (a theoretical project that proved inadequate, although by no means false); it slithers away from the responsibilities of a serious critique of Marxism and the development of "laissez-faire" capitalism toward state capitalism, while pretending to retain continuity with the Marxian project.

Ultimately, this highly mixed stratum was destroyed not by the guns of the Versaillese but by the advance of industrialism.

The Paris Commune of 1871 was largely a city council, established to coordinate municipal administration under conditions of revolutionary unrest. The Russian soviets of 1905 were largely fighting organizations, established to coordinate near-insurrectionary strikes in St. Petersburg. These councils were based almost entirely on factories and trade unions: there was a delegate for every five hundred workers (where individual factories and shops contained a smaller number, they were grouped together for voting purposes), and additionally, delegates from trade unions and political parties. The soviet mode of organization took on its clearest and most stable form in St. Petersburg, where the soviet contained about four hundred delegates at its high point, including representatives of the newly organized professional unions. The St. Petersburg soviet rapidly developed from a large strike committee into a parliament of all oppressed classes, broadening its representation, demands and responsibilities. Delegates were admitted from cities outside St. Petersburg, political demands began to dominate economic ones, and links were established with peasant organizations and their delegates admitted into the deliberations of the body. Inspired by St. Petersburg, soviets sprang up in all the major cities and towns of Russia and developed into an incipient revolutionary power counterposed to all the governmental institutions of the autocracy.

The St. Petersburg soviet lasted less than two months. Most of its members were arrested in December 1905. To a large extent, the soviet was deserted by the St. Petersburg proletariat, which never rose in armed insurrection and whose strikes diminished in size and militancy as trade revived in the late autumn. Ironically, the last stratum to advance beyond the early militancy of the soviet were the Moscow students, who rose in insurrection on December 22 and during five days of brilliantly conceived urban guerrilla warfare reduced local police and military forces to near impotence. The students received very little aid from the workers in the city. Their street battles might have continued indefinitely, even in the face of massive proletarian apathy, had the czar's guard not been transported to Moscow by the railway workers on one of the few operating lines to the city.

The soviets of 1917 were the true heirs of the soviets of 1905, and to distinguish the two from each other, as some writers occasionally do, is spurious. Like their predecessors of twelve years earlier, the 1917 soviets were based largely on factories, trade unions and party organizations, but they were expanded to include delegates from army groups and a sizeable number of stray radical intellectuals. The soviets of 1917 reveal all the limitations of "sovietism." Though the soviets were invaluable as *local* fighting organizations, their *national* congresses proved to be increasingly unrepresentative bodies. The congresses were organized along very hierarchical lines. Local soviets in cities, towns and villages elected delegates to district and regional bodies; these elected delegates to the actual nationwide congresses. In larger cities, representation to the congresses was less indirect, but it was indirect nonetheless—from the voter in a large city to the municipal soviet and from the municipal soviet to the congress. In either case the congress was separated from the mass of voters by one or more representative levels.

The soviet congresses were scheduled to meet every three months. This permitted far too long a time span to exist between sessions. The first congress, held in June 1917, had some eight hundred delegates; later congresses were even larger, numbering a thousand or more delegates. To "expedite" the work of the congresses and to provide continuity of function between the tri-monthly sessions, the congresses elected an executive committee, fixed at not more than two hundred in 1918 and expanded to a maximum of three hundred in 1920. This body was to remain more or less in permanent session, but it too was regarded as unwieldy and most of its responsibilities after the October revolution were turned over to a small Council of People's Commissars. Having once acquired control of the Second Congress of Soviets (in October 1917), the Bolsheviks found it easy to centralize power in the Council of Commissars and later in the Political Bureau of the Communist Party. Opposition groups in the soviets either left the Second Congress or were later expelled from all soviet organs. The tri-monthly meetings of the congresses were permitted to lapse: the completely Bolshevik Executive Committee and Council of People's Commissars simply did not summon them. Finally, the congresses were held only once a year. Similarly, the intervals between the meetings of district and regional soviets grew increasingly longer and even the meetings of the Executive Committee, created by the congresses as a body in permanent session, became increasingly infrequent until finally they were held only three times a year. The power of the local soviets passed into the hands of the Executive Committee, the power of the Executive Committee passed into the hands of the Council of People's Commissars, and finally, the power of the Council of People's Commissars passed into the hands of the Political Bureau of the Communist Party.

That the Russian soviets were incapable of providing the anatomy for a truly popular democracy is to be ascribed not only to their hierarchical structure, but also to their limited social roots. The insurgent military battalions, from which the soviets drew their original striking power, were highly unstable, especially after the final collapse of the czarist armies. The newly formed Red Army was recruited, disciplined, centralized and tightly controlled by the Bolsheviks. Except for partisan bands and naval forces, soviet military bodies remained politically inert throughout the civil war. The peasant villages turned inward toward their local concerns, and were apathetic about national problems. This left the factories as the most important political base of the soviets. Here we encounter a basic contradiction in *class* concepts of revolutionary power: proletarian socialism, precisely because it emphasizes that power must be based exclusively on the factory, creates the conditions for a centralized, hierarchical political structure.

However much its social position is strengthened by a system of "self-management," the factory is not an autonomous social organism. The amount of social control the factory can exercise is fairly limited, for every factory is highly dependent for its operation and its very existence upon other factories and sources of raw materials. Ironically, the soviets, by basing themselves primarily in the factory and isolating the factory from its local environment, shifted power from the community and the region to the nation, and eventually from the base of society to its summit. The soviet system consisted of an elaborate skein of mediated social relationships, knitted along nationwide class lines.

Perhaps the only instance where a system of working class self-management succeeded as a mode of *class* organization was in Spain, where anarcho-syndicalism attracted a large number of workers and peasants to its banner. The Spanish anarcho-syndicalists *consciously* sought to limit the tendency toward centralization. The CNT (Confederación Nacional del Trabajo), the large anarcho-syndicalist union in Spain, created a dual organization with an elected committee system to act as a control on local bodies and national congresses. The assemblies had the power to revoke their delegates to the council and countermand council decisions. For all practical purposes the "higher" bodies of the CNT functioned as coordinating bodies. Let there be no mistake about the effectiveness of this scheme of organization: it imparted to each member of the CNT a weighty sense of responsibility, a sense of direct, immediate and personal influence in the activities and policies of the union. This responsibility was exercised with a high mindedness that made the CNT the most militant as well as the largest revolutionary movement in Europe during the interwar decades.

The Spanish Revolution of 1936 put the CNT system to a practical test, and it worked fairly well. In Barcelona, CNT workers seized the factories, transportation facilities and utilities, and managed them along anarcho-syndicalist lines. It remains a matter of record, attested to by visitors of almost every political persuasion, that the city's economy operated with remarkable success and efficiency—despite the systematic sabotage practiced by the bourgeois Republican government and the Spanish Communist Party. The experiment finally collapsed in shambles when the central government's assault troops occupied Barcelona in May 1937, following an uprising of the proletariat.

Despite their considerable influence, the Spanish anarchists had virtually no roots outside certain sections of the working class and peasantry. The movement was limited primarily to industrial Catalonia, the coastal Mediterranean areas, rural Aragon, and Andalusia. What destroyed the experiment was its isolation within Spain itself and the overwhelming forces—Republican as well as fascist, and Stalinist as well as bourgeois—that were mobilized against it.*

It would be fruitless to examine in detail the council modes of organization that emerged in Germany in 1918, in the Asturias in 1934, and in Hungary in 1956. The German councils were hopelessly perverted: the so-called "majority" (reformist) social democrats succeeded in gaining control of the newly formed councils and using them for counterrevolutionary ends. In Hungary and Asturias the councils were quickly destroyed by counterrevolution, but there is no reason to believe that, had they

* *This is not to ignore the disastrous political errors made by many "leading" Spanish anarchists. Although the leading anarchists were faced with the alternative of establishing a dictatorship in Catalonia, which they were not prepared to do (and rightly so!), this was no excuse for practicing opportunistic tactics all along the way.

developed further, they would have avoided the fate of the Russian soviets. History shows that the Bolsheviks were not the only ones to distort the council mode of operation. Even in anarcho-syndicalist Spain there is evidence that by 1937 the committee system of the CNT was beginning to clash with the assembly system; whatever the outcome might have been, the whole experiment was ended by the assault of the Communists and the Republican government against Barcelona.

The fact remains that council modes of organization are not immune to centralization, manipulation and perversion. These councils are still particularistic, one-sided and mediated forms of social management. At best, they can be the stepping stones to a decentralized society—at worst, they can easily be integrated into hierarchical forms of social organization.

ASSEMBLY AND COMMUNITY

Let us turn to the popular assembly for an insight into unmediated forms of social relations. The assembly probably formed the structural basis of early clan and tribal society until its functions were pre-empted by chiefs and councils. It appeared as the ecclesia in classical Athens; later, in a mixed and often perverted form, it reappeared in the medieval and Renaissance towns of Europe. Finally, as the "sections," assemblies emerged as the insurgent bodies in Paris during the Great Revolution. The ecclesia and the Parisian sections warrant the closest study. Both developed in the most complex cities of their time and both assumed a highly sophisticated form, often welding individuals of different social origins into a remarkable, albeit temporary, community of interests. It does not minimize their limitations to say that they developed methods of functioning so successfully libertarian in character that even the most imaginative utopias have failed to match in speculation what they achieved in practice.

The Athenian ecclesia was probably rooted in the early assemblies of the Greek tribes. With the development of property and social classes, it was replaced by a feudal social structure, lingering only in the social memory of the people. For a time, Athenian society seemed to be charting the disastrous course toward internal decay that Rome was to follow several centuries later. A large class of heavily mortgaged peasants, a growing number of serf-like sharecroppers, and a large body of urban laborers and slaves were polarized against a small number of powerful land magnates and a parvenu commercial middle class. By the sixth century B.C., all the conditions in Athens and Attica (the surrounding agricultural region) had ripened for a devastating social war.

The course of Athenian history was reversed by the reforms of Solon. In a series of drastic measures, the peasantry was restored to an economically viable condition, the landowners were shorn of most of their power, the ecclesia was revived, and a reasonably equitable system of justice was established. The trend toward a popular democracy continued to unfold for nearly a century and a half, until it achieved a form that has never quite been equaled elsewhere. By Periclean times the Athenians had perfected their polis to a point where it represented a triumph of rationality within the material limitations of the ancient world.

Structurally, the basis of the Athenian polis was the ecclesia. Shortly after sunrise at each prytany (the tenth day of the year), thousands of male citizens from all over Attica began to gather on the Pnyx, a hill directly outside Athens, for a meeting of the assembly. Here, in the open air, they leisurely disported themselves among groups of friends until the solemn intonation of prayers announced the opening of the meeting. The agenda, arranged under the three headings of "sacred," "profane" and "foreign affairs," had been distributed days earlier with the announcement of the assembly. Although the ecclesia could not add or bring forward anything that the agenda did not contain, its subject matter could be rearranged at the will of the assembly. No quorum was necessary, except for proposed decrees affecting individual citizens.

The ecclesia enjoyed complete sovereignty over all institutions and offices in Athenian society. It decided questions of war and peace, elected and removed generals, reviewed military campaigns, debated and voted upon domestic and foreign policy, redressed grievances, examined and passed upon the operations of administrative boards, and banished undesirable citizens. Roughly one man out of six in the citizen body was occupied at any given time with the administration of the community's affairs. Some fifteen hundred men, chosen mainly by lot, staffed the boards responsible for the collection of taxes, the management of shipping, food supply and public facilities, and the preparation of plans for public construction. The army, composed entirely of conscripts from each of the ten tribes of Attica, was led by elected officers; Athens was policed by citizen-bowmen and Scythian state slaves.

The agenda of the ecclesia was prepared by a body called the Council of 500. Lest the council gain any authority over the ecclesia, the Athenians carefully circumscribed its composition and functions. Chosen by lot from rosters of citizens who, in turn, were elected annually by the tribes, the Council was divided into ten subcommittees, each of which was on duty for a tenth of the year. Every day a president was selected by lot from among the fifty members of the subcommittee that was on duty to the polis. During his twenty-four hours of office, the Council's president held the state seal and the keys to the citadel and public archives and functioned as acting head of the country. Once he had been chosen, he could not occupy the position again.

Each of the ten tribes annually elected six hundred citizens to serve as "judges"—what we would call jurymen—in the Athenian courts. Every morning, they trudged up to the temple of Theseus, where lots were drawn for the trials of the day. Each court consisted of at least 201 jurymen and the trials were fair by any historical standard of juridical practice.

Taken as a whole, this was a remarkable system of social management; run almost entirely by amateurs, the Athenian polis reduced the formulation and administration of public policy to a completely public affair. "Here is no privileged class, no class of skilled politicians, no bureaucracy; no body of men, like the Roman Senate, who alone understood the secrets of State, and were looked up to and trusted as the gathered wisdom of the whole community," observes W. Warde Fowler. "At Athens there was no disposition, and in fact no need, to trust the experience of any one; each man entered intelligently into the details of his own temporary duties, and discharged them, as far as we can tell, with industry and integrity."[26] Overdrawn as this view may be for a class society that required slaves and denied women any role in the polis, the fact remains that Fowler's account is *essentially* accurate.

Indeed, the greatness of the achievement lies in the fact that Athens, despite the slave, patriarchal and class features it shared with classical society, as a whole developed into a working democracy in the literal sense of the term. No less significant, and perhaps consoling for our own time, is the fact that this achievement occurred when it seemed that the polis had charted a headlong course toward social decay. At its best, Athenian democracy greatly modified the more abusive and inhuman features of ancient society. The burdens of slavery were small by comparison with other historical periods, except when slaves were employed in capitalist enterprises. Generally, slaves were allowed to accumulate their own funds; on the yeoman farmsteads of Attica they generally worked under the same conditions and shared the same food as their masters; in Athens, they were indistinguishable in dress, manner and bearing from citizens—a source of ironical comment by foreign visitors. In many crafts, slaves not only worked side by side with freemen, but occupied supervisory positions over free workers as well as other slaves.

On balance, the image of Athens as a slave economy which built its civilization and generous humanistic outlook on the backs of human chattels is false—"false in its interpretation of the past and in its confident pessimism as to the future, willfully false, above all, in its cynical estimate of human nature," observes Edward Zimmerman. "Societies, like men, cannot live in compartments. They cannot hope to achieve greatness by making amends in their use of leisure for the lives they have brutalized in acquiring it. Art, literature, philosophy, and all other great products of a nation's genius, are no mere delicate growths of a sequestered hothouse culture; they must be sturdily rooted, and find continual nourishment, in the broad common soil of national life. That, if we are looking for lessons, is one we might learn from ancient Greece."[27]

In Athens, the popular assembly emerged as the final product of a sweeping social transition. In Paris, more than two millennia later, it emerged as the lever of social transition itself, as a revolutionary form and an insurrectionary force.

The Parisian sections of the early 1790s played the same role as organs of struggle as the soviets of 1905 and 1917, with the decisive difference that relations within the sections were not mediated by a hierarchical structure. Sovereignty rested with the revolutionary assemblies themselves, not above them. The Parisian sections emerged directly from the voting system established for elections to the Estates General. In 1789 the monarchy had divided the capital into sixty electoral districts, each of which formed an assembly of so called "active" or taxpaying citizens, the eligible voters of the city. These primary assemblies were expected to elect a body of electors which, in turn, was to choose the sixty representatives of the capital. After performing their electoral functions, the assemblies were required to disappear, but they remained on in defiance of the monarchy and constituted themselves into permanent municipal bodies. By degrees they turned into neighborhood assemblies of all "active" citizens, varying in form, scope and power from one district to another.

The municipal law of May 1790 reorganized the sixty districts into forty-eight sections. The law was intended to circumscribe the popular assemblies, but the sections simply ignored it. They continued to broaden their base and extend their control over Paris. On July 30, 1792, the Théâtre-Francais section swept aside the distinction between "active" and "passive" citizens, inviting the poorest and most destitute of the *sans-culottes* to participate in the assembly. Other sections followed the Théâtre-Francais, and from this period the sections became authentic popular organs—indeed the very soul of the Great Revolution. It was the sections which constituted the new revolutionary Commune of August 10, which organized the attack on the Tuileries and finally eliminated the Bourbon monarchy; it was the sections which decisively blocked the efforts of the Girondins to rouse the provinces against revolutionary Paris; it was the sections which, by ceaseless prodding, by their unending delegations and by armed demonstrations, provided the revolution with its remarkable leftward momentum after 1791.

The sections, however, were not merely fighting organizations; they represented genuine forms of self-management. At the high point of their development, they took over the complete administration of the city. Individual sections policed their own neighborhoods, elected their own judges, were responsible for the distribution of food, provided public aid to the poor, and contributed to the maintenance of the National Guard. With the declaration of war in April 1792 the sections took on the added tasks of enrolling volunteers for the revolutionary army and caring for their families, collecting donations for the war effort, and equipping and provisioning entire battalions. During the period of the "maximum," when controls were established over prices and wages to prevent a runaway inflation, the sections took responsibility for the maintenance of government-fixed prices. To provision Paris, the sections sent their representatives to the countryside to buy and transport food and see to its distribution at fair prices.

It must be borne in mind that this complex of extremely important activities was undertaken not by professional bureaucrats but, for the most part, by ordinary shopkeepers and craftsmen. The bulk of the sectional responsibilities were discharged after working hours, during the free time of the section members. The popular assemblies of the sections usually met during the evenings in neighborhood churches. Assemblies were ordinarily open to all the adults of the neighborhood. In periods of emergency, assembly meetings were held daily; special meetings could be called at the request of fifty members. Most administrative responsibilities were discharged by committees, but the popular assemblies established all the policies of the sections, reviewed and passed upon the work of all the committees, and replaced officers at will.

The forty-eight sections were coordinated through the Paris Commune, the municipal council of the capital. When emergencies arose, sections often cooperated with each other directly, through ad hoc delegates. This form of cooperation from below never crystalized into a permanent relationship. The Paris Commune of the Great Revolution never became an overbearing, ossified institution; it changed with almost every important political emergency, and its stability, form and functions depended largely upon the wishes of the sections. In the days preceding the uprising of August 10, 1792, for example, the sections simply suspended the old municipal council, confined Petion, the mayor of Paris, and, in the persons of their insurrectionary commissioners, took over all the authority of the Commune and the command of the National Guard. Almost the same procedure was followed nine months later when the Girondin deputies were expelled from the Convention, with the difference that the Commune, and Pache, the mayor of Paris, gave their consent (after some persuasive "gestures") to the uprising of the radical sections.

Having relied on the sections to fasten their hold on the Convention, the Jacobins began to rely on the Convention to destroy the sections. In September 1793 the Convention limited section assemblies to two a week; three months later the sections were deprived of the right to elect justices of the peace and divested of their role in organizing relief work. The sweeping centralization of France, which the Jacobins undertook between 1793 and 1794, completed the destruction of the sections.* The sections were denied control over the police and their administrative responsibilities were placed in the hands of salaried bureaucrats. By January 1794 the

* Marx, it may be noted, greatly admired the Jacobins for "centralizing" France and in the famous "Address of the Central Council" (1850) modeled his tactics for Germany on their policies. This was short-sightedness of incredible proportions—and institutional emphasis that revealed a gross insensitivity to the self-activity and the self-remaking of a people in revolutionary motion. See "Listen, Marxist!"

vitality of the sections had been thoroughly sapped. As Michelet observes: "The general assemblies of the sections were dead, and all their power had passed to their revolutionary committees, which, themselves being no longer elected bodies, but simply groups of officials nominated by the authorities, had not much life in them either." The sections had been subverted by the very revolutionary leaders they had raised to power in the Convention. When the time came for Robespierre, Saint-Just and Lebas to appeal to the sections against the Convention, the majority did virtually nothing in their behalf. Indeed, the revolutionary Gravilliers section—the men who had so earnestly supported Jacques Roux and the *enragés* in 1793—vindictively placed their arms at the service of the Thermidorians and marched against the Robespierrists—the Jacobin leaders, who, a few months earlier, had driven Roux to suicide and guillotined the spokesmen of the left.

FROM "HERE" TO "THERE"

The factors which undermined the assemblies of classical Athens and revolutionary Paris require very little discussion. In both cases the assembly mode of organization was broken up not only from without, but also from within—by the development of class antagonisms. There are no forms, however cleverly contrived, that can overcome the content of a given society. Lacking the material resources, the technology and the level of economic development to overcome class antagonisms as such, Athens and Paris could achieve an approximation of the forms of freedom only temporarily—and only to deal with the more serious threat of complete social decay. Athens held on to the ecclesia for several centuries, mainly because the polis still retained a living contact with tribal forms of organization; Paris developed its sectional mode of organization for a period of several years, largely because the *sans-culottes* had been precipitously swept to the head of the revolution by a rare combination of fortunate circumstances. Both the ecclesia and the sections were undermined by the very conditions they were intended to check—property, class antagonisms and exploitation—but which they were incapable of eliminating. What is remarkable about them is that they worked at all, considering the enormous problems they faced and the formidable obstacles they had to overcome.

It must be borne in mind that Athens and Paris were large cities, not peasant villages; indeed, they were complex, highly sophisticated urban centers by the standards of their time. Athens supported a population of more than a quarter of a million, Paris over seven hundred thousand. Both cities were engaged in worldwide trade; both were burdened by complex logistical problems; both had a multitude of needs that could be satisfied only by a fairly elaborate system of public administration. Although each had only a fraction of the population of present-day New York or London, their advantages on this score were more than canceled out by their extremely crude systems of communication and transportation, and by the need, in Paris at least, for members of the assembly to devote the greater part of the day to brute toil. Yet Paris, no less than Athens, was administered by amateurs: by men who, for several years and in their spare time, saw to the administration of a city in revolutionary ferment. The principal means by which they made their revolution, organized its conquests, and finally sustained it against counterrevolution at home and invasion abroad, was the neighborhood public assembly. There is no evidence that these assemblies and the committees they produced were inefficient or technically incompetent. On the contrary, they awakened a popular initiative, a resoluteness in action, and a sense of revolutionary purpose that no professional bureaucracy, however radical its pretensions, could ever hope to achieve. Indeed, it is worth emphasizing that Athens founded Western philosophy, mathematics, drama, historiography and art, and that revolutionary Paris contributed more than its share to the culture of the time and the political thought of the Western world. The arena for these achievements was not the traditional state, structured around a bureaucratic apparatus, but a system of unmediated relations, a face-to-face democracy organized into public assemblies.

The sections provide us with a rough model of assembly organization in a large city and during a period of revolutionary transition from a centralized political state to a potentially decentralized society. The ecclesia provides us with a rough model of assembly organization in a decentralized society. The word “model” is used deliberately. The ecclesia and the sections were lived experiences, not theoretical visions. But precisely because of this they validate in practice many anarchic theoretical speculations that have often been dismissed as “visionary” and “unrealistic.”

The goal of dissolving propertied society, class rule, centralization and the state is as old as the historical emergence of property, classes and states. In the beginning, the rebels could look backward to clans, tribes and federations; it was still a time when the past was closer at hand than the future. Then the past receded completely from man's vision and memory, except perhaps as a lingering dream of the "golden age" or the "Garden of Eden."* At this point the very notion of liberation becomes speculative and theoretical, and like all strictly theoretical visions its content was permeated with the social material of the present. Hence the fact that utopia, from More to Bellamy, is an image not of a hypothetical future, but of a present drawn to the logical conclusion of rationality—or absurdity. Utopia has slaves, kings, princes, oligarchs, technocrats, elites, suburbanites and a substantial petty bourgeoisie. Even on the left, it became customary to define the goal of a propertyless, stateless society as a series of approximations, of stages in which the end in view was attained by the use of the state. Mediated power entered into the vision of the future; worse, as the development of Russia indicates, it was strengthened to the point where the state today is not merely the "executive committee" of a specific class but a human condition. Life itself has become bureaucratized.

In envisioning the complete dissolution of the existing society, we cannot get away from the question of *power*—be it power over our own lives, the "seizure of power," or the dissolution of power. In going from the present to the future, from "here" to "there," we must ask: what is power? Under what conditions is it dissolved? And what does its dissolution mean? How do the forms of freedom, the unmediated relations of social life, emerge from a statified society, a society in which the state of unfreedom is carried to the point of absurdity—to domination for its own sake?

We begin with the historical fact that nearly all the major revolutionary upheavals began spontaneously:† witness the three days of "disorder" that preceded the takeover of the Bastille in July 1789, the defense of the artillery in Montmartre that led to the Paris Commune of 1871, the famous "five days" of February 1917 in Petrograd, the uprising of Barcelona in July 1936, the takeover of Budapest and the expulsion of the

* It was not until the 1860s, with the work of Bachofen and Morgan, that humanity rediscovered its communal past. By that time the discovery had become a purely critical weapon directed against the bourgeois family and property.

† Here, indeed, "history" has something to teach us—precisely because these spontaneous uprisings are not history but various manifestations of the same phenomenon: revolution. Whosoever calls himself a revolutionist and does not study these events on their *own* terms, thoroughly and without theoretical preconceptions, is a dilettante who is playing at revolution.

Russian army in 1956. Nearly all the great revolutions came from *below*, from the molecular movement of the "masses," their progressive individuation and their explosion—an explosion which invariably took the authoritarian "revolutionists" completely by surprise.

There can be no separation of the revolutionary process from the revolutionary goal. *A society based on self-administration must be achieved by means of self-administration.* This implies the forging of a self (yes, literally a forging in the revolutionary process) and a mode of administration which the self can possess.* If we define "power" as the power of man over man, power can only be destroyed by the very process in which man acquires power over his own life and in which he not only "discovers" himself but, more meaningfully, formulates his selfhood in all its social dimensions.

Freedom, so conceived, cannot be "delivered" to the individual as the "end product" of a "revolution"—much less as a "revolution" achieved by social-philistines who are hypnotized by the trappings of authority and power. The assembly and community cannot be legislated or decreed into existence. To be sure, a revolutionary group can purposively and consciously seek to promote the creation of these forms; but if assembly and community are not allowed to emerge organically, if their growth is not instigated, developed and matured by the social processes at work, they will not be really popular forms. Assembly and community must arise from within the revolutionary process itself; indeed, the revolutionary process must *be* the formation of assembly and community, and with it, the destruction of power. Assembly and community must become "fighting words," not distant panaceas. They must be created as *modes of struggle* against the existing society, not as theoretical or programmatic abstractions.

It is hardly possible to stress this point strongly enough. The future assemblies of people in the block, the neighborhood or the district—the revolutionary sections to come—will stand on a higher social level than all the present-day committees, syndicates, parties and clubs adorned by the most resounding "revolutionary" titles. They will be the living nuclei of utopia in the decomposing body of bourgeois society. Meeting in auditoriums, theaters, courtyards, halls, parks and—like their forerunners, the

* What Wilhelm Reich and, later, Herbert Marcuse have made clear is that "selfhood" is not only a personal dimension but also a social one. The self that finds expression in the assembly and community is, literally, the assembly and community that has found self-expression—a complete congruence of form and content.

sections of 1793—in churches, they will be the arenas of demassification, for the very *essence* of the revolutionary process is people acting as individuals.

At this point the assembly may be faced not only with the power of the bourgeois state—the famous problem of "dual power"—but with the danger of the incipient state. Like the Paris sections, it will have to fight not only against the Convention, but also against the tendency to create mediated social forms.* The factory committees, which will almost certainly be the forms that will take over industry, must be managed directly by workers' assemblies in the factories. By the same token, neighborhood committees, councils and boards must be rooted completely in the neighborhood assembly. They must be answerable at every point to the assembly; they and their work must be under continual review by the assembly; and finally, their members must be subject to immediate recall by the assembly. The specific gravity of society, in short, must be shifted to its base—the armed people in permanent assembly.

As long as the arena of the assembly is the modern bourgeois city, the revolution is faced with a recalcitrant environment. The bourgeois city, by its very nature and structure, fosters centralization, massification and manipulation. Inorganic, gargantuan, and organized like a factory, the city tends to inhibit the development of an organic, rounded community. In its role as the universal solvent, the assembly must try to dissolve the city itself.

We can envision young people renewing social life just as they renew the human species. Leaving the city, they begin to found the nuclear ecological communities to which older people repair in increasing numbers. Large resource pools are mobilized for their use; careful ecological surveys and suggestions are placed at their disposal by the most competent and imaginative people available. The modern city begins to shrivel, to contract and to disappear, as did its ancient progenitors millennia earlier. In the new, rounded ecological community, the assembly finds its authentic environment and true shelter. Form and content now correspond completely. The journey from "here" to "there," from sections to ecclesia, from cities to communities, is completed. No longer is the factory a particularized phenomenon; it now becomes an organic part of the community. In

* Together with disseminating ideas, the most important job of the anarchists will be to defend the spontaneity of the popular movement by continually engaging the authoritarians in a theoretical and organizational duel.

this sense, it is no longer a factory. The dissolution of the factory into the community completes the dissolution of the last vestiges of propertied, of class, and, above all, of mediated society into the new polis. And now the real drama of human life can unfold, in all its beauty, harmony, creativity and joy.

New York
January 1968

All the old crap of the thirties is coming back again—the shit about the "class line," the "role of the working class," the "trained cadres", the "vanguard party," and the "proletarian dictatorship." It's all back again, and in a more vulgarized form than ever. The Progressive Labor Party is not the only example, it is merely the worst. One smells the same shit in various offshoots of SDS, and in the Marxist and Socialist clubs on campuses, not to speak of the Trotskyist groups, the International Socialist Clubs, and Youth Against War and Fascism.

In the thirties, at least it was understandable. The United States was paralyzed by a chronic economic crisis, the deepest and longest in its history. The only living forces that seemed to be battering at the walls of capitalism were the great organizing drives of the CIO, with their dramatic sitdown strikes, their radical militancy, and their bloody clashes with the police. The political atmosphere throughout the entire world was charged by the electricity of the Spanish Civil War, the last of the classical workers' revolutions, when every radical sect in the American left could identify with its own militia columns in Madrid and Barcelona. That was thirty years ago. It was a time when anyone who cried out "Make love, not war" would have been regarded as a freak; the cry then was "Make jobs, not war"—the cry of an age burdened by scarcity, when the achievement of socialism entailed "sacrifices" and a "transition period" to an economy of material abundance. To an eighteen-year-old kid in 1937 the very concept of cybernation would have seemed like the wildest science fiction, a fantasy comparable to visions of space travel. That eighteen-year-old kid has now reached fifty years of age, and his roots are planted in an era so remote as to differ *qualitatively* from the realities of the present period in the United States. Capitalism itself has changed since then, taking on increasingly statified forms that could be anticipated only dimly thirty years ago. And now we are being asked to go back to the "class line," the "strategies," the "cadres" and the organizational forms of that distant period in almost blatant disregard of the new issues and possibilities that have emerged.

When the hell are we finally going to create a movement that looks to the future instead of to the past? When will we begin to learn from what is being born instead of what is dying? Marx, to his lasting credit, tried to do that in his own day; he tried to evoke a futuristic spirit in the revolutionary movement of the 1840s and 1850s. "The tradition of all the dead generations weighs like a nightmare on the brain of the living," he wrote in *The Eighteenth Brumaire of Louis Bonaparte.* "And just when they seem to be engaged in revolutionizing themselves and things, in creating something entirely new, precisely in such epochs of revolutionary crisis they anxiously conjure up the spirits of the past to their service and borrow from them names, battle slogans and costumes in order to present the new scene of world history in this time-honored disguise and borrowed language. Thus Luther donned the mask of the Apostle Paul, the revolution of 1789 to 1814 draped itself alternately as the Roman Republic and the Roman Empire, and the revolution of 1848 knew nothing better than to parody, in turn, 1789 and the tradition of 1793 to 1795... The social revolution of the nineteenth century cannot draw its poetry from the past, but only from the future. It cannot begin with itself before it has stripped off all superstition in regard to the past... In order to arrive at its content, the revolution of the nineteenth century must let the dead bury their dead. There the phrase went beyond the content; here the content goes beyond the phrase."[28]

Is the problem any different today, as we approach the twenty-first century? Once again the dead are walking in our midst—ironically, draped in the name of Marx, the man who tried to bury the dead of the nineteenth century. So the revolution of our own day can do nothing better than parody, in turn, the October Revolution of 1917 and the civil war of 1918–1920, with its "class line," its Bolshevik Party, its "proletarian dictatorship," its puritanical morality, and even its slogan, "soviet power." The complete, all-sided revolution of our own day that can finally resolve the historic "social question," born of scarcity, domination and hierarchy, follows the tradition of the partial, the incomplete, the one-sided revolutions of the past, which merely changed the form of the "social question," replacing one system of domination and hierarchy by another. At a time when bourgeois society itself is in the process of disintegrating all the social classes that once gave it stability, we hear the hollow demands for a "class line." At a time when all the political institutions of hierarchical society are entering a period of profound decay, we hear the hollow demands for a "political party" and a "workers' state." At a time when hierarchy as such is being brought into question, we hear the hollow demands for "cadres," "vanguards" and "leaders." At a time when centralization and the state have been brought to the most explosive point of historical negativity, we hear the hollow demands for a "centralized movement" and a "proletarian dictatorship."

This pursuit of security in the past, this attempt to find a haven in a fixed dogma and an organizational hierarchy as substitutes for creative thought and praxis is bitter evidence of how little many revolutionaries are capable of "revolutionizing themselves and things," much less of revolutionizing society as a whole. The deep-rooted conservatism of the PLP* "revolutionaries" is almost painfully evident; the authoritarian leader and hierarchy replace the patriarch and the school bureaucracy; the discipline of the Movement replaces the discipline of bourgeois society; the authoritarian code of political obedience replaces the state; the credo of "proletarian morality" replaces the mores of puritanism and the work ethic. The old substance of exploitative society reappears in new forms, draped in a red flag, decorated by portraits of Mao (or Castro or Che) and adorned with the little "Red Book" and other sacred litanies.

The majority of the people who remain in the PLP today deserve it. If they can live with a movement that cynically dubs its own slogans into photographs of DRUM pickets;† if they can read a magazine that asks whether Marcuse is a "copout or cop"; if they can accept a "discipline" that reduces them to poker-faced, programmed automata; if they can use the most disgusting techniques (techniques borrowed from the cesspool of bourgeois business operations and parliamentarianism) to manipulate other organizations; if they can parasitize virtually every action and situation merely to promote the growth of their party—even if this means defeat for the action itself—then they are beneath contempt. For these people to call themselves reds and describe attacks upon them as redbaiting is a form of McCarthyism in reverse. To rephrase Trotsky's juicy description of Stalinism, they are the syphilis of the radical youth movement today. And for syphilis there is only one treatment—an antibiotic, not an argument.

Our concern here is with those honest revolutionaries who have turned to Marxism, Leninism or Trotskyism because they earnestly seek a

* These lines were written when the Progressive Labor Party (PLP) exercised a great deal of influence in SDS. Although the PLP has now lost most of its influence in the student movement, the organization still provides a good example of the mentality and values prevalent in the Old Left. The above characterization is equally valid for most Marxist-Leninist groups, hence this passage and other references to the PLP have not been substantially altered.

† The Dodge Revolutionary Union Movement, part of the Detroit based League of Revolutionary Black Workers.

coherent social outlook and an effective strategy of revolution. We are also concerned with those who are awed by the theoretical repertory of Marxist ideology and are disposed to flirt with it in the absence of more systematic alternatives. To these people we address ourselves as brothers and sisters and ask for a serious discussion and a comprehensive re-evaluation. We believe that Marxism has ceased to be applicable to our time not because it is too visionary or revolutionary, but because it is not visionary or revolutionary enough. We believe it was born of an era of scarcity and presented a brilliant critique of that era, specifically of industrial capitalism, and that a new era is in birth which Marxism does not adequately encompass and whose outlines it only partially and onesidedly anticipated. We argue that the problem is not to "abandon" Marxism or to "annul" it, but to transcend it dialectically, just as Marx transcended Hegelian philosophy, Ricardian economics, and Blanquist tactics and modes of organization. We shall argue that in a more advanced stage of capitalism than Marx dealt with a century ago, and in a more advanced stage of technological development than Marx could have clearly anticipated, a new critique is necessary, which in turn yields new modes of struggle, of organization, of propaganda and of lifestyle. Call these new modes whatever you will, even "Marxism" if you wish. We have chosen to call this new approach post-scarcity anarchism, for a number of compelling reasons which will become evident in the pages that follow.

THE HISTORICAL LIMITS OF MARXISM

The idea that a man whose greatest theoretical contributions were made between 1840 and 1880 could "foresee" the entire dialectic of capitalism is, on the face of it, utterly preposterous. If we can still learn much from Marx's insights, we can learn even more from the unavoidable errors of a man who was limited by an era of material scarcity and a technology that barely involved the use of electric power. We can learn how different our own era is from that of *all* past history, how qualitatively new are the potentialities that confront us, how unique are the issues, analyses and praxis that stand before us if we are to make a revolution and not another historical abortion.

The problem is not that Marxism is a "method" which must be reapplied to "new situations" or that "neo-Marxism" has to be developed to overcome the limitations of "classical Marxism." The attempt to rescue the Marxian pedigree by emphasizing the method over the system or by adding "neo" to a sacred word is sheer mystification if all the *practical* conclusions of the system flatly contradict these efforts.* Yet this is precisely the state of affairs in Marxian exegesis today. Marxists lean on the fact that the system provides a brilliant interpretation of the past while willfully ignoring its utterly misleading features in dealing with the present and future. They cite the coherence that historical materialism and the class analysis give to the interpretation of history, the economic insights of *Capital* provides into the development of industrial capitalism, and the brilliance of Marx's analysis of earlier revolutions and the tactical conclusions he established, without once recognizing that qualitatively new problems have arisen which never existed in his day. Is it conceivable that historical problems and methods of class analysis based entirely on unavoidable scarcity can be transplanted into a new era of potential abundance? Is it conceivable that an economic analysis focused primarily on a "freely competitive" system of industrial capitalism can be transferred to a managed system of capitalism, where state and monopolies combine to manipulate economic life? Is it conceivable that a strategic and tactical repertory formulated in a period when coal and steel constituted the basis of industrial technology can be transferred to an age based on radically new sources of energy, on electronics, on cybernation?

As a result of this transfer, a theoretical corpus which was liberating a century ago is turned into a straitjacket today. We are asked to focus on the working class as the "agent" of revolutionary change at a time when capitalism visibly antagonizes and produces revolutionaries among virtually all strata of society, particularly the young. We are asked to guide our tactical methods by the vision of a "chronic economic crisis" despite the fact that no such crisis has been in the offing for thirty years.† We are asked to accept a "proletarian dictatorship"—a long "transitional period" whose function is not merely the suppression of counterrevolutionaries

* Marxism is above all a theory of praxis, or to place this relationship in its correct perspective, a praxis of theory. This is the very meaning of Marx's transformation of dialectics, which took it from the subjective dimension (to which the Young Hegelians still tried to confine Hegel's outlook) into the objective, from philosophical critique into social action. If theory and praxis become divorced, Marxism is not killed, it commits suicide. This is its most admirable and noble feature. The attempts of the cretins who follow in Marx's wake to keep the system alive with a patchwork of emendations, exegesis, and half-assed "scholarship" a la Maurice Dobb and George Novack are degrading insults to Marx's name and a disgusting pollution of everything he stood for.

† In fact Marxists do very little talking about the "chronic [economic] crisis of capitalism" these days—despite the fact that this concept forms the focal point of Marx's economic theories.

but above all the development of a technology of abundance—at a time when a technology of abundance is at hand. We are asked to orient our "strategies" and "tactics" around poverty and material immiseration at a time when revolutionary sentiment is being generated by the banality of life under conditions of material abundance. We are asked to establish political parties, centralized organizations, "revolutionary" hierarchies and elites, and a new state at a time when political institutions as such are decaying and when centralization, elitism and the state are being brought into question on a scale that has never occurred before in the history of hierarchical society.

We are asked, in short, to return to the past, to diminish instead of grow, to force the throbbing reality of our times, with its hopes and promises, into the deadening preconceptions of an outlived age. We are asked to operate with principles that have been transcended not only theoretically but by the very development of society itself. History has not stood still since Marx, Engels, Lenin and Trotsky died, nor has it followed the simplistic direction which was charted out by thinkers—however brilliant—whose minds were still rooted in the nineteenth century or in the opening years of the twentieth. We have seen capitalism itself perform many of the tasks (including the development of a technology of abundance) which were regarded as socialist; we have seen it "nationalize" property, merging the economy with the state wherever necessary. We have seen the working class neutralized as the "agent of revolutionary change," albeit still struggling within a *bourgeois* framework for more wages, shorter hours and "fringe" benefits. The class struggle in the *classical* sense has not disappeared; it has suffered a more deadening fate by being co-opted into capitalism. The revolutionary struggle within the advanced capitalist countries has shifted to a historically new terrain: it has become a struggle between a generation of youth that has known no chronic economic crisis and the culture, values and institutions of an older, conservative generation whose perspective on life has been shaped by scarcity, guilt, renunciation, the work ethic and the pursuit of material security. Our enemies are not only the visibly entrenched bourgeoisie and the state apparatus but also an outlook which finds its support among liberals, social democrats, the minions of a corrupt mass media, the "revolutionary" parties of the past, and, painful as it may be to the acolytes of Marxism, the worker dominated by the factory hierarchy, by the industrial routine, and by the work ethic. The point is that the divisions now cut across virtually all the traditional class lines and they raise a spectrum of problems that none of the Marxists, leaning on analogies with scarcity societies, could foresee.

THE MYTH OF THE PROLETARIAT

Let us cast aside all the ideological debris of the past and cut to the theoretical roots of the problem. For our age, Marx's greatest contribution to revolutionary thought is his dialectic of social development. Marx laid bare the great movement from primitive communism through private property to communism in its higher form—a communal society resting on a liberatory technology. In this movement, according to Marx, man passes on from the domination of man by nature, to the domination of man by man, and finally to the domination of nature by man* and from social domination as such. Within this larger dialectic, Marx examines the dialectic of capitalism itself—a social system which constitutes the last historical "stage" in the domination of man by man. Here, Marx makes not only profound contributions to contemporary revolutionary thought (particularly in his brilliant analysis of the commodity relationship) but also exhibits those limitations of time and place that play so confining a role in our own time.

The most serious of these limitations emerges from Marx's attempt to explain the transition from capitalism to socialism, from a class society to a classless society. It is vitally important to emphasize that this explanation was reasoned out almost entirely by analogy with the transition of feudalism to capitalism—that is, *from one class society to another class society*, from one system of property to another. Accordingly, Marx points out that just as the bourgeoisie developed within feudalism as a result of the split between town and country (more precisely, between crafts and agriculture), so the modern proletariat developed within capitalism as a result of the advance of industrial technology. Both classes, we are told, develop social interests of their own—indeed, revolutionary social interests that throw them against the old society in which they were spawned. If the bourgeoisie gained control over economic life long before it overthrew feudal society, the proletariat, in turn, gains its own revolutionary power by

* For ecological reasons, we do not accept the notion of the "domination of nature by man" in the simplistic sense that was passed on by Marx a century ago. For a discussion of this problem, see "Ecology and Revolutionary Thought."

the fact that it is "disciplined, united, organized" by the factory system.* In both cases, the development of the productive forces becomes incompatible with the traditional system of social relations. "The integument is burst asunder." The old society is replaced by the new.

The critical question we face is this: can we explain the transition from a class society to a classless society by means of the same dialectic that accounts for the transition of one class society to another? This is not a textbook problem that involves the juggling of logical abstractions but a very real and concrete issue for our time. There are profound differences between the development of the bourgeoisie under feudalism and the development of the proletariat under capitalism which Marx either failed to anticipate or never faced clearly. The bourgeoisie controlled economic life long before it took state power; it had become the dominant class materially, culturally and ideologically before it asserted its dominance politically. The proletariat does not control economic life. Despite its indispensable role in the industrial process, the industrial working class is not even a majority of the population, and its strategic economic position is being eroded by cybernation and other technological advances.† Hence it requires an act of high consciousness for the proletariat to use its power to achieve a social revolution. Until now, the achievement of this consciousness has been blocked by the fact that the factory milieu is one of the most well-entrenched arenas of the work ethic, of hierarchical systems of management, of obedience to leaders, and in recent times of production committed to superfluous commodities and armaments. The factory serves not only to "discipline," "unite," and "organize" the workers, but also to do so in a thoroughly bourgeois fashion. In the factory, capitalistic

* It is ironic that Marxists who talk about the "economic power" of the proletariat are actually echoing the position of the anarcho-syndicalists, a position that Marx bitterly opposed. Marx was not concerned with the "economic power" of the proletariat but with its *political* power; notably the fact that it would become the majority of the population. He was convinced that the *industrial* workers would be driven to revolution primarily by material destitution which would follow from the tendency of capitalist accumulation; that, *organized* by the factory system and *disciplined* by industrial routine, they would be able to constitute trade unions and, above all, political parties, which in some countries would be obliged to use insurrectionary methods and in others (England, the United States, and in later years Engels added France) might well come to power in elections and legislate socialism into existence. Characteristically, many Marxists have been as dishonest with their Marx and Engels as the Progressive Labor Party has been with the readers of *Challenge*, leaving important observations untranslated or grossly distorting Marx's meaning.

† This is as good a place as any to dispose of the notion that anyone is a "proletarian" who has nothing to sell but his labor power. It is true that Marx defined the proletariat in these terms, but he also worked out a historical dialectic in the development of the proletariat. The proletariat developed out of a propertyless exploited class, reaching its most advanced form in the *industrial* proletariat, which corresponded to the most advanced form of capital. In the later years of his life, Marx came to despise the Parisian workers, who were engaged preponderantly in the production of luxury goods, citing "our German workers"—the most robot-like in Europe—as the "model" proletariat of the world.

production not only renews the social relations of capitalism with each working day, as Marx observed, it also renews the psyche, values and ideology of capitalism.

Marx sensed this fact sufficiently to look for reasons more compelling than the mere fact of exploitation or conflicts over wages and hours to propel the proletariat into revolutionary action. In his general theory of capitalist accumulation he tried to delineate the harsh, objective laws that force the proletariat to assume a revolutionary role. Accordingly he developed his famous theory of immiseration: competition between capitalists compels them to undercut each others' prices, which in turn leads to a continual reduction of wages and the absolute impoverishment of the workers. The proletariat is compelled to revolt because with the process of competition and the centralization of capital there "grows the mass of misery, oppression, slavery, degradation."*

But capitalism has not stood still since Marx's day. Writing in the middle years of the nineteenth century, Marx could not be expected to grasp the full consequences of his insights into the centralization of capital and the development of technology. He could not be expected to foresee that capitalism would develop not only from mercantilism into the dominant industrial form of his day—from state-aided trading monopolies into highly competitive industrial units—but further, that with the centralization of capital, capitalism returns to its mercantilist origins on a higher level of development and reassures the state-aided monopolistic form. The economy tends to merge with the state and capitalism begins to "plan" its development instead of leaving it exclusively to the interplay of competition and market forces. To be sure, the system does not abolish the traditional class struggle, but manages to contain it, using its immense technological resources to assimilate the most strategic sections of the working class.

Thus the full thrust of the immiseration theory is blunted and in the United States the traditional class struggle fails to develop into the class

* The attempt to describe Marx's immiseration theory in international terms instead of national (as Marx did) is sheer subterfuge. In the first place, this theoretical legerdemain simply tries to sidestep the question of why immiseration has not occurred within the industrial strongholds of capitalism, the *only areas which form a technologically adequate point of departure for a classless society.* If we are to pin our hopes on the colonial world as "the proletariat," this position conceals a very real danger: genocide. America and her recent ally Russia have all the technical means to bomb the underdeveloped world into submission. A threat lurks on the historical horizon—the development of the United States into a truly fascist imperium of the nazi type. It is sheer rubbish to say that this country is a "paper tiger." It is a thermonuclear tiger and the American ruling class, lacking any cultural restraints, is capable of being even more vicious than the German.

war. It remains entirely within bourgeois dimensions. Marxism, in fact, becomes ideology. It is assimilated by the most advanced forms of the state capitalist movement—notably Russia. By an incredible irony of history, Marxian "socialism" turns out to be in large part the very state capitalism that Marx failed to anticipate in the dialectic of capitalism.* The proletariat, instead of developing into a revolutionary class within the womb of capitalism, turns out to be an organ within the body of bourgeois society.

The question we must ask at this late date in history is whether a social revolution that seeks to achieve a classless society can emerge from a conflict between traditional classes in a class society, or whether such a social revolution can only emerge from the decomposition of the traditional classes, indeed from the emergence of an entirely new "class" *whose very essence is that it is a non-class,* a growing stratum of revolutionaries. In trying to answer this question, we can learn more by returning to the broader dialectic which Marx developed for human society as a whole than from the model he borrowed from the passage of feudal into capitalist society. Just as primitive kinship clans began to differentiate into classes, so in our own day there is a tendency for classes to decompose into entirely new subcultures which bear a resemblance to non-capitalist forms of relationships. These are not strictly economic groups any more; in fact, they reflect the tendency of the social development to transcend the economic categories of scarcity society. They constitute, in effect, a crude, ambiguous *cultural* preformation of the movement of scarcity into post-scarcity society.

The process of class decomposition must be understood in all its dimensions. The word "process" must be emphasized here: the traditional classes do not disappear, nor for that matter does the class struggle. Only a social revolution could remove the prevailing class structure and the conflicts it engenders. The point is the traditional class struggle ceases to have revolutionary implications; it reveals itself as the physiology of the prevailing society, not as the labor pains of birth. In fact the traditional class struggle stabilizes capitalist society by "correcting" its abuses (in wages, hours, inflation, employment, etc.). The unions in capitalist society constitute themselves into a counter- "monopoly" to the industrial

* Lenin sensed this and described "socialism" as "nothing but state capitalist monopoly *made to benefit the whole people.*"[29] This is an extraordinary statement if one thinks out its implications, and a mouthful of contradictions.

monopolies and are incorporated into the neomercantile statified economy as an estate. Within this estate there are lesser or greater conflicts, but taken as a whole the unions strengthen the system and serve to perpetuate it.

To reinforce this class structure by babbling about the "role of the working class," to reinforce the traditional class struggle by imputing a "revolutionary" content to it, to infect the new revolutionary movement of our time with "workeritis" is *reactionary to the core.* How often do the Marxian doctrinaires have to be reminded that the history of the class struggle is the history of a disease, of the wounds opened by the famous "social question," of man's one-sided development in trying to gain control over nature by dominating his fellow man? If the byproduct of this disease has been technological advance, the main products have been repression, a horrible shedding of human blood, and a terrifying distortion of the human psyche.

As the disease approaches its end, as the wounds begin to heal in their deepest recesses, the process now unfolds toward wholeness; the *revolutionary* implications of the traditional class struggle lose their meaning as theoretical constructs and as social reality. The process of decomposition embraces not only the traditional class structure but also the patriarchal family, authoritarian modes of upbringing, the influence of religion, the institutions of the state, and the mores built around toil, renunciation, guilt and repressed sexuality. *The process of disintegration, in short, now becomes generalized and cuts across virtually all the traditional classes, values and institutions. It creates entirely new issues, modes of struggle and forms of organization and calls for an entirely new approach to theory and praxis.*

What does this mean concretely? Let us contrast two approaches, the Marxian and the revolutionary. The Marxian doctrinaire would have us approach the worker—or better, "enter" the factory—and proselytize him in "preference" to anyone else. The purpose?—to make the worker "class conscious." To cite the most neanderthal examples from the old left, one cuts one's hair, grooms oneself in conventional sports clothing, abandons pot for cigarettes and beer, dances conventionally, affects "rough" mannerisms, and develops a humorless, deadpan and pompous mien.*

* On this score, the Old Left projects its own neanderthal image on the American worker. Actually this image more closely approximates the character of the union bureaucrat or the Stalinist commissar.

One becomes, in short, what the worker is at his most caricaturized worst: not a "petty bourgeois degenerate," to be sure, but a *bourgeois* degenerate. One becomes an imitation of the worker insofar as the worker is an imitation of his masters. Beneath this metamorphosis of the student into the "worker" lies a vicious cynicism. One tries to use the discipline inculcated by the factory milieu to discipline the worker to the party milieu. One tries to use the worker's respect for the industrial hierarchy to wed the worker to the party hierarchy. This disgusting process, which if successful could lead only to the substitution of one hierarchy for another, is achieved by pretending to be concerned with the worker's economic day-to-day demands. Even Marxian theory is degraded to accord with this debased image of the worker. (See almost any copy of *Challenge*—the *National Enquirer* of the left. Nothing bores the worker more than this kind of literature.) In the end, the worker is shrewd enough to know that he will get better results in the day-to-day class struggle through his union bureaucracy than through a Marxian party bureaucracy. The forties revealed this so dramatically that within a year or two, with hardly any protest from the rank-and-file, unions succeeded in kicking out by the thousands "Marxians" who had done spade-work in the labor movement for more than a decade, even rising to the top leadership of the old CIO internationals.

The worker becomes a *revolutionary* not by becoming more of a worker but by undoing his "workerness." And in this he is not alone; the same applies to the farmer, the student, the clerk, the soldier, the bureaucrat, the professional—and the Marxist. The worker is no less a "bourgeois" than the farmer, student, clerk, soldier, bureaucrat, professional—and Marxist. His "workerness" is the *disease* he is suffering from, the social affliction telescoped to individual dimensions. Lenin understood this in *What Is to Be Done?* but he smuggled in the old hierarchy under a red flag and some revolutionary verbiage. The worker begins to become a revolutionary when he undoes his "workerness," when he comes to detest his class status here and now, when he begins to shed exactly those features which the Marxists most prize in him—his work ethic, his character structure derived from industrial discipline, his respect for hierarchy, his obedience to leaders, his consumerism, his vestiges of puritanism. In this sense, the worker becomes a revolutionary to the degree that he sheds his class status and achieves an *un*-class consciousness. He degenerates—and he degenerates magnificently. What he is shedding are precisely those class shackles that bind him to *all* systems of domination. He abandons those *class* interests that enslave him to consumerism, suburbia, and a bookkeeping conception of life.*

The most promising development in the factories today is the emergence of young workers who smoke pot, fuck off on their jobs, drift into and out of factories, grow long or longish hair, demand more leisure time rather than more pay, steal, harass all authority figures, go on wildcats, and turn on their fellow workers. Even more promising is the emergence of this human type in trade schools and high schools, the reservoir of the industrial working class to come. To the degree that workers, vocational students and high school students link their lifestyles to various aspects of the anarchic youth culture, to that degree will the proletariat be transformed from a force for the conservation of the established order into a force for revolution.

A qualitatively new situation emerges when man is faced with a transformation from a repressive class society, based on material scarcity, into a liberatory classless society, based on material abundance. From the decomposing traditional class structure a new human type is created in ever-increasing numbers—the *revolutionary*. This revolutionary begins to challenge not only the economic and political premises of hierarchical society, but hierarchy as such. He not only raises the need for social revolution but also tries to *live* in a revolutionary manner to the degree that this is possible in the existing society.† He not only attacks the forms

* The worker, in this sense, begins to approximate the socially transitional human types who have provided history with its most revolutionary elements. Generally, the "proletariat" has been most revolutionary in transitional periods, when it was least "proletarianized " psychically by the industrial system. The great focuses of the classical workers' revolutions were Petrograd and Barcelona, where the workers had been directly uprooted from a peasant background, and Paris, where they were still anchored in crafts or came directly from a craft background. These workers had the greatest difficulty in acclimating themselves to industrial domination and became a continual source of social and revolutionary unrest. By contrast, the stable hereditary working class tended to be surprisingly non-revolutionary. Even in the case of the German workers who were cited by Marx and Engels as models for the European proletariat, the majority did not support the Spartacists in 1919. They returned large majorities of official Social Democrats to the Congress of Workers' Councils, and to the Reichstag in later years, and rallied consistently behind the Social Democratic Party right up to 1933.

† This revolutionary lifestyle may develop in the factories as well as on the streets, in schools as well as in crashpads, in the suburbs as well as on the Bay Area-East Side axis. Its essence is defiance, and a personal "propaganda of the deed" that erodes all the mores, institutions and shibboleths of domination. As society begins to approach the threshold of the revolutionary period, the factories, schools and neighborhoods become the actual arena of revolutionary "play"—a "play" that has a very serious core. Strikes become a chronic condition and are called for their own sake to break the veneer of routine, to defy the society on an almost hourly basis, to shatter the mood of bourgeois normality. This new mood of the workers, students and neighborhood people is a vital precursor to the actual moment of revolutionary transformation. Its most conscious expression is the demand for "self-management"; the worker refuses to be a "managed" being, a *class* being. This process was most evident in Spain, on the eve of the 1936 revolution, when workers in almost every city and town called strikes "for the hell of it"—to express their independence, their sense of awakening, their break with the social order and with bourgeois conditions of life. It was also an essential feature of the 1968 general strike in France.

created by the legacy of domination, but also improvises new forms of liberation which take their poetry from the future.

This preparation for the future, this experimentation with liberatory post-scarcity forms of social relations, may be illusory if the future involves a substitution of one class society by another; it is indispensable, however, if the future involves a classless society built on the *ruins* of a class society. What, then, will be the "agent" of revolutionary change? It will be literally the great majority of society, drawn from all the different traditional classes and fused into a common revolutionary force by the decomposition of the institutions, social forms, values and lifestyles of the prevailing class structure. Typically, its most advanced elements are the youth—a generation that has known no chronic economic crisis and that is becoming less and less oriented toward the myth of material security so widespread among the generation of the thirties.

If it is true that a social revolution cannot be achieved without the active or passive support of the workers, it is no less true that it cannot be achieved without the active or passive support of the farmers, technicians and professionals. Above all, a social revolution cannot be achieved without the support of the youth, from which the ruling class recruits its armed forces. If the ruling class retains its armed might, the revolution is lost *no matter how many workers rally to its support.* This has been vividly demonstrated not only by Spain in the thirties but by Hungary in the fifties and Czechoslovakia in the sixties. The revolution of today—by its very nature, indeed, by its *pursuit of wholeness*—wins not only the soldier and the worker, *but the very generation from which soldiers, workers, technicians, farmers, scientists, professionals and even bureaucrats have been recruited.* Discarding the tactical handbooks of the past, the revolution of the future follows the path of least resistance, eating its way into the most susceptible areas of the population irrespective of their "class position." It is nourished by *all* the contradictions in bourgeois society, not simply by the contradictions of the 1860s and 1917. Hence it attracts all those who feel the burdens of exploitation, poverty, racism, imperialism and, yes, those whose lives are frustrated by consumerism, suburbia, the mass media, the family, school, the supermarket and the prevailing system of repressed sexuality. Here the form of the revolution becomes as total as its content—classless, propertyless, hierarchyless, and *wholly* liberating.

To barge into this revolutionary development with the worn recipes of Marxism, to babble about a "class line" and the "role of the working class," amounts to a subversion of the present and the future by the past. To elaborate this deadening ideology by babbling about "cadres," a "vanguard party," "democratic centralism" and the "proletarian dictatorship" is sheer counterrevolution. It is to this matter of the "organizational question"—this vital contribution of Leninism to Marxism—that we must now direct some attention.

THE MYTH OF THE PARTY

Social revolutions are not made by parties, groups or cadres, they occur as a result of deep-seated historic forces and contradictions that activate large sections of the population. They occur not merely because the "masses" find the existing society intolerable (as Trotsky argued) but also because of the tension between the actual and the possible, between what-is and what-could-be. Abject misery alone does not produce revolutions; more often than not, it produces an aimless demoralization, or worse, a private, personalized struggle to survive.

The Russian Revolution of 1917 weighs on the brain of the living like a nightmare because it was largely the product of "intolerable conditions," of a devastating imperialistic war. Whatever dreams it had were virtually destroyed by an even bloodier civil war, by famine, and by treachery. What emerged from the revolution were the ruins not of an old society but of whatever hopes existed to achieve a new one. The Russian Revolution failed miserably; it replaced czarism by state capitalism.* The Bolsheviks

* A fact which Trotsky never understood. He never followed through the consequences of his own concept of "combined development" to its logical conclusions. He saw (quite correctly) that czarist Russia, the latecomer in the European bourgeois development, necessarily acquired the most advanced industrial and class forms instead of recapitulating the entire bourgeois development from its beginnings. He neglected to consider that Russia, torn by tremendous internal upheaval, might even run ahead of the capitalist development elsewhere in Europe. Hypnotized by the formula "nationalized property equals socialism," he failed to recognize that monopoly capitalism itself tends to amalgamate with the state by its own inner dialectic. The Bolsheviks, having cleared away the traditional forms of bourgeois social organization (which still act as a rein on the state capitalist development in Europe and America), inadvertently prepared the ground for a "pure" state capitalist development in which the state finally becomes the ruling class. Lacking support from a technologically advanced Europe, the Russian Revolution became an internal counterrevolution; Soviet Russia became a form of state capitalism that does not "benefit the whole people." Lenin's analogy between "socialism" and state capitalism became a terrifying reality under Stalin. Despite its humanistic core, Marxism failed to comprehend how much its concept of "socialism" approximates a later stage of capitalism itself—the return to mercantile forms on a higher industrial level. The failure to understand this development led to devastating theoretical confusion in the contemporary revolutionary movement, as witness the splits among the Trotskyists over this question.

were the tragic victims of their own ideology and paid with their lives in great numbers during the purges of the thirties. To attempt to acquire any unique wisdom from this scarcity revolution is ridiculous. What we can learn from the revolutions of the past is what all revolutions have in common and their profound limitations compared with the enormous possibilities that are now open to us.

The most striking feature of the past revolutions is that they began spontaneously. Whether one chooses to examine the opening phases of the French Revolution of 1789, the revolutions of 1848, the Paris Commune, the 1905 revolution in Russia, the overthrow of the czar in 1917, the Hungarian revolution of 1956, or the French general strike of 1968, the opening stages are generally the same; a period of ferment explodes spontaneously into a mass upsurge. Whether the upsurge is successful or not depends on its resoluteness and on whether the troops go over to the people.

The "glorious party," when there is one, almost invariably lags behind the events. In February 1917 the Petrograd organization of the Bolsheviks opposed the calling of strikes precisely on the eve of the revolution which was destined to overthrow the czar. Fortunately, the workers ignored the Bolshevik "directives" and went on strike anyway. In the events which followed, no one was more surprised by the revolution than the "revolutionary" parties, including the Bolsheviks. As the Bolshevik leader Kayurov recalled: "Absolutely no guiding initiatives from the party were felt...the Petrograd committee had been arrested and the representative from the Central Committee, Comrade Shliapnikov, was unable to give any directives for the coming day."[30] Perhaps this was fortunate. Before the Petrograd committee was arrested, its evaluation of the situation and its own role had been so dismal that, had the workers followed its guidance, it is doubtful that the revolution would have occurred when it did.

The same kind of story could be told of the upsurges which preceded 1917 and those which followed—to cite only the most recent, the student uprising and general strike in France during May–June 1968. There is a convenient tendency to forget that close to a dozen "tightly centralized" Bolshevik-type organizations existed in Paris at this time. It is rarely mentioned that virtually every one of these "vanguard" groups disdained the student uprising up to May 7, when the street fighting broke out in earnest. The Trotskyist Jeunesse Communiste Révolutionnaire was a notable exception—and it merely coasted along, essentially following the initiatives of the March 22nd Movement.* Up to May 7 all the Maoist groups criticized the student uprising as peripheral and unimportant; the Trotskyist Fédération des Etudiants Révolutionnaires regarded it as "adventuristic" and tried to get the students to leave the barricades on May 10; the Communist Party, of course, played a completely treacherous role. Far from leading the popular movement, the Maoists and Trotskyists were its captives throughout. Ironically, most of these Bolshevik groups used manipulative techniques shamelessly in the Sorbonne student assembly in an effort to "control" it, introducing a disruptive atmosphere that demoralized the entire body. Finally, to complete the irony, all of these Bolshevik groups were to babble about the need for "centralized leadership" when the popular movement collapsed—a movement that occurred despite their "directives" and often in opposition to them.

Revolutions and uprisings worthy of any note not only have an initial phase that is magnificently anarchic *but also tend spontaneously to create their own forms of revolutionary self-management.* The Parisian sections of 1793–94 were the most remarkable forms of self-management to be created by any of the social revolutions in history.† More familiar in form were the councils or "soviets" which the Petrograd workers established in 1905. Although less democratic than the sections, the councils were to reappear in a number of later revolutions. Still another form of revolutionary self-management were the factory committees which the anarchists established in the Spanish Revolution of 1936. Finally, the sections reappeared as student assemblies and action committees in the May–June uprising and general strike in Paris in 1968.‡

At this point we must ask what role the "revolutionary" party plays in all these developments. In the beginning, as we have seen, it tends to have an inhibitory function, not a "vanguard" role. Where it exercises influence,

* The March 22nd Movement functioned as a catalytic agent in the events, not as a leadership. It did not command; it instigated, leaving a free play to the events. This free play, which allowed the students to push ahead on their own momentum, was indispensable to the dialectic of the uprising, for without it there would have been no barricades on May 10, which in turn triggered off the general strike of the workers.

† See "The Forms of Freedom."

‡ With a sublime arrogance that is attributable partly to ignorance, a number of Marxist groups were to dub virtually all of the above forms of self-management as "soviets." The attempt to bring all of these different forms under a single rubric is not only misleading but willfully obscurantist. The actual soviets were the least democratic of the revolutionary forms and the Bolsheviks shrewdly used them to transfer the power to their own party. The soviets were not based on face-to-face democracy, like the Parisian sections or the student assemblies of 1968. Nor were they based on economic self-management, like the Spanish anarchist factory committees. The soviets actually formed a workers' parliament, hierarchically organized, which drew its representation from factories and later from military units and peasant villages.

it tends to slow down the flow of events, not "coordinate" the revolutionary forces. This is not accidental. The party is structured along hierarchical lines *that reflect the very society it professes to oppose.* Despite its theoretical pretensions, it is a bourgeois organism, a miniature state, with an apparatus and a cadre whose function it is to *seize* power, not *dissolve* power. Rooted in the prerevolutionary period, it assimilates all the forms, techniques and mentality of bureaucracy. Its membership is schooled in obedience and in the preconceptions of a rigid dogma and is taught to revere the leadership. The party's leadership, in turn, is schooled in habits born of command, authority, manipulation and egomania. This situation is worsened when the party participates in parliamentary elections. In election campaigns, the vanguard party models itself completely on existing bourgeois forms and even acquires the paraphernalia of the electoral party. The situation assumes truly critical proportions when the party acquires large presses, costly headquarters and a large inventory of centrally controlled periodicals, and develops a paid "apparatus"—in short, a bureaucracy with vested material interests.

As the party expands, the distance between the leadership and the ranks invariably increases. Its leaders not only become "personages," they lose contact with the living situation below. The local groups, which know their own immediate situation better than any remote leader, are obliged to subordinate their insights to directives from above. The leadership, lacking any direct knowledge of local problems, responds sluggishly and prudently. Although it stakes out a claim to the "larger view," to greater "theoretical competence," the competence of the leadership tends to diminish as one ascends the hierarchy of command. The more one approaches the level where the real decisions are made, the more conservative is the nature of the decision-making process, the more bureaucratic and extraneous are the factors which come into play, the more considerations of prestige and retrenchment supplant creativity, imagination, and a disinterested dedication to revolutionary goals.

The party becomes less efficient from a revolutionary point of view the more it seeks efficiency by means of hierarchy, cadres and centralization. Although everyone marches in step, the orders are usually wrong, especially when events begin to move rapidly and take unexpected turns—as they do in all revolutions. The party is efficient in only one respect—in molding society in its own hierarchical image if the revolution is successful. It recreates bureaucracy, centralization and the state. It fosters the bureaucracy, centralization and the state. It fosters the very social conditions which justify this kind of society. Hence, instead of "withering away," the state controlled by the "glorious party" preserves the very conditions which "necessitate" the existence of a state—and a party to "guard" it.

On the other hand, this kind of party is extremely vulnerable in periods of repression. The bourgeoisie has only to grab its leadership to destroy virtually the entire movement. With its leaders in prison or in hiding, the party becomes paralyzed; the obedient membership has no one to obey and tends to flounder. Demoralization sets in rapidly. The party decomposes not only because of the repressive atmosphere but also because of its poverty of inner resources.

The foregoing account is not a series of hypothetical inferences, it is a composite sketch of all the mass Marxian parties of the past century—the Social Democrats, the Communists, and the Trotskyist party of Ceylon (the only mass party of its kind). To claim that these parties failed to take their Marxian principles seriously merely conceals another question: why did this failure happen in the first place? The fact is, these parties were co-opted into bourgeois society because they were structured along bourgeois lines. The germ of treachery existed in them from birth.

The Bolshevik Party was spared this fate between 1964 and 1917 for only one reason: it was an illegal organization during most of the years leading up to the revolution. The party was continually being shattered and reconstituted, with the result that until it took power it never really hardened into a fully centralized, bureaucratic, hierarchical machine. Moreover, it was riddled by factions; the intensely factional atmosphere persisted throughout 1917 into the civil war. Nevertheless, the Bolshevik leadership was ordinarily extremely conservative, a trait that Lenin had to fight throughout 1917—first in his efforts to reorient the Central Committee against the provisional government (the famous conflict over the "April Theses"), later in driving the Central Committee toward insurrection in October. In both cases he threatened to resign from the Central Committee and bring his views to "the lower ranks of the party."

In 1918, factional disputes over the issue of the Brest-Litovsk treaty became so serious that the Bolsheviks nearly split into two warring communist parties. Oppositional Bolshevik groups like the Democratic Centralists and the Workers' Opposition waged bitter struggles within the party throughout 1919 and 1920, not to speak of oppositional movements that developed within the Red Army over Trotsky's propensity for centralization. The complete centralization of the Bolshevik Party—the achievement of "Leninist unity," as it was to be called later—did not occur until 1921, when Lenin succeeded in persuading the Tenth Party Congress to ban factions. By this time, most of the White Guards had been crushed and the foreign interventionists had withdrawn their troops from Russia.

It cannot be stressed too strongly that the Bolsheviks tended to centralize their party to the degree that they became isolated from the working class. This relationship has rarely been investigated in latter-day Leninist circles, although Lenin was honest enough to admit it. The story of the Russian Revolution is not merely the story of the Bolshevik Party and its supporters. Beneath the veneer of official events described by Soviet historians there was another, more basic, development—the spontaneous movement of the workers and revolutionary peasants, which later clashed sharply with the bureaucratic policies of the Bolsheviks. With the overthrow of the czar in February 1917, workers in virtually all the factories of Russia spontaneously established factory committees, staking out an increasing claim on industrial operations. In June 1917 an all-Russian conference of factory committees was held in Petrograd which called for the "organization of thorough control by labor over production and distribution." The demands of this conference are rarely mentioned in Leninist accounts of the Russian Revolution, despite the fact that the conference aligned itself with the Bolsheviks. Trotsky, who describes the factory committees as "the most direct and indubitable representation of the proletariat in the whole country," deals with them peripherally in his massive three-volume history of the revolution. Yet so important were these spontaneous organisms of self-management that Lenin, despairing of winning the soviets in the summer of 1917, was prepared to jettison the slogan "All Power to the Soviets" for "All Power to the Factory Committees." This demand would have catapulted the Bolsheviks into a completely anarcho-syndicalist position, although it is doubtful that they would have remained there very long.

With the October Revolution, all the factory committees seized control of the plants, ousting the bourgeoisie and completely taking control of industry. In accepting the concept of workers' control, Lenin's famous decree of November 14, 1917, merely acknowledged an accomplished fact; the Bolsheviks dared not oppose the workers at this early date. But they began to whittle down the power of the factory committees. In January 1918, a scant two months after "decreeing" workers' control, Lenin began to advocate that the administration of the factories be placed under trade union control. The story that the Bolsheviks "patiently" experimented with workers' control, only to find it "inefficient" and "chaotic," is a myth. Their "patience" did not last more than a few weeks. Not only did Lenin oppose direct workers' control within a matter of weeks after the decree of November 14, even union control came to an end shortly after it had been established. By the summer of 1918, almost all of Russian industry had been placed under bourgeois forms of management. As Lenin put it, the "revolution demands... precisely in the interests of socialism that the masses *unquestionably obey the single will* of the leaders of the labor process."* Thereafter, workers' control was denounced not only as "inefficient," "chaotic" and "impractical," but also as "petty bourgeois"!

The Left Communist Osinsky bitterly attacked all of these spurious claims and warned the party: "Socialism and socialist organization must be set up by the proletariat itself, or they will not be set up at all; something else will be set up—state capitalism."[31] In the "interests of socialism" the Bolshevik party elbowed the proletariat out of every domain it had conquered by its own efforts and initiative. The party did not coordinate the revolution or even lead it; it dominated it. First workers' control and later union control were replaced by an elaborate hierarchy as monstrous as any structure that existed in prerevolutionary times. As later years were to demonstrate, Osinsky's prophecy became reality.

The problem of "who is to prevail"—the Bolsheviks or the Russian "masses"—was by no means limited to the factories. The issue reappeared in the countryside as well as the cities. A sweeping peasant war had buoyed up the movement of the workers. Contrary to official Leninist accounts,

* V.I. Lenin, "The Immediate Tasks of the Soviet Government," in *Selected Works*, vol. 7 (International Publishers; New York, 1943), p. 342. In this harsh article, published in April 1918, Lenin completely abandoned the libertarian perspective he had advanced the year before in *State and Revolution*. The main themes of the article are the needs for "discipline," for authoritarian control over the factories, and for the institution of the Taylor system (a system Lenin had denounced before the revolution as enslaving men to the machine). The article was written during a comparatively peaceful period of Bolshevik rule some two months after the signing of the Brest-Litovsk Treaty and a month before the revolt of the Czech Legion in the Urals—the revolt that started the civil war on a wide scale and opened the period of direct Allied intervention in Russia. Finally, the article was written nearly a year before the defeat of the German revolution. It would be difficult to account for the "immediate Tasks" merely in terms of the Russian civil war and the failure of the European revolution.

the agrarian upsurge was by no means limited to a redistribution of the land into private plots. In the Ukraine, peasants influenced by the anarchist militias of Nestor Makhno and guided by the communist maxim "From each according to his ability; to each according to his needs," established a multitude of rural communes. Elsewhere, in the north and in Soviet Asia, several thousand of these organisms were established, partly on the initiative of the Left Social Revolutionaries and in large measure as a result of traditional collectivist impulses which stemmed from the Russian village, the *mir*. It matters little whether these communes were numerous or embraced large numbers of peasants; the point is that they were authentic popular organisms, the nuclei of a moral and social spirit that ranged far above the dehumanizing values of bourgeois society.

The Bolsheviks frowned upon these organisms from the very beginning and eventually condemned them. To Lenin, the preferred, the more "socialist," form of agricultural enterprise was represented by the state farm—an agricultural factory in which the state owned the land and farming equipment, appointing managers who hired peasants on a wage basis. One sees in these *attitudes* toward workers' control and agricultural communes the essentially bourgeois spirit and mentality that permeated the Bolshevik Party—a spirit and mentality that emanated not only from its theories, but also from its corporate mode of organization. In December 1918 Lenin launched an attack against the communes on the pretext that peasants were being "forced" to enter them. Actually, little if any coercion was used to organize these communistic forms of self-management. As Robert G. Wesson, who studied the Soviet communes in detail, concludes: "Those who went into communes must have done so largely of their own volition."[32] The communes were not suppressed but their growth was discouraged until Stalin merged the entire development into the forced collectivization drives of the late twenties and early thirties.

By 1920 the Bolsheviks had isolated themselves from the Russian working class and peasantry. Taken together, the elimination of workers' control, the suppression of the Makhnovtsy, the restrictive political atmosphere in the country, the inflated bureaucracy, and the crushing material poverty inherited from the civil war years generated a deep hostility toward Bolshevik rule. With the end of hostilities, a movement surged up from the depths of Russian society for a "third revolution"—not to restore the past, as the Bolsheviks claimed, but to realize the very goals of freedom, economic as well as political, that had rallied the masses around the Bolshevik program of 1917. The new movement found its most conscious form in the Petrograd proletariat and among the Kronstadt sailors. It also found expression in the party: the growth of anticentralist and anarcho-syndicalist tendencies among the Bolsheviks reached a point where a bloc of oppositional groups, oriented toward these issues, gained 124 seats at a Moscow provincial conference as against 154 for supporters of the Central Committee.

On March 2, 1921, the "red sailors" of Kronstadt rose in open rebellion, raising the banner of a "Third Revolution of the Toilers." The Kronstadt program centered around demands for free elections to the soviets, freedom of speech and press for the anarchists and the left socialist parties, free trade unions, and the liberation of all prisoners who belonged to socialist parties. The most shameless stories were fabricated by the Bolsheviks to account for this uprising, acknowledged in later years as brazen lies. The revolt was characterized as a "White Guard plot" despite the fact that the great majority of Communist Party members in Kronstadt joined the sailors—*precisely as Communists*—in denouncing the party leaders as betrayers of the October Revolution. As Robert Vincent Daniels observes in his study of Bolshevik oppositional movements: "Ordinary Communists were indeed so unreliable... that the government did not depend upon them either in the assault on Kronstadt itself or in keeping order in Petrograd, where Kronstadt's hopes for support chiefly rested. The main body of troops employed were Chekists and officer cadets from Red Army training schools. The final assault on Kronstadt was led by the top officialdom of the Communist Party—a large group of delegates to the Tenth Party Congress was rushed from Moscow for this purpose."[33] So weak was the regime internally that the elite had to do its own dirty work.

Even more significant than the Kronstadt revolt was the strike movement that developed among the Petrograd workers, a movement that sparked the uprising of the sailors. Leninist histories do not recount this critically important development. The first strikes broke out in the Troubotchny factory on February 23, 1921. Within a matter of days the movement swept one factory after another, until by February 28 the famous Putilov works—the "crucible of the Revolution"—went on strike. Not only were economic demands raised, the workers raised distinctly political ones, anticipating all the demands that were to be raised by the

Kronstadt sailors a few days later. On February 24, the Bolsheviks declared a "state of siege" in Petrograd and arrested the strike leaders, suppressing the workers' demonstrations with officer cadets. The fact is, the Bolsheviks did not merely suppress a "sailors' mutiny"; they crushed the working class itself. It was at this point that Lenin demanded the banning of factions in the Russian Communist Party. Centralization of the party was now complete—and the way was paved for Stalin.

We have discussed these events in detail because they lead to a conclusion that the latest crop of Marxist-Leninists tend to avoid: the Bolshevik Party reached its maximum degree of centralization in Lenin's day *not to achieve a revolution or suppress a White Guard counterrevolution, but to effect a counterrevolution of its own against the very social forces it professed to represent.* Factions were prohibited and a monolithic party created not to prevent a "capitalist restoration" but to contain a mass movement of workers for soviet democracy and social freedom. The Lenin of 1921 stood opposed to the Lenin of 1917.

Thereafter, Lenin simply floundered. This man who above all sought to anchor the problems of his party in social contradictions found himself literally playing an organizational "numbers game" in a last-ditch attempt to arrest the very bureaucratization he had himself created. There is nothing more pathetic and tragic than Lenin's last years. Paralyzed by a simplistic body of Marxist formulas, he can think of no better countermeasures than organizational ones. He proposes the formation of the Workers' and Peasants' Inspection to correct bureaucratic deformations in the party and state—and this body falls under Stalin's control and becomes highly bureaucratic in its own right. Lenin then suggests that the size of the Workers' and Peasants' Inspection be reduced and that it be merged with the Control Commission. He advocates enlarging the Central Committee. Thus it rolls along: this body to be enlarged, that one to be merged with another, still a third to be modified or abolished. The strange ballet of organizational forms continues up to his very death, as though the problem could be resolved by organizational means. As Mosche Lewin, an obvious admirer of Lenin, admits, the Bolshevik leader "approached the problems of government more like a chief executive of a strictly 'elitist' turn of mind. He did not apply methods of social analysis to the government and was content to consider it purely in terms of organizational methods."[34]

If it is true that in the bourgeois revolutions the "phrase went beyond the content," in the Bolshevik revolution the forms replaced the content. The soviets replaced the workers and their factory committees, the party replaced the soviets, the Central Committee replaced the Party, and the Political Bureau replaced the Central Committee. In short, means replaced ends. This incredible substitution of form for content is one of the most characteristic traits of Marxism-Leninism. In France during the May–June events, all the Bolshevik organizations were prepared to destroy the Sorbonne student assembly in order to increase their influence and membership. Their principal concern was not the revolution or the authentic social forms created by the students, but the growth of their own parties.

Only one force could have arrested the growth of bureaucracy in Russia: a social force. Had the Russian proletariat and peasantry succeeded in increasing the domain of self-management through the development of viable factory committees, rural communes and free soviets, the history of the country might have taken a dramatically different turn. There can be no question that the failure of socialist revolutions in Europe after the First World War led to the isolation of the revolution in Russia. The material poverty of Russia, coupled with the pressure of the surrounding capitalist world, clearly militated against the development of a socialist or a consistently libertarian society. But by no means was it ordained that Russia had to develop along state capitalist lines; contrary to Lenin's and Trotsky's initial expectations, the revolution was defeated by internal forces, not by invasion of armies from abroad. Had the movement from below restored the initial achievements of the revolution in 1917, a multifaceted social structure might have developed, based on workers' control of industry, on a freely developing peasant economy in agriculture, and on a living interplay of ideas, programs and political movements. At the very least, Russia would not have been imprisoned in totalitarian chains and Stalinism would not have poisoned the world revolutionary movement, paving the way for fascism and the Second World War.

The development of the Bolshevik Party, however, precluded this development—Lenin's or Trotsky's "good intentions" notwithstanding. By destroying the power of the factory committees in industry and by crushing the Makhnovtsy, the Petrograd workers and the Kronstadt sailors, the Bolsheviks virtually guaranteed the triumph of the Russian bureaucracy over Russian society. The centralized party—a completely bourgeois institution—became the refuge of counterrevolution in its most sinister form. This was covert counterrevolution that draped itself in the red flag and the terminology of Marx. Ultimately, what the Bolsheviks suppressed in 1921 was not an "ideology" or a "White Guard conspiracy," but an *elemental struggle of the Russian people* to free themselves of their shackles and take control of their own destiny.* For Russia, this meant the nightmare of Stalinist dictatorship; for the generation of the thirties it meant the horror of fascism and the treachery of the Communist parties in Europe and the United States.

THE TWO TRADITIONS

It would be incredibly naive to suppose that Leninism was the product of a single man. The disease lies much deeper, not only in the limitations of Marxian theory but in the limitations of the social era that produced Marxism. If this is not clearly understood, we will remain as blind to the dialectic of events today as Marx, Engels, Lenin and Trotsky were in their own day. For us this blindness will be all the more reprehensible because behind us lies a wealth of experience that these men lacked in developing their theories.

Karl Marx and Friedrich Engels were centralists—not only politically, but socially and economically. They never denied this fact and their writings are studded with glowing encomiums to political, organizational and economic centralization. As early as March 1850, in the famous "Address of the Central Council to the Communist League," they call upon the workers to strive not only for "the single and indivisible German republic, but also strive in it for the most decisive centralization of power in the hands of the state authority." Lest the demand be taken lightly, it is repeated continually in the same paragraph, which concludes; "As in France in 1793, so today in Germany the carrying through of the strictest centralization is the task of the really revolutionary party."

* In interpreting this elemental movement of the Russian workers and peasants as a series of "White Guard conspiracies," "acts of kulak resistance," and "plots of international capital," the Bolsheviks reached an incredible theoretical low and deceived no one but themselves. A spiritual erosion developed within the party that paved the way for the politics of the secret police, for character assassination, and finally for the Moscow trials and the annihilation of the Old Bolshevik cadre. One sees the return of this odious mentality in PL articles like "Marcuse: Cop-out or Cop?"—the theme of which is to establish Marcuse as an agent of the CIA. (See *Progressive Labor*, February 1969.) The article has a caption under a photograph of demonstrating Parisians which reads: "Marcuse got to Paris too late to stop the May action," opponents of the PLP are invariably described by this rag as "redbaiters" and as "anti-worker." If the American left does not repudiate this police approach and character assassination it will pay bitterly in the years to come.

The same theme reappears continually in later years. With the outbreak of the Franco-Prussian War, for example, Marx writes to Engels: "The French need a thrashing. If the Prussians win, the centralization of state power will be useful for the centralization of the German working class."[35]

Marx and Engels, however, were not centralists because they believed in the virtues of centralism per se. Quite the contrary: both Marxism and anarchism have always agreed that a liberated, communist society entails sweeping decentralization, the dissolution of bureaucracy, the abolition of the state, and the breakup of the large cities. "Abolition of the antithesis between town and country is not merely possible," notes Engels in *Anti-Duhring.* "It has become a direct necessity…the present poisoning of the air, water and land can be put to an end only by the fusion of town and country…" To Engels this involves a "uniform distribution of the population over the whole country"[36]—in short, the physical decentralization of the cities.

The origins of Marxian centralism are in problems arising from the formation of the national state. Until well into the latter half of the nineteenth century, Germany and Italy were divided into a multitude of independent duchies, principalities and kingdoms. The consolidation of these geographic units into unified nations, Marx and Engels believed, was a *sine qua non* for the development of modern industry and capitalism. Their praise of centralism was engendered not by any centralistic mystique but by the events of the period in which they lived—the development of technology, trade, a unified working class, and the national state. Their concern on this score, in short, is with the emergence of capitalism, with the tasks of the bourgeois revolution in an era of unavoidable material scarcity. Marx's approach to a "proletarian revolution," on the other hand, is markedly different. He enthusiastically praises the Paris Commune as a "model to all the industrial centers of France." "This regime," he writes, "once established in Paris and the secondary centers, the old centralized government would in the provinces, too, have to give way to the *self-government of the producers.*" (Emphasis added.) The unity of the nation, to be sure, would not disappear, and a central government would exist during the transition to communism, but its functions would be limited.

Our object is not to bandy about quotations from Marx and Engels but to emphasize how key tenets of Marxism—which are accepted so uncritically today—were in fact the product of an era that has long been transcended by the development of capitalism in the United States and Western Europe. In his day Marx was occupied not only with the problems of the "proletarian revolution" but also with the problems of the bourgeois revolution, particularly in Germany, Spain, Italy and Eastern Europe. He dealt with the problems of transition from capitalism to socialism in capitalist countries which had not advanced much beyond the coal-steel technology of the Industrial Revolution, and with the problems of transition from feudalism to capitalism in countries which had scarcely advanced much beyond handicrafts and the guild system. To state these concerns broadly, Marx was occupied above all with the *preconditions* of freedom (technological development, national unification, material abundance) rather than with the *conditions* of freedom (decentralization, the formation of communities, the human scale, direct democracy). His theories were still anchored in the realm of survival, not the realm of *life.*

Once this is grasped it is possible to place Marx's theoretical legacy in meaningful perspective—to separate its rich contributions from its historically limited, indeed paralyzing, shackles on our own time. The Marxian dialectic, the many seminal insights provided by historical materialism, the superb critique of the commodity relationship, many elements of the economic theories, the theory of alienation, and above all the notion that freedom has material preconditions—these are lasting contributions to revolutionary thought.

By the same token, Marx's emphasis on the industrial proletariat as the "agent" of revolutionary change, his "class analysis" in explaining the transition from a class to a classless society, his concept of the proletarian dictatorship, his emphasis on centralism, his theory of capitalist development (which tends to jumble state capitalism with socialism), his advocacy of political action through electoral parties—these and many related concepts are false in the context of our time and were misleading, as we shall see, even in his own day. They emerge from the limitations of his vision—more properly, from the limitations of his time. They make sense only if one remembers that Marx regarded capitalism as historically progressive, as an indispensable stage to the development of socialism, and they have practical applicability only to a time when Germany in particular was confronted by bourgeois-democratic tasks and national unification. (We are not trying to say that Marx was correct in holding this approach, merely that the approach makes sense when viewed in its time and place.)

Just as the Russian Revolution included a subterranean movement of the "masses" which conflicted with Bolshevism, so there is a subterranean movement in history which conflicts with all systems of authority. This movement has entered into our time under the name of "anarchism," although it has never been encompassed by a single ideology or body of sacred texts. Anarchism is a libidinal movement of humanity against coercion in any form, reaching back in time to the very emergence of propertied society, class rule and the state. From this period onward, the oppressed have resisted all forms that seek to imprison the spontaneous development of social order. Anarchism has surged to the foreground of the social arena in periods of major transition from one historical era to another. The decline of the ancient and feudal world witnessed the upsurge of mass movements, in some cases wildly Dionysian in character, that demanded an end to all systems of authority, privilege and coercion.

The anarchic movements of the past failed largely because material scarcity, a function of the low level of technology, vitiated an organic harmonization of human interests. Any society that could promise little more materially than equality of poverty invariably engendered deep-seated tendencies to restore a new system of privilege. In the absence of a technology that could appreciably reduce the working day, the need to work vitiated social institutions based on self-management. The Girondins of the French Revolution shrewdly recognized that they could use the working day against revolutionary Paris. To exclude radical elements from the sections, they tried to enact legislation which would end all assembly meetings before 10 p.m., the hour when Parisian workers returned from their jobs. Indeed, it was not only the manipulative techniques and the treachery of the "vanguard" organizations that brought the anarchic phases of past revolutions to an end, it was also the material limits of past eras. The" masses" were always compelled to return to a lifetime of toil and rarely were they free to establish organs of self-management that could last beyond the revolution.

Anarchists such as Bakunin and Kropotkin, however, were by no means wrong in criticizing Marx for his emphasis on centralism and his elitist notions of organization. Was centralism absolutely necessary for technological advances in the past? Was the nation-state indispensable to the expansion of commerce? Did the workers' movement benefit by the emergence of highly centralized economic enterprises and the "indivisible" state? We tend to accept these tenets of Marxism too uncritically, largely because capitalism developed within a centralized political arena. The anarchists of the last century warned that Marx's centralistic approach, insofar as it affected the events of the time, would so strengthen the bourgeoisie and the state apparatus that the overthrow of capitalism would be extremely difficult. The revolutionary party, by duplicating these centralistic, hierarchical features would reproduce hierarchy and centralism in the post revolutionary society.

Bakunin, Kropotkin, and Malatesta were not so naive as to believe that anarchism could be established over night. In imputing this notion to Bakunin, Marx and Engels willfully distorted the Russian anarchist's views. Nor did the anarchists of the last century believe that the abolition of the state involved "laying down arms" immediately after the revolution, to use Marx's obscurantist choice of terms, thoughtlessly repeated by Lenin in *State and Revolution*. Indeed, much of that passes for "Marxism" in *State and Revolution* is pure anarchism—for example, the substitution of revolutionary militias for professional armed bodies and the substitution of organs of self-management for parliamentary bodies. What is authentically Marxist in Lenin's pamphlet is the demand for "strict centralism," the acceptance of a "new" bureaucracy, and the identification of soviets with a state.

The anarchists of the last century were deeply preoccupied with the question of achieving industrialization without crushing the revolutionary spirit of the "masses" and rearing new obstacles to emancipation. They feared that centralization would reinforce the ability of the bourgeoisie to resist the revolution and instill in the workers a sense of obedience. They tried to rescue all those precapitalist communal forms (such as the Russian *mir* and the Spanish *pueblo)* which might provide a springboard to a free society, not only in a structural sense but also a spiritual one. Hence they emphasized the need for decentralization even under capitalism. In contrast to the Marxian parties, their organizations gave considerable attention to what they called "integral education"—the development of the *whole* man—to counteract the debasing and banalizing influence of bourgeois society. The anarchists tried to live by the values of the future to the extent that this was possible under capitalism. They believed in direct action to foster the initiative of the "masses," to preserve the spirit of revolt, to encourage spontaneity. They tried to develop organizations based on mutual aid and brotherhood, in which control would be exercised from below upward, not downward from above.

We must pause here to examine the nature of anarchist organizational forms in some detail, if only because the subject has been obscured by an appalling amount of rubbish. Anarchists, or at least anarcho-communists, accept the need for organization.* It should be as absurd to have to repeat this point as to argue over whether Marx accepted the need for social revolution.

The real question at issue here is not organization versus non-organization, but rather what *kind* of organization the anarcho-communists try to establish. What the different kinds of anarcho-communist organizations have in common is organic developments from below, not bodies engineered into existence from above. They are social movements, combining a creative revolutionary lifestyle with a creative revolutionary theory, not political parties whose mode of life is indistinguishable from the surrounding bourgeois environment and whose ideology is reduced to rigid "tried and tested programs." As much as is humanly possible, they try to reflect the liberated society they seek to achieve, not slavishly duplicate the prevailing system of hierarchy, class and authority. They are built around intimate groups of brothers and sisters—affinity groups—whose ability to act in common is based on initiative, on convictions freely arrived at, and on a deep personal involvement, not around a bureaucratic apparatus fleshed out by a docile membership and manipulated from above by a handful of all-knowing leaders.

The anarcho-communists do not deny the need for coordination between groups, for discipline, for meticulous planning, and for unity in action. But they believe that coordination, discipline, planning, and unity in action must be achieved *voluntarily*, by means of a self-discipline nourished by conviction and understanding, not by coercion and a mindless, unquestioning obedience to orders from above. They seek to achieve the effectiveness imputed to centralism by means of voluntarism and insight, not by establishing a hierarchical, centralized structure. Depending upon

* The term "anarchist" is a generic word like the term "socialist," and there are probably as many different kinds of anarchists as there are socialists. In both cases, the spectrum ranges from individuals whose views derive from an extension of liberalism (the "individualist anarchists," the social-democrats) to revolutionary communists (the anarcho-communists, the revolutionary Marxists, Leninists and Trotskyists).

needs or circumstances, affinity groups can achieve this effectiveness through assemblies, action committees, and local, regional or national conferences. But they vigorously oppose the establishment of an organizational structure that becomes an end in itself, of committees that linger on after their practical tasks have been completed, of a "leadership" that reduces the "revolutionary" to a mindless robot.

These conclusions are not the result of flighty "individualist" impulses; quite to the contrary, they emerge from an exacting study of past revolutions, of the impact centralized parties have had on the revolutionary process, and of the nature of social change in an era of potential material abundance. Anarcho-communists *seek to preserve and extend the anarchic phase that opens all the great social revolutions.* Even more than Marxists, they recognize that revolutions are produced by deep historical processes. No central committee "makes" a social revolution; at best it can stage a *coup d'état,* replacing one hierarchy by another—or worse, arrest a revolutionary process if it exercises any widespread influence. A central committee is an organ for acquiring power, for *recreating* power, for gathering to itself what the "masses" have achieved by their own revolutionary efforts. One must be blind to all that has happened over the past two centuries not to recognize these essential facts.

In the past, Marxists could make an intelligible (although invalid) claim for the need for a centralized party, because the anarchic phase of the revolution was nullified by material scarcity. Economically, the "masses" were always compelled to return to a daily life of toil. The revolution closed at ten o'clock, quite aside from the reactionary intentions of the Girondins of 1793; it was arrested by the low level of technology. Today even this excuse has been removed by the development of a post-scarcity technology, notably in the U.S. and Western Europe. A point has now been reached where the "masses" can begin, almost overnight, to expand drastically the "realm of freedom" in the Marxian sense—to acquire the leisure time needed to achieve the highest degree of self-management.

What the May–June events in France demonstrated was not the need for a Bolshevik-type party but the need for greater consciousness among the "masses." Paris demonstrated that an organization is needed to propagate ideas systematically—and not ideas alone, but *ideas which promote the concept of self-management.* What the French "masses" lacked was not a central committee or a Lenin to "organize" or "command" them, but the conviction that they could have *operated* the factories instead of merely occupying them. It is noteworthy that *not a single Bolshevik-type party in France raised the demand of self-management.* The demand was raised only by the anarchists and the Situationists.

There is a need for a revolutionary organization—but its function must always be kept clearly in mind. Its first task is propaganda, to "patiently explain," as Lenin put it. In a revolutionary situation, the revolutionary organization presents the most advanced demands: it is prepared at every turn of events to formulate—in the most concrete fashion—the immediate task that should be performed to advance the revolutionary process. It provides the boldest elements in action and in the decision-making organs of the revolution.

In what way, then, do anarcho-communist groups differ from the Bolshevik type of party? Certainly not on such issues as the need for organization, planning, coordination, propaganda in all its forms or the need for a social program. Fundamentally, they differ from the Bolshevik type of party in their belief that genuine revolutionaries must function *within the framework of the forms created by the revolution,* not within the forms created by the party. What this means is that their commitment is to the revolutionary organs of self-management, not to the revolutionary "organization"; to the *social* forms, not the *political* forms. Anarcho-communists seek to persuade the factory committees, assemblies or soviets to make themselves into *genuine organs of popular self-management,* not to dominate them, manipulate them, or hitch them to an all-knowing political party. Anarcho-communists do not seek to rear a state structure over these popular revolutionary organs but, on the contrary, to dissolve all the organizational forms developed in the prerevolutionary period (including their own) into these genuine revolutionary organs.

These differences are decisive. Despite their rhetoric and slogans, the Russian Bolsheviks never believed in the soviets; they regarded them as instruments of the Bolshevik Party, an attitude which the French Trotskyists faithfully duplicated in their relations with the Sorbonne students' assembly, the French Maoists with the French labor unions, and the Old Left groups with SDS. By 1921, the soviets were virtually dead, and all decisions were made by the Bolshevik Central Committee and Political Bureau. Not only do anarcho-communists seek to prevent Marxist parties from repeating this; they also wish to prevent their own organization from playing a similar role. Accordingly, they try to prevent bureaucracy, hierarchy and elites from emerging in their midst. No less important, they attempt to *remake themselves*; to root out from their own personalities those authoritarian traits and elitist propensities that are assimilated in hierarchical society almost from birth. The concern of the anarchist movement with lifestyle is not merely a preoccupation with its own integrity, but with the integrity of the revolution itself.*

In the midst of all the confusing ideological crosscurrents of our time, one question must always remain in the foreground: what the hell are we trying to make a revolution for? Are we trying to make a revolution to recreate hierarchy, dangling a shadowy dream of future freedom before the eyes of humanity? Is it to promote further technological advance, to create an even greater abundance of goods than exists today? Is it to "get even" with the bourgeoisie? Is it to bring PL to power? Or the Communist Party? Or the Socialist Workers Party? Is it to emancipate abstractions such as "The Proletariat," "The People," "History," "Society"?

Or is it finally to dissolve hierarchy, class rule and coercion—*to make it possible for each individual to gain control of his everyday life*? Is it to make each moment as marvelous as it could be and the life span of each individual an utterly fulfilling experience? If the true purpose of revolution is to bring the neanderthal men of PL to power, it is not worth making. We need hardly argue the inane questions of whether individual development can be severed from social and communal development; obviously the two go together. The basis for a whole human being is a rounded society; the basis for a free human being is a free society.

These issues aside, we are still faced with the question that Marx raised in 1850: when will we begin to take our poetry from the future instead of the past? The dead must be permitted to bury the dead. Marxism is dead because it was rooted in an era of material scarcity, limited in its possibilities by material want. The most important social message of Marxism is that freedom has material preconditions—we must survive in order to live. With the development of a technology that could

* It is this goal, we may add, that motivates anarchist dadaism, the anarchist flipout that produces the creases of consternation on the wooden faces of PLP types. The anarchist flipout attempts to shatter the internal values inherited from hierarchical society, to explode the rigidities instilled by the bourgeois socialization process. In short, it is an attempt to break down the superego that exercises such a paralyzing effect upon spontaneity, imagination and sensibility and to restore a sense of desire, possibility and the marvelous—of revolution as a liberating, joyous festival.

not have been conceived by the wildest science fiction of Marx's day, the possibility of a post-scarcity society now lies before us. All the institutions of propertied society—class rule, hierarchy, the patriarchal family, bureaucracy, the city, the state—have been exhausted. Today, decentralization is not only desirable as a means of restoring the human scale, it is necessary to recreate a viable ecology, to preserve life on this planet from destructive pollutants and soil erosion, to preserve a breathable atmosphere and the balance of nature. The promotion of spontaneity is necessary if the social revolution is to place each individual in control of his everyday life.

The old forms of struggle do not totally disappear with the decomposition of class society, but they are being transcended by the issues of a classless society. There can be no social revolution without winning the workers, hence they must have our active solidarity in every struggle they wage against exploitation. We fight against social crimes wherever they appear—and industrial exploitation is a profound social crime. But so are racism, the denial of the right to self-determination, imperialism and poverty profound social crimes—and for that matter so are pollution, rampant urbanization, the malignant socialization of the young, and sexual repression. As for the problem of winning the working class to the revolution, we must bear in mind that a precondition for the existence of the bourgeoisie is the development of the proletariat. Capitalism as a social system presupposes the existence of *both* classes and is perpetuated by the development of both classes. We begin to undermine the premises of class rule to the degree that we foster the declassifying of the non-bourgeois classes, at least institutionally, psychologically and culturally.

For the first time in history, the anarchic phase that opened all the great revolutions of the past can be preserved as a permanent condition by the advanced technology of our time. The anarchic institutions of that phase—the assemblies, the factory committees, the action committees—can be stabilized as the elements of a liberated society, as the elements of a new system of self-management. Will we build a movement that can defend them? Can we create an organization of affinity groups that is capable of dissolving into these revolutionary institutions? Or will we build a hierarchical, centralized, bureaucratic party that will try to dominate them, supplant them, and finally destroy them?

Listen, Marxist: The organization we try to build is the kind of society our revolution will create. Either we will shed the past—in ourselves as well as in our groups—or there will simply be no future to win.

New York
May 1969

A Note on Affinity Groups

The term "affinity group" is the English translation of the Spanish *grupo de afinidad,* which was the name of an organizational form devised in pre-Franco days as the basis of the redoubtable Federación Anarquista Ibérica, the Iberian Anarchist Federation. (The FAI consisted of the most idealistic militants in the CNT, the immense anarcho-syndicalist labor union.) A slavish imitation of the FAI's forms of organization and methods would be neither possible nor desirable. The Spanish anarchists of the thirties were faced with entirely different social problems from those which confront American anarchists today. The affinity group form, however, has features that apply to any social situation, and these have often been intuitively adopted by American radicals, who call the resulting organizations "collectives," "communes" or "families."

The affinity group could easily be regarded as a new type of extended family, in which kinship ties are replaced by deeply empathetic human relationships—relationships nourished by common revolutionary ideas and practice. Long before the word "tribe" gained popularity in the American counterculture, the Spanish anarchists called their congresses *asambleas de las tribus*—assemblies of the tribes. Each affinity group is deliberately kept small to allow for the greatest degree of intimacy between those who compose it. Autonomous, communal and directly democratic, the group combines revolutionary theory with revolutionary lifestyle in its everyday behavior. It creates a free space in which revolutionaries can remake themselves individually, and also as social beings.

Affinity groups are intended to function as catalysts within the popular movement, not as "vanguards"; they provide initiative and consciousness, not a "general staff" and a source of "command." The groups proliferate on a molecular level and they have their own "Brownian movement." Whether they link together or separate is determined by living situations, not by bureaucratic fiat from a distant center. Under conditions of political repression, affinity groups are highly resistant to police infiltration. Owing to the intimacy of the relationships between the participants, the groups are often difficult to penetrate and, even if penetration occurs, there is no centralized apparatus to provide the infiltrator with an overview of the movement as a whole. Even under such demanding conditions, affinity groups can still retain contact with each other through their periodicals and literature.

During periods of heightened activity, on the other hand, nothing prevents affinity groups from working together closely on any scale required by a living situation. They can easily federate by means of local, regional or national assemblies to formulate common policies and they can create temporary action committees (like those of the French students and workers in 1968) to coordinate specific tasks. Affinity groups, however, are always rooted in the popular movement. Their loyalties belong to the social forms created by the revolutionary people, not to an impersonal bureaucracy. As a result of their autonomy and localism, the groups can retain a sensitive appreciation of new possibilities. Intensely experimental and variegated in lifestyles, they act as a stimulus on each other as well as on the popular movement. Each group tries to acquire the resources needed to function largely on its own. Each group seeks a rounded body of knowledge and experience in order to overcome the social and psychological limitations imposed by bourgeois society on individual development. Each group, as a nucleus of consciousness and experience, tries to advance the spontaneous revolutionary movement of the people to a point where the group can finally disappear into the organic social forms created by the revolution.

Robert B. Carson, in an article published in the April 1970 issue of Monthly Review, *writes that the "major thrust" of 'Listen, Marxist!' is to "destroy a class-based analysis of society and revolutionary activity." This criticism has been made by many Marxists who read the article.**

Carson's accusation is quite absurd. I seriously doubt if he did more than skim the article. Carson goes on to say that my approach is "ahistorical" and that I try to promote a "crude kind of individualistic anarchism"—this despite the fact that a large portion of the article attempts to draw important historical lessons from earlier revolutions and despite the fact that the article is unequivocally committed to anarcho-communism.

The most interesting thing about Carson's criticism is what it reveals about the theoretical level of many Marxists. Apparently Carson regards a *futuristic* approach as "ahistorical." He also seems to regard my belief that freedom exists only when each individual controls his daily life as "a crude kind of individualistic anarchism." Here we get to the nub of the problem. Futurism and individual freedom are indeed the "main thrust" of the pamphlet. Carson's reply confirms *precisely* what the pamphlet set out to prove about Marxism today, namely that Marxism (I do not speak of Marx here) is *not* futuristic and that its perspectives are oriented not toward concrete, existential freedom, but toward an abstract freedom—freedom for "Society," for the "Proletariat," for *categories* rather than for people. Carson's first charge, I might emphasize, should be leveled not only at me but at Marx—at his futurism in the *Eighteentb Brumaire of Louis Napoleon.*

As to the charge that I am opposed to a "class-based analysis of society and revolutionary activity," need I say that a "class analysis" permeates the pamphlet? Is it conceivable that I could have terms like "capitalist" and "bourgeois" without working with a "class-based analysis"? Originally I thought there could have been no doubt about the matter. I have since changed the expression "class analysis" in the text to "class line," and perhaps I had better explain the difference this change is meant to convey.

What Carson is *really* saying is that I do not have a *Marxist* "class analysis"—a "class analysis" in which the industrial proletariat is driven to revolution by destitution and immiseration. Carson apparently assumes that Marx's traditional "class *line*" exhausts all there is to say about the class struggle. And in this respect, he assumes far too much. One need

* This is an edited summary of several discussions on "Listen, Marxist!," most of which occurred at my anarcho-communism class at Alternate U, New York's liberation school. I have selected the most representative and recurrent questions raised by readers of the pamphlet.

only turn to Bakunin, for example, to find a class analysis that was quite different from Marx's—and more relevant today. Bakunin believed that the industrial proletariat by no means constitutes the most revolutionary class in society. He never received the credit due him for predicting the *embourgeoisement* of the industrial working class with the development of capitalist industry. In Bakunin's view, the most revolutionary class was not the industrial proletariat—"a class always increasing in numbers, and disciplined, united, organized by the very mechanisms of capitalist production itself" (Marx)—but the uprooted peasantry and urban *déclassés*, the rural and urban lumpen elements Marx so heartily despised. We need go no further than the urban centers of America—not to speak of the rice paddies of Asia—to find how accurate Bakunin was by comparison with Marx.

As it turned out, the development of capitalist industry not only "disciplined," "united" and "organized" the working class but, *by these very measures,* denatured the proletariat for generations. By contrast, the transitional and lumpenized classes of society today (such as blacks, drop-out youth, people like students, intellectuals and artists who are not rooted in the factory system, and young workers whose allegiance to the work ethic has been shaken by cultural factors) are the most radical elements in the world today.

A "class analysis" does not necessarily begin and end with Marx's nineteenth-century version, a version I regard as grossly inaccurate. The class struggle, moreover, does not begin and end at the point of production. It may emerge from the poverty of the unemployed and unemployables, many of whom have never done a day's work in industry; it may emerge from a new sense of possibility that slowly pervades society—the tension between "what is" and "what could be"—which percolates through virtually all traditional classes; it may emerge from the cultural and physical decomposition of the traditional class structure on which the social stability of capitalism was based. Finally, every class struggle is not necessarily revolutionary. The class struggle between the original Roman *proletarius* and *patricius* was decidedly reactionary and eventually ended, as Marx observed in the opening lines of the *Communist Manifesto,* "in the common ruin of the contending classes."[37]

Today, not only poverty but also a relative degree of affluence is causing revolutionary unrest—a factor Marx never anticipated. Capitalism, having started out by proletarianizing the urban *déclassés,* is now ending its lifecycle by creating new urban *déclassés,* including "shiftless" young industrial workers who no longer take the jobs, the factory discipline or the work ethic seriously. This stratum of *déclassés* rests on a new economic base—a post-scarcity technology, automation, a relative degree of material abundance—and it prefigures culturally the classless society the Marxists so devoutly envision as humanity's future. One would have thought that this remarkable dialectic, this "negation of the negation," would have stirred a flicker of understanding in the heavy thinkers of the Marxist movement.

It would be difficult to conceive of a revolution in any industrially advanced capitalist country without the support of the industrial proletariat.

Of course. And "Listen, Marxist!" makes no claim that a social revolution is possible without the participation of the industrial proletariat. The article, in fact, tries to show how the proletariat can be won to the revolutionary movement by stressing issues that concern the quality of life and work. I agree, of course, with the libertarian Marxists and anarcho-syndicalists, who raise the slogan "workers' management of production." I wonder, however, if this slogan goes far enough now. My suspicion is that the workers, when they get into revolutionary motion, will demand even more than control of the factories. I think they will demand the elimination of toil, or, what amounts to the same thing, freedom from work. Certainly a dropout outlook is growing among kids from working-class families—high school kids who are being influenced by the youth culture.

Although many other factors may contribute to the situation, it remains true that the workers will develop revolutionary views to the degree that they shed their traditional working-class traits. Young workers, I think, will increasingly demand leisure and the abolition of alienated labor. The young Marx, I might add, was not indifferent to the development of unconventional values in the proletariat. In *The Holy Family,* he cites with obvious favor a Parisian working-class girl in Eugene Sue's *The Wandering Jew* who gives of her love and loyalty spontaneously, disdaining marriage and bourgeois conventions. He notes, "she constitutes a really human contrast to the hypocritical, narrow-hearted, self-seeking wife of the bourgeois, to the whole circle of the bourgeosie, that is, to the official circle."[38] The working class, in the young Marx's view, is the negation of capitalism not only in that it suffers total alienation, abasement and dehumanization, but also in that it affirms life forces and human values. Unfortunately, observations of this kind tend to fade away as Marx's socialism becomes increasingly "objectivist" and "scientific" (the admirers of Marx's famous-but untranslated and little-read-*Gründrisse* notwithstanding). The later Marx begins to prize the bourgeois traits of the worker—the worker's "discipline," "practicality," and "realism"—as the characteristics necessary for a revolutionary class.

The approach which Marx followed in *The Holy Family* was, I think, the correct one. Trapped by the notion that the working class, *qua* class, implied the liquidation of class society, Marx failed to see that this class was the alter ego of the bourgeoisie. Only a new cultural movement could rework the outlook of the proletariat—and deproletarianize it. Ironically, the Parisian working-class girls of Marx's youth were not industrial workers, but rather people of transitional classes who straddled small and large-scale production. They were largely lumpenized elements, like the *sans-culottes* of the French Revolution.

If the analysis in "Listen, Marxist!" is "class-based," what is the nature of the class struggle?

The class struggle does not center around material exploitation alone but also around spiritual exploitation. In addition, entirely new issues emerge: coercive attitudes, the quality of work, ecology (or, stated in more general terms, psychological and environmental oppression). Moreover, the alienated and oppressed sectors of society are now the *majority* of the people, not a single class defined by its relationship to the means of production; the more radical as well as more liberatory sensibilities appear in the younger, not in the more "mature," age groups. Terms like "classes" and "class struggle," conceived of almost entirely as economic categories and relations, are too one-sided to express the *universalization* of the struggle. Use these limited expressions if you like (the target is still a ruling class and a class society), but this terminology, with its traditional connotations, does not reflect the sweep and the multi-dimensional nature of the struggle. Words like "class struggle" fail to encompass the cultural and spiritual revolt that is taking place along with the economic struggle.

"Listen, Marxist!" speaks a great deal about the potentialities of a post-scarcity society, but what of the actualities? There is still a great deal of poverty and hunger in the U.S. Inflation is a growing problem, not to speak of unemployment, bad housing, racial discrimination, work speed-ups, trade union bureaucracy, and the danger of fascism, imperialism and war.

"Listen, Marxist!" was written to deal with the simplifications of social problems (the economic and Third World oriented "either/or" notions) that were developing in the "New Left." The post-scarcity viewpoint advanced in the pamphlet was not designed to replace one simplification (class struggle) by another (utopia). Yes, these economic, racial and bureaucratic actualities exist for millions of people in the U.S. and abroad. Any revolutionary movement that fails to deal energetically and militantly with them will be as distorted as a movement that deals with them, singly or severally, to the exclusion of all others. My writings on post-scarcity possibilities, ecology, utopia, the youth culture and alienation are intended to help fill a major gap in radical theory and praxis, not to create another gap.

The really important problem we face is how the actualities of the present scarcity society are related to—and conditioned by—the potentialities for a future post-scarcity society. So far as this really dialectical problem is concerned, the heavy thinkers of the "left" show themselves to be incredibly light-minded and narrowly empirical. In the industrialized Western world, scarcity has to be enforced, so great is the productive potential of technology. Today economic planning has one basic purpose: to confine a highly advanced technology within a commodity framework. Many of the social problems which were endured almost passively a generation ago are now regarded as intolerable because the tension between "what is" and "what could be" has reached a point where "what is" seems utterly irrational. This tension adds an explosive character to many actualities that evoked only a flicker of protest a quarter of a century ago. Moreover, the tension between "what is" and "what could be" conditions all the traditional economic and social issues that have occupied radical movements for generations. We can no longer deal with these issues adequately unless we view them in the light of the economic, social and cultural possibilities of post-scarcity.

Let me present a concrete example. Assume there is a struggle by welfare mothers to increase their allotments. In the past, the mothers were organized by liberal groups or Stalinists; petitions were drawn up, demonstrations were organized, and *perhaps* a welfare center or two was occupied. Almost invariably, one of the groups or parties trotted out a "reform candidate" who promised that, if elected, he would fight "unflinchingly" for higher welfare expenditures. The entire struggle was contained within the organizational forms and institutions of the system: formal meetings of the mothers (with the patronizing "organizers" pulling the strings), formal modes of actions (petitions, demonstrations, elections for public office), and maybe a modest amount of direct action. The issue pretty much came to an end with a compromise on allotment increases and perhaps a lingering formal organization to oversee (and later sell out) future struggles around welfare issues.

Here actuality triumphed completely over potentiality. At best, a few mothers might be "radicalized," which meant that they joined (or were shamelessly used by) organizations such as the Communist Party to promote their political influence. For the rest, most of the welfare mothers returned to the shabbiness of their daily lives and to varying degrees of passivity as human beings. Nothing was really changed for those who did not ego trip as "leaders," "politicals" and "organizers."

To revolutionaries with a "post-scarcity consciousness" (to use Todd Gitlin's phrase), this kind of situation would be intolerable. Without losing sight of the concrete issues that initially motivated the struggle, revolutionaries would try to catalyze an order of relationships between the mothers entirely different from relationships the usual organizational format imposes. They would try to foster a deep sense of community, a rounded human relationship that would transform the very subjectivity of the people involved. Groups would be small; in order to achieve the full participation of everyone involved. Personal relationships would be intimate, not merely issue-oriented. People would get to *know* each other, to *confront* each other; they would *explore* each other with a view toward achieving the most complete, unalienated relationships. Women would discuss sexism as well as their welfare allotments, child-rearing as well as harassment by landlords, their dreams and hopes as human beings as well as the cost of living.

From this intimacy there would grow, hopefully, a supportive system of kinship, mutual aid, sympathy and solidarity in daily life. The women might collaborate to establish a rotating system of baby sitters and child-care attendants, the cooperative buying of good food at greatly reduced prices, the common cooking and partaking of meals, the mutual learning of survival skills and new social ideas, the fostering of creative talents, and many other shared experiences. Every aspect of life that could be explored and changed would be one part of the new kinds of relationships. This "extended family"—based on explored affinities and collective activities—would replace relationships mediated by "organizers," "chairmen," an "executive committee," *Robert's Rules of Order,* elites, and political manipulators.

The struggle for increased allotments would expand beyond the welfare system to the schools, the hospitals, the police, the physical, cultural, aesthetic and recreational resources of the neighborhood, the stores, the houses, the doctors and lawyers in the area, and so on—into the very ecology of the district.

What I have said on this issue could be applied to every issue—unemployment, bad housing, racism, work conditions—in which an insidious assimilation of bourgeois modes of functioning is masked as "realism" and "actuality." The new order of relationships that could be developed from a welfare struggle is utopian only in the sense that actuality is informed and conditioned by post-scarcity consciousness. The future penetrates the present; it recasts the way people "organize" and the goals for which they strive.

Perhaps a post-scarcity perspective is possible in the U.S. and Europe, but it is hard to see how a post-scarcity approach has any relevance for the Third World, where technological development is grossly inadequate to meet the most elementary needs of the people. It would seem that the libertarian revolution and the non-coercive, unmediated social forms that are possible for the U.S. and Europe would have to be supplanted by the rigorous planning of highly centralized, coercive institutions in Asia, Africa and Latin America. Carl Oglesby has even argued that to help these continents catch up with the U.S., it will be necessary for Americans to work ten or twelve hours daily to produce the goods needed.

I think we must dispel the confusion that exists about the Third World. This confusion, due partly to the superficiality of knowledge about the Third World, has done enormous harm to radical movements in the First

World. "Third World" ideology in the U.S., by promoting a mindless imitation of movements in Asia and Latin America, leads to a bypassing of the social tasks in the First World. The result is that American radicals have often eased the tasks of American imperialism by creating an alien movement that does not speak to issues at home. The "Movement" (whatever *that* is) is isolated and the American people are fair game for every tendency, reactionary as well as liberal, that speaks to their problems.

I think we should begin with some essentials. The Third World is *not* engaged in a "socialist revolution." One must be grossly ignorant of Marxism—the favored ideology of the Third World fetishists—in order to overlook the *real* nature of the struggle in Asia, Africa and Latin America. These areas are still taking up the tasks that capitalism resolved for the U.S. and Europe more than a century ago—national unification, national independence and industrial development. The Third World takes up these tasks in an era when state capitalism is becoming predominant in the U.S. and Europe, with the result that its own social forces have a highly statified character. Socialism and advanced forms of state capitalism are not easy to distinguish from each other, especially if one's conception of "socialism" is highly schematic. Drape hierarchy with a red flag, submerge the crudest system of primitive accumulation and forced collectivization in rhetoric about the interests of "the People" or "the Proletariat," cover up hierarchy, elitism and a police state with huge portraits of Marx, Engels and Lenin, print little "Red Books" that invite the most authoritarian adulation and preach the most inane banalities in the name of "dialectics" and "socialism"—and any gullible liberal who is becoming disenchanted with his ideology, yet is totally unconscious of the bourgeois conditioning he has acquired from the patriarchal family and authoritarian school, can suddenly become a flaming "revolutionary" socialist.

The whole process is disgusting—all the more so because it stands at odds with every aspect of reality. One is tempted to scream; "Look, motherfucker! Help the Third World by fighting capitalism at home! Don't cop out by hiding under Ho's and Mao's skirts when your real job is to overthrow domestic capitalism by dealing with the real possibilities of an American revolution! Develop a revolutionary project at home because every revolutionary project here is *necessarily* internationalist and anti-imperialist, no matter how much its goals and language are limited to the American condition." Oglesby's hostility to a post-scarcity approach on the grounds that we will have to work ten or twelve hours daily to meet the Third World's needs is simply preposterous. To assume that the working day will be increased by an American revolution is to invite its defeat before the first blow is struck. If, in some miraculous way, Oglesby's "revolution" were to be victorious, surely he doesn't think that the American people would accept an increased working day without a strong, centralized state apparatus cracking its whip over the entire population. In which case, one wonders what kind of "aid" such a regime would "offer" to the Third World?

Like many of the "Third World" zealots, Oglesby seems to have an incomplete knowledge of America's industrial capacity and the real needs of the Third World. Roughly seventy percent of the American labor force does absolutely no productive work that could be translated into terms of real output or the maintenance of a rational system of distribution. Their work is largely limited to servicing the commodity economy—filing, billing, bookkeeping for a profit and loss statement, sales promotion, advertising, retailing, finance, the stock market, government work, military work, police work, etc, *ad nauseam.* Roughly the same percentage of the goods produced is such pure garbage that people would voluntarily stop consuming it in a rational society. Working hours could be reduced enormously after a revolution without losing high productive output, provided that the available labor supply and raw materials were used rationally. The quality of the productive output, moreover, could be so improved that its durability and usefulness would more than cancel out any reduction in productive capacity.

On the other side, let us look more closely at the material needs of the Third World. As Westerners, "we" tend to assume out of hand that "they" want or need the same kind of technologies and commodities that capitalism produced in America and Europe. This crude assumption is bolstered by the fear consciously generated by imperialist ideology, that millions of black, brown, and yellow people are hungrily eyeing "our" vast resources and standard of living. This ideology reminds us how lucky "we" are to be Americans or Europeans, enjoying the blessings of "free enterprise," and how menacing "they" are, festering in poverty, misery and the ills of overpopulation. Ironically, the "Third World" zealots share this ideology in the sense that they, too, conceive of Asian, African and Latin American needs in Western terms—an approach that might be called the Nkrumah mentality of technological gigantism. Whatever is living and vital in the precapitalist society of the Third World is sacrificed to industrial *machismo*, oozing with the egomaniacal elitism of the newly converted male radical.

Perhaps no area of the world is more suitable for an eco-technology than the Third World.* Most of Asia, Africa and Latin America lie in the "solar belt," between latitudes 40 degrees north and south, where solar energy can be used with the greatest effectiveness for industrial and domestic purposes. New, small-scale technologies are more easily adapted for use in the underdeveloped areas than elsewhere. The small-scale gardening technologies, in fact, are indispensable for the productive use of the soil types that are prevalent in semi-tropical, tropical, and highland biomes. The peasantry in these areas have a long tradition of technological know-how in terracing and horticulture, for which small machines are already available or easily designable. Great strides have been made in developing an irrigation technology to provide year-round water resources for agriculture and industry. A unique combination could be made of machine and handcrafts, crafts in which these areas still excel. With advances in the standard of living and in education, the population of these areas could be expected to stabilize sufficiently to remove pressure on the land. What the Third World needs above all is a rational, sophisticated communications network to redistribute food and manufactures from areas of plentiful supply to those in need.

A technology of this kind could be developed for the Third World fairly rapidly by American and European industry without placing undue strain on the resources of the West. The rational use of such a technology presupposes a sweeping social revolution in the Third World itself—a revolution, I believe, that would almost immediately follow a social revolution in the U.S. With the removal of imperialism's mailed fist, a new perspective could open for the Third World. The village would acquire a new sense of unity with the elimination of the local hierarchies appointed by the central governments which have so heavily parasitized the regions. An exchange economy would continue to exist in the Third World, although its base would probably be collectivist. In any case, the exploitation of labor and the domination of women by men would be eliminated,

* The alternatives to a "Western"-type technology for the Third World and the resolution of the "population problem" in this area are discussed in some detail in my book, *The Ecology of Freedom*, published by AK Press.

thus imposing severe restrictions on the use of income differentials for exploitative purposes.* The resources of the First World could be used to promote the most revolutionary social alternatives—a people's movement as against an authoritarian one, decentralized, immediate relations as against centralized mediated institutions.

It would be difficult to say what kind of institutional structure would emerge from revolutionary changes in the Third World following a complete social revolution in the First World. Until now, the Third World has been obliged to fight imperialism largely on its own. Although there has been a great deal of international solidarity from millions of people in Europe and the U.S. for Third World struggles, there has been no real, disinterested material support from these key industrial areas. One wonders what will happen when a revolutionary United States and Europe begin to aid the Third World fully and disinterestedly, with nothing but the well being of the African, Asian and Latin American peoples at issue. I believe that the social development in the Third World will take a more benign and libertarian form than we suspect; and that surprisingly little coercion will be needed to deal with material scarcity in these areas.

In any case, there is no reason to fear that a quasi-statist development in the Third World would be more than temporary or that it would affect the world development. If the U.S. and Europe took a libertarian direction, their strategic industrial position in the world economy would, I think, favor a libertarian alternative for the world as a whole. Revolution is contagious, even when it occurs in a relatively small and economically insignificant country. I cannot imagine that Eastern Europe could withstand the effects of a libertarian revolution in Western Europe and the U.S. The revolution would almost certainly engulf the Soviet Union, where massive dissatisfaction exists, and finally the entire Asian continent. If one doubts the fulfillment of this possibility, let him consider the impact of the French Revolution on Europe at a time when the world economy was far less interdependent than it is today.

After the revolution the planet would be dealt with as a whole. The relocation of populations in areas of high density, the development of rational, humanistic birth control programs oriented toward improving

* More can be learned, I think, from the impact the Spanish anarchist movement had on the village economy than from Mao or Ho and the movements they spoke for. Unfortunately, very little information on this development is available in English. The spontaneous takeover and collectivization of the land by Spanish *pueblos* during the early weeks of Franco's rebellion provides us with one of the most remarkable accounts of how the peasantry can respond to libertarian influence.

the quality of life, and the modification of technology along ecological lines—all of these programs would be on the agenda of history. Aside from suggesting some basic guidelines drawn from ecology, I can do no more than speculate about how the resources and land areas of the world could be used to improve life in a postrevolutionary period. These programs will be solved in practice and by human communities that stand on a far higher level, culturally, psychologically and materially, than any community that exists today.

"Listen, Marxist!" seems to be quite relevant as a critique of the vulgar Marxists—Progressive Labor, the Trotskyists, and other "Old Left" movements. But what of the more sophisticated Marxists—people such as Marcuse, Gorz and the admirers of Gramsci? Surely "Listen, Marxist!" imputes too much to the "Old Left" in taking it as the point of departure for a critique of Marxism.

Marcuse is the most original of the thinkers who still call themselves Marxists, and I must confess that even on those points where I may have disagreements with him, I am stimulated by what he has to say.

With this exception, I would differ with the claim that "Listen, Marxist!" is relevant only as a critique of the "Old Left." The article is relevant to all types of Marxist ideology. Two things trouble me about Marx's mature writings; their pseudo-objectivity and the obstacles they raise to utopian thinking. The Marxian project, as it was formulated by Marx himself, deepened the early socialist tradition but also narrowed it, and in the long run this has produced a net setback rather than a net gain.

By Marx's pseudo-objectivity I mean the astonishing extent to which Marx identified "scientific socialism" with the scientism of the nineteenth century. Although there is a tendency today for the more sophisticated "neoMarxists" to cast the Marxian project in terms of alienation, the project (as it developed in Marx's hands) was above all an attempt to make socialism "scientific," to provide it with the authority of a scientific critique. This led to an emphasis on "objectivity" that increasingly subverted the humanistic goals of socialism. Freedom and eros (where the latter was taken up at all) were anchored so completely in the material preconditions for freedom that even the loss of freedom, if it promoted the material development, was viewed as an "advance" of freedom. Marx, for example, welcomed state centralization as a step in the development of the productive forces without once considering how this process enhanced the capacity of the bourgeoisie to resist revolution. He disclaimed any moral evaluation of society and in his later years became increasingly captive to scientism and to mathematical criteria of truth.

The result of this development has been a major loss for the humanistic and imaginative elements of socialism. Marxism has damaged the left enormously by anchoring it in a pseudo-objectivity that is almost indistinguishable from the juridical mentality. Whenever I hear "New Left" Marxists denounce a position as "objectively counterrevolutionary," "objectively racist," or "objectively sexist," my flesh crawls. The charge, flung randomly against all opponents, circumvents the need for an analytic or a dialectical critique. One simply traces "counterrevolution," "racism" or "sexism" to be the preconceived "objective effects." Marx rarely exhibited the crudity of the "Old Left" and "New Left" in his use of this approach, but he used the approach often enough—and often as a substitute for a multi-dimensional analysis of phenomena.

You must see how consequential this is. Freedom is divested of its autonomy, of its sovereignty over the human condition. It is turned into a means instead of an end. Whether freedom is desirable or not depends upon whether it furthers the "objective" development. Accordingly, any authoritarian organization, any system of repression, any manipulatory tactic can become acceptable, indeed admirable, if it favors the "building of socialism" or "resistance to imperialism"—as though "socialism" or "anti-imperialism" is meaningful when it is poisoned by manipulation, repression, and authoritarian forms of organization. Categories replace realities; abstract goals replace real goals; "History" replaces everyday life. The universal, which requires a complex, many-sided analysis to be grasped, is replaced by the particular; the total, by the one-sided.

No less serious is the rejection of utopian thought—the imaginative forays of Charles Fourier and William Morris. What Martin Buber called the "utopian element in socialism" is rejected for a "hardheaded" and "objective" treatment of "reality." But, in fact, this approach shrivels reality by limiting one's purview of social experience and data. The hidden potential of a given reality is either subverted by an emphasis on the "objective" actualities or, at least, diminished by a one-sided treatment. The revolutionary becomes a captive to experience not as it exists dialectically, in *all* its actualities and potentialities, but as it is defined in advance by "scientific socialism." Not surprisingly, the New Left, like the Old Left, has never grasped the revolutionary potential of the ecology issue, nor has it used ecology as a basis for understanding the problems of communist reconstruction and utopia. At best the issue is given lip service, with some drivel about how "pollution is profitable"; at worst it is denounced as spurious, diversionary and "objectively counterrevolutionary." Most of the sophisticated Marxists are as captive to these limiting features of Marxism as their New Left brethren. The difference is that they are simply more sophisticated.

In contrast to most radical works, "Listen, Marxist!" continually speaks of "hierarchical society" instead of "class society" of "domination" instead of "exploitation." What significance do these differences in language have?

A difference is definitely intended. Pre-Marxian socialism was, in many ways, much broader than the Marxian variety. Not only was it more utopian, it was also occupied more with the general than the particular. Varlet, the last of the great *enragés,* who survived the death of his comrade Jacques Roux and Robespierre's purge of the left, concluded that government and revolution are utterly "incompatible." What a splendid insight! In this one observation revolutionary consciousness expanded from a critique of a specific class society to a critique of hierarchical society as such. The pre-Marxian socialist and radical theorists began to occupy themselves with domination, not only exploitation; with hierarchy, not only class rule. With Fourier, consciousness advanced to the point where the goal of society was viewed as pleasure, not simply happiness.

You must see what an enormous gain this was. Exploitation, class rule and happiness are the *particular* within the more *generalized* concepts of domination, hierarchy and pleasure. It is theoretically—and, in great part, actually—possible to eliminate exploitation and class rule or to achieve happiness, as these concepts are defined by Marxism, without achieving a life of pleasure or eliminating domination and hierarchy. Marx, by "scientifically" anchoring exploitation, classes, and happiness in the economic domain, actually provided the rationale for a theoretical regression from the original socialist values. Marxian economic solutions, such as nationalization of property, may even create the illusion that hierarchy has disappeared. One has only to study the torment of the Trotskyist movement over the nature of the Russian state to see how obfuscating Marxian theory can be.

This particularization of the general is precisely what Marxism achieved. As I noted in reply to the previous question, socialism was given greater theoretical depth by the acquisition of dialectical philosophy, but it was narrowed disastrously by Marx's economic emphasis. Even Marx's writings shrivel in content as the man "matures." They increasingly center on the "objective" economic elements of society, until Marx sinks into a grotesque fetishization of economic theory of the kind we find in volume two of *Capital*. With Marx's death, an immense exegetical literature emerges on capitalist circulation, accumulation and "realization theory." Even Rosa Luxemburg was caught in this swamp, not to speak of the Keynesian Marxists who churn out their papers for the *American Economic Review* and *Science and Society*.

Marxism created a stupendous intellectual furniture that one must clear away to make contact with reality. The field abounds with "experts" and heavies, with academics and authorities whose bullshit makes original, indeed dialectical, thought virtually impossible. Once we rescue the essentials, this theoretical garbage must be junked. It is vitally necessary that we return to the generalized terrain that pre-Marxian socialism established, and then go forward again.

The youth culture has already posed the "social question" in its richest and most meaningful terms—"Life versus death." I would say, with an eye towards the insights of Marxism, "Life versus survival." In any case, we have to get away from the one-sided, repressive jargon of Marxism, which defines our perspective in a limiting manner. I am reminded of a fine passage from Paul Avrich's recent book, *Kronstadt 1921,* in which the language of the revolutionary Kronstadt sailors is contrasted with that of the Bolsheviks. "Rebel agitators," Avrich notes, speaking of the sailors, "wrote and spoke (as an interviewer later noted) in a homespun language free of Marxist jargon and foreign sounding expressions. Eschewing the word 'proletariat,' they called, in true populist fashion, for a society in which all the 'toilers'—peasants, workers and the 'toiling intelligentsia'—would play a dominant role. They were inclined to speak of a 'social' rather than a 'socialist' revolution, viewing class conflict not in the narrow sense of industrial workers versus bourgeoisie, but in the traditional *narodnik* sense of the laboring masses as a whole pitted against all who throve on their misery and exploitation, including politicians and bureaucrats as well as landlords and capitalists. Western ideologies—Marxism and liberalism alike—had little place in their mental outlook."[39]

The point, of course, is not Western ideologies versus Russian, or "homespun" versus "foreign-sounding" language. The real point is the *broader* concepts with which the "masses" worked almost intuitively—concepts drawn from the experience of their own oppression. Note how the sailors had a broader view of the "laboring masses" and their "oppressors" than the Bolsheviks, a view that included the elitist Bolsheviks among the oppressors. Note well, too, how Marxist jargon made it possible for the Bolsheviks to exclude themselves as oppressors in flat denial of the real situation. For my part, I am delighted that the New Left in America has replaced the words "workers" and "proletariat" by "people." Indeed, it is significant that even professedly Marxian groups like the Panthers and Weathermen have been obliged to use a populist language, for this language reflects the changed reality and problems of our times.

To sum up: what I am talking about is a human condition reflected by the word "power." We must finally resolve the historic and everyday dichotomies: man's power over woman, man's power over man, and man's power over nature. For inherent in the issue of power—of domination—are the contradictory, destructive effects of power: the corruption of life-giving sexuality, of a life-nourishing society, of a life-orienting ego, and of a life-sustaining ecology. The statement "power corrupts" is not a truism because it has never been fully understood. It may yet become understood because power now *destroys.* No amount of theoretical exegesis can place power in the service of history or of a revolutionary organization. The only act of power that is excusable any longer is that one act—popular revolution—that will finally dissolve power as such by giving each individual power over his or her everyday life.

New York
August 1970

The May–June Events in France: 1

France: A Movement for Life

THE QUALITY OF EVERYDAY LIFE

The 1968 May–June uprising was one of the most important events to occur in France since the Paris Commune of 1871. Not only did it shake the foundations of bourgeois society in France, it raised issues and posed solutions of unprecedented importance for modern industrial society. It deserves the closest study and the most thoroughgoing discussion by revolutionaries everywhere.

The May–June uprising occurred in an industrialized, consumption-oriented country—less developed than the United States, but essentially in the same economic category. The uprising exploded the myth that the wealth and resources of modern industrial society can be used to absorb all revolutionary opposition. The May–June events showed that contradictions and antagonisms in capitalism are not eliminated by statification and advanced forms of industrialism, but changed in form and character.

The fact that the uprising took everyone by surprise, including the most sophisticated theoreticians in the Marxist, Situationist and anarchist movements, underscores the importance of the May–June events and raises the need to re-examine the sources of revolutionary unrest in modern society. The graffiti on the walls of Paris—"Power to the Imagination," "It is forbidden to forbid," "Life without dead times," "Never work"—represent a more probing analysis of these sources than all the theoretical tomes inherited from the past. The uprising revealed that we are at the end of an old era and well into the beginning of a new one. The motive forces of revolution today, at least in the industrialized world, are not simply scarcity and material need, but also *the quality of everyday life, the demand for the liberation of experience, the attempt to gain control over one's own destiny.* It matters little that the graffiti on the walls of Paris were initially scrawled by a small minority. From everything I have seen, it is clear that the graffiti (which now form the content of several books) have captured the imagination of many thousands in Paris. They have touched the revolutionary nerve of the city.

THE SPONTANEOUS MAJORITY MOVEMENT

The revolt was a majority movement in the sense that it cut across nearly all the class lines in France. It involved not only students and workers, but technicians, engineers and clerical people in nearly every stratum of the state, industrial and commercial bureaucracy. It swept in professionals and laborers, intellectuals and football players, television broadcasters and subway workers. It even touched the gendarmerie of Paris, and almost certainly affected the great mass of conscript soldiers in the French army.

The revolt was initiated primarily by the young. It was begun by university students, then it was taken up by young industrial workers, unemployed youth, and the "leather jackets"—the so-called "delinquent youth" of the cities. Special emphasis must be given to high school students and adolescents, who often showed more courage and determination than the university students. But the revolt swept in older people as well—blue and white-collar workers, technicians and professionals. Although it was catalyzed by conscious revolutionaries, especially by anarchist affinity groups whose existence no one had even faintly supposed, the flow, the movement of the uprising was spontaneous. No one had "summoned it forth"; no one had "organized" it; no one succeeded in "controlling" it.

A festive atmosphere prevailed throughout most of the May–June days, an awakening of solidarity, of mutual aid, indeed of a selfhood and self-expression that had not been seen in Paris since the Commune. People literally discovered themselves and their fellow human beings anew or remade themselves. In many industrial towns, workers clogged the squares, hung out red flags, read avidly and discussed every leaflet that fell into their hands. A fever for life gripped millions, a reawakening of senses that people never thought they possessed, a joy and elation they never thought they could feel. Tongues were loosened, ears and eyes acquired a new acuity. There was singing with new, and often ribald, verses added to old tunes. Many factory floors were turned into dance floors. The sexual inhibitions that had frozen the lives of so many young people in France were shattered in a matter of days. This was not a solemn revolt, a *coup d'état* bureaucratically plotted and manipulated by a "vanguard" party; it was witty, satirical, inventive and creative—and therein lay its strength, its capacity for immense self-mobilization, its infectiousness.

Many people transcended the narrow limitations that had impeded their social vision. For thousands of students, the revolution destroyed the prissy, tight-assed sense of "studenthood"—that privileged, pompous state that is expressed in America by the "position paper" and by the stuffy sociologese of the "analytical" document. The individual workers who came to the action committees at Censier* ceased to be "workers" as such. They became revolutionaries. And it is precisely on the basis of this new identity that people whose lives had been spent in universities, factories and offices could meet freely, exchange experiences and engage in common actions without any self-consciousness about their social "origins" or "background."

The revolt had created the beginnings of its own classless, nonhierarchical society. Its primary task was to extend this qualitatively new realm to the country at large—to every corner of French society. Its hope lay in the extension of self-management in all its forms—the general assemblies and their administrative forms, the action committees, the factory strike committees—to all areas of the economy, indeed to all areas of life itself. The most advanced consciousness of this task seems to have appeared not so much among the workers in the more traditional industries, where the Communist-controlled CGT exercises great power, as among those in newer, more technically advanced industries, such as electronics. (Let me emphasize that this is a tentative conclusion, drawn from a number of scattered but impressive episodes that were related to me by young militants in the student-worker action committees.)

AUTHORITY AND HIERARCHY

Of paramount importance is the light that the May–June revolt cast on the problem of authority and hierarchy. In this respect it challenged not only the conscious processes of individuals, but also their most important unconscious, socially conditioned habits. (It does not have to be argued at any great length that the habits of authority and hierarchy are instilled in the individual at the very outset of life—in the family milieu of infancy, in childhood "education" at home and in school, in the organization of work, "leisure" and everyday life. This shaping of the character structure of the individual by what seem like "archetypal" norms of obedience and command constitutes the very essence of what we call the "socialization" of the young.)

The mystique of bureaucratic "organization," of imposed, formalized hierarchies and structures, pervades the most radical movements in

* The new building of the Sorbonne Faculty of Letters.

nonrevolutionary periods. The remarkable susceptibility of the left to authoritarian and hierarchical impulses reveals the deep roots of the radical movement in the very society it professedly seeks to overthrow. In this respect, nearly every revolutionary organization is a potential source of counterrevolution. Only if the revolutionary organization is so "structured" that its forms reflect the direct, decentralized forms of freedom initiated by the revolution, only if the revolutionary organization fosters in the revolutionist the lifestyles and personality of freedom, can this potential for counterrevolution be diminished. Only then is it possible for the revolutionary movement to dissolve into the revolution, to disappear into its new, directly democratic social forms like surgical thread into a healing wound.

The act of revolution rips apart all the tendons that hold authority and hierarchy together in the established order. The direct entry of the people into the social arena is the very *essence* of revolution. Revolution is the most advanced form of direct action. By the same token, direct action in "normal" times is the indispensable preparation for revolutionary action. In both cases, there is a substitution of social action from below for political action within the established, hierarchical framework. In both cases, there are molecular changes of "masses," classes and social strata into revolutionary individuals. This condition must become permanent if the revolution is to be successful—if it is not to be transformed into a counterrevolution masked by revolutionary ideology. Every formula, every organization, every "tried-and-tested" program, must give way to the demands of the revolution. There is no theory, program or party that has greater significance than the revolution itself.

Among the most serious obstacles to the May–June uprising were not only de Gaulle and the police, but also the hardened organizations of the left—the Communist Party that suffocated initiative in many factories and the Leninist and Trotskyist groups that created such a bad odor in the general assembly of the Sorbonne. I speak here not of the many individuals who romantically identified themselves with Che, Mao, Lenin or Trotsky (often with all four at once), but of those who surrendered their entire identity, initiative and volition to tightly disciplined, hierarchical organizations. However well-intentioned these people may have been, it became their task to "discipline" the revolt, more precisely, to de-revolutionize it by imbuing it with the habits of obedience and authority that their organizations have assimilated from the established order. These habits, fostered by participation in highly structured organizations—organizations modeled, in fact, on the very society the "revolutionaries" profess to oppose—led to parliamentary maneuvering, secret caucusing, and attempts to "control" the revolutionary forms of freedom created by the revolution. They produced in the Sorbonne assembly a poisonous vapor of manipulation. Many students to whom I spoke were absolutely convinced that these groups were prepared to destroy the Sorbonne assembly if they could not "control" it. The groups were concerned not with the vitality of the revolutionary forms but with the growth of their own organizations. Having created authentic forms of freedom in which everyone could freely express his viewpoint, the assembly would have been perfectly justified to have banned all bureaucratically organized groups from its midst.

It remains to the lasting credit of the March 22nd Movement that it merged into the revolutionary assemblies and virtually disappeared as an organization, except in name. In its own assemblies, March 22nd arrived at all its decisions by the "sense of the assembly," and it permitted all tendencies within its midst to freely test their views in practice. Such tolerance did not impair its "effectiveness"; this anarchic movement, by the common agreement of nearly all observers, did more to catalyze the revolt than any other student group. What distinguishes March 22nd and groups such as the anarchists and Situationists from all others is that they worked not for the "seizure of power" but for its dissolution.

THE DIALECTIC OF MODERN REVOLUTION

The French events of May and June reveal, vividly and dramatically, the remarkable dialectic of revolution. The everyday misery of a society is highlighted by the possibilities for the realization of desire and freedom. The greater these possibilities, the more intolerable the everyday misery. For this reason, it matters little that French society has been more affluent in recent years than at any time in its history. Affluence in its highly distorted bourgeois form merely indicates that the material conditions for freedom have developed, that the technical possibilities for a new, liberated life are overripe.

It is plain, now, that these possibilities have haunted French society for a long time, even if unperceived by most people. The insensate consumption of goods graphs, in its own warped way, the tension between the shabby reality of French society and the liberatory possibilities of a revolution today, just as a sedating diet and extravagant obesity reveal the tension in an individual. A time is finally reached when the diet of goods becomes tasteless, when the social obesity becomes intolerable. The breaking point is unpredictable. In the case of France, it was the barricades of May 10, a day which shook the conscience of the entire country and posed a question to the workers: "If the students, 'those children of the bourgeoisie', can do it, why can't we?" It is clear that a molecular process was going on in France, completely invisible to the most conscious revolutionaries, a process that the barricades precipitated into revolutionary action. After May 10, the tension between the mediocrity of everyday life and the possibilities of a liberatory society exploded into the most massive general strike in history.

The scope of the strike shows that nearly all strata of French society were profoundly disaffected and that the revolution was anchored not in a particular class but in everyone who felt dispossessed, denied, and cheated of life. The revolutionary thrust came from a stratum which, more than any other, should have "accommodated" itself to the existing order—the young. It was the young who had been nourished on the pap of Gaullist "civilization," who had not experienced the contrasts between the relatively attractive features of the prewar civilization and the shabbiness of the new one. But the pap didn't work. Its power to co-opt and absorb, in fact, is weaker than was suspected by most critics of French society. The pap-fed society could not withstand the drive for life, particularly in the young.

No less important, the lives of young people in France, as in America, had never been burdened by the Depression years and the quest for material security that shaped the lives of their elders. The prevailing reality of French life was taken by the young people for what it is—shabby, ugly, egotistical, hypocritical and spiritually annihilating. This single fact—the revolt of the young—is the most damning evidence of the system's inability to prevail on its own terms.

The tremendous internal decay of Gaullist society, a decay long antedating the revolt itself, took forms that do not fit into any of the traditional, economically oriented formulas of "revolution." Much had been written about "consumerism" in French society to the effect that it was a polluting form of social stabilization. The fact that objects, *commodities*, were replacing the traditional subjective loyalties fostered by the church, the school, the mass media and the family, should have been seen as evidence of greater social decomposition than was suspected. The fact that traditional class consciousness was declining in the working class should have been evidence that conditions were maturing for a majority *social* revolution, not a minority *class* revolution. The fact that "lumpen" values in dress, music, art and lifestyle were spreading among French youth should have been evidence that the potential for "disorder" and direct action was ripening behind the facade of conventional political protest.

By a remarkable twist of dialectic irony, a process of "debourgeoisification" was going on precisely when France had attained unprecendented heights of material affluence. Whatever may have been the personal popularity of de Gaulle, a process of deinstitutionalization was going on precisely when state capitalism seemed more entrenched in the social structure than at any time in the recent past. The tension between drab reality and the liberatory possibilities was increasing precisely when French society seemed more quiescent than at any time since the 1920s. A process of alienation was going on precisely when it seemed that the verities of bourgeois society were more secure than at any time in the history of the republic.

The point is that the issues that make for social unrest had changed qualitatively. The problems of survival, scarcity and renunciation had changed into those of life, abundance and desire. The "French dream," like the "American dream" was eroding and becoming demystified. Bourgeois society had given all it could give on the only terms it was capable of "giving" anything—a plethora of shabby material goods acquired by meaningless, deadening work. Experience itself (not "vanguard parties" and "tried-and-tested programs") became the mobilizing agent and source of creativity for the May–June uprising. And this is as it should be. Not only is it natural that an uprising *breaks out* spontaneously—a feature of all the great revolutions in history—but it is also natural that it *unfolds* spontaneously. This hardly means that revolutionary groups stand mute before the events. If they have ideas and suggestions, it is their responsibility to present them. But to use the social forms created by the revolution for manipulatory purposes, to operate secretly behind the back of the revolution, to distrust it and try to replace it by the "glorious party," is wantonly criminal and unforgivable. Either the revolution eventually absorbs *all* political organisms, or the political organisms become ends in themselves—the inevitable sources of bureaucracy, hierarchy and human enslavement.

To diminish the spontaneity of a revolution, to break the continuum between *self*-mobilization and *self*-emancipation, to remove the *self* from the process in order to mediate it with political organizations and institutions borrowed from the past, is to vitiate the revolution's liberatory goals. If the revolution does not start from below, if it does not enlarge the "base" of society until it becomes the society itself, then it is a mere *coup d'état.* If it does not produce a society in which each individual controls his daily life, instead of daily life controlling each individual, then it is a counterrevolution. Social liberation can only occur if it is simultaneously self-liberation—if the "mass" movement is a self-activity that involves the highest degree of individuation and self-awakening.

In the molecular movement below that prepares the condition for revolution, in the self-mobilization that carries the revolution forward, in the joyous atmosphere that consolidates the revolution—in *all* of these successive steps, we have a *continuum* of individuation, a process in which power is dissolved, an expansion of personal experience and freedom almost aesthetically congruent with the possibilities of our time. To see this process and articulate it, to catalyze the process and pose the next practical tasks, to deal unequivocally with the ideological movements that seek to "control" the revolutionary process—these, as the French events have shown, are the primary responsibilities of the revolutionary today.

Paris
July 1968

THE MAKING OF A REVOLUTION: WHAT HAPPENED... WHAT COULD HAVE HAPPENED...

You ask how the May–June revolt could have developed into a successful social revolution.* I shall try to give you my own views as clearly as possible. My answer applies not only to France, but to any industrialized country in the world. For what happened in France could be regarded as a model of social revolution in any advanced bourgeois country today. It astonishes me that there is so little discussion about France in the United States. The May–June events are the first really clear illustration of how a revolution can unfold in an industrially developed country in the present historical period, and they should be studied with the greatest care.

The general strike, let me point out, occurred not only because of the wage grievances that were piling up in France, but also—and mainly, in my opinion—because the people were fed up. Intuitively, unconsciously, and often quite consciously, the strikers were disgusted with the whole system, and they showed it in countless ways. A cartoon published in France after the May–June events shows a CGT official addressing the strikers: "What do you want?" he shouts. "Better pay? Shorter hours? Longer vacations?" Each time this Stalinist hack asks one of these questions, the strikers respond with silence. Finally, the CGT official cries out in anger; "Tell me, damn it! I am your representative!" And the strikers answer with a huge cry. "We want the revolution!"

To a very large extent, this response is accurate. The cartoon expressed a sentiment which was still very diffuse, of course, but was nevertheless quite real. That is why the cartoon was so popular in France when it came out. it expressed what many workers (especially young workers) felt in a vague way—and perhaps not so vaguely.

The student barricades of May 10 precipitated the general strike, the largest general strike in history. The workers (mainly the young workers) said to themselves, "if the students can do it, so can we." And out of the Sud-Aviation plant in Nantes, a city with the strongest anarcho-syndicalist tendencies in France, came the general strike. The strike swept into Paris and brought out almost everybody, not only industrial workers. Insurance

* This is an excerpt from a letter written shortly after the May–June events.

employees went out, as well as postal workers, department store clerks, professionals, teachers, scientific researchers. Yes, even the football players took over the building of their professional association and put out a banner that proclaimed, "Football belongs to the people!" It was not only a workers' strike; it was a *people's* strike that cut across almost all class lines. You must understand this, for it is a very important fact about the possibilities of our time. At Nantes, peasants brought their tractors into the city to help the movement and longshoremen emptied the holds of the ships to feed the strikers. The most advanced demands, I should emphasize, were raised in the *newer* industries—for example, in the electronics plants. In one such plant, a firm composed largely of highly skilled technicians, the employees declared publicly, "We have everything we want. We won large wage increases and longer vacations in negotiations we conducted last month [April]. We are now striking for only one demand: workers' control of industry—and not only in our plant, but for all the plants in France."

What an astonishing development! And this demand was precisely the key to the whole situation. The workers had occupied the plants. The economy was in their hands. Whether this sweeping movement would become a complete social revolution depended upon one thing-would the workers not only occupy the plants, but *work* them? This was the barrier that had to be surmounted. Had the workers begun to work the plants under workers' management, the revolt would have advanced into a full-scale social revolution.

Let us now try to imagine what would have happened if the workers had actually surmounted this barrier. Each plant would elect its own factory committee from among its own workers to *administer* the plant. (Here the workers could have counted on a great deal of cooperation from the technical staff, most of whom would have gone over to the revolution.) I emphasize "administer" because policy would be made by the workers in the plant, by an assembly of the workers on the factory floor. The factory committee would merely execute and coordinate these policies. Here you have true revolutionary democracy, and in the arena of production, where the means of life are made.

Let us go further (and what I shall describe was absolutely possible). The factory committees of all the local plants could now link together to form an area administrative council, whose function would be to deal with whatever supply problems exist. Each member of this council would be rigorously controlled by the workers in the plant from which he or she came and would be fully accountable to the factory assembly. The tasks of the council, I must emphasize, would be entirely administrative; many of its technical functions could be taken over by computers, and membership on the council would be rotated as often as possible.

Together with these industrial forms of organization, there would also be neighborhood organizations—assemblies corresponding to the French revolutionary sections of 1793, as well as action committees to perform the administrative tasks of the neighborhood assemblies. They too would form an administrative council, which would work with the factory committee council, the two meeting together periodically to deal with common problems. One of the most important functions of the neighborhood assemblies—the new "sections"—would be to recycle employment from nonproductive areas of the economy (sales, insurance, advertising, "government," and other socially useless areas) into productive areas. The goal here would be to shorten the work week as rapidly as possible. In this way, everyone would benefit almost immediately from the new arrangement of society—both the industrial worker and, say, the ex-salesman whom the worker trains in the factory. All would get the means of life for a fraction of the time they devote to work under bourgeois conditions. The revolution would thus undercut the position of many counterrevolutionary elements who, from time immemorial, have argued that the old conditions of life were better than the new.

What is essential here is not the fine detail of this structure, which could be worked out in practice, but the dissolution of power into the assemblies, both factory and neighborhood. In the past, very little attention has been given to the role and importance of unmediated relations and popular assemblies. So strongly was the notion of "representation" fixed in the thinking of revolutionary groups and the people that the assemblies, where they existed, arose almost accidentally. Apart from the Greek ecclesia, they emerged, in most cases, not as a result of conscious design, but rather of fortuitous circumstances. Ordinarily, the various councils and committees in earlier revolutions were given enormous powers in formulating policy; the demarcation between administrative work and policy decisions was murky at best, or simply nonexistent. As a result, the committees and councils became social agencies exercising enormous political powers *over* society; they became a nascent state apparatus that rapidly acquired control over society as a whole. This can now be avoided, partly by making all committees and councils *directly* answerable to assemblies, partly by using the new technology to shorten the work week radically, thereby freeing the whole people for active participation in the management of society.

At first the various committees, councils and assemblies would use the existing mechanism of supply and distribution to meet the material needs of society. Steel would come to Paris the way it always has: by means of the same ordering methods and the same railways and trucks, probably operated by the same engineers and truck drivers. The postal, cable and telephone networks that were used before the revolution to request materials would be used again after the revolution. Finally, finished goods would be distributed by the same warehouses and retail outlets except that the cash registers would be removed. The principal functions of the new factory committee councils and neighborhood councils would be to deal with any bottlenecks and obstructive practices that might emerge and to propose changes that would lead to a more rational use of existing resources.

Capitalism has already established the physical mechanism of circulation—of distribution and transportation that is needed to maintain society without any state apparatus. This physical mechanism of circulation can be vastly improved upon, to be sure, but it would still be as workable the day after the revolution as it was the day before the revolution. It needs no police, jails, armies or courts to maintain it. The state is superimposed on this technical system of distribution and actually serves to distort it by maintaining an artificial system of scarcity. (This, today, is the real meaning of the "sanctity of property.")

I must emphasize again that since we are concerned with human needs, not with profit, a vast number of people who are needed to operate the profit system could be freed from their idiotic work. So could many people who are occupied with working for the state. These people could join their brothers and sisters in productive jobs, thus drastically shortening everyone's work week. In this new system, the producers and the community could jointly manage the economy from below, coordinating their administrative operations through factory committees, councils of factory committee representatives, and neighborhood action committees—all directly accountable to the plant and neighborhood assemblies, all recallable for their actions. At this point, society takes direct control of its affairs. The state, its bureaucracy, its armies, police, judges and jails, can disappear.

You may object that the old system of production and distribution is still centralized structurally and based on a national division of labor. Agreed; you are perfectly correct. But does its *control* have to be centralized? As long as policy is made from below and everyone who executes that policy is controlled locally, administration is socially decentralized although the means of production are structurally fairly centralized as yet. A computer used to coordinate the operations of a vast plant, for example, is an instrument for structural centralization. However, if the people who program and operate the computer are completely answerable to the workers in the plant, their operations are socially decentralized.

To pass from a narrow analogy to the broader problems of administration, let us suppose that a board of highly qualified technicians is established to propose changes in the steel industry. This board, we may suppose, advances proposals to rationalize the industry by closing some plants and expanding the operations of others in different parts of the country. Is this a "centralized" body or not? The answer is both yes and no. Yes, only in the sense that the board is dealing with problems that concern the country as a whole; no, because it can make no decisions that *must* be executed for the country as a whole. The board's plan must be examined by all the workers in the plants that are to be closed down, and those whose operations are to be expanded. The plan itself may be accepted, modified, or simply rejected. The board has no power to enforce "decisions"; it merely offers recommendations. Additionally, its personnel are controlled by the plant in which they work and the locality in which they live.

Similar boards, I may add, could be established to plan the physical decentralization of the society—boards composed of ecologists as well as technologists. They could develop plans for entirely new patterns of land use in different areas of the country. Like the technicians who are dealing with the existing steel industry, they would have no decision-making powers. The adoption, modification or rejection of their plans would rest entirely with the communities involved.

But I've already traveled too much into the "future." Let us return to the May–June events of 1968. What of de Gaulle, the generals, the army, the police? Here we come to another crucial problem that faced the May–June revolt. Had the armament workers not merely occupied the arms factories but worked them to arm the revolutionary people, had the railroad workers transported these arms to the revolutionary people in the cities, towns and villages, had the action committees organized armed militias—then the situation in France would have changed drastically. An armed people, organized into militias by its own action committees (and there are plenty of reservists among the young people to train them), would have confronted the state. Most of the militants I spoke to do not believe that the bulk of the army, composed overwhelmingly of conscripts, would have fired on the people. If the people were armed, every street could have been turned into a bastion and every factory into a fortress. Whether de Gaulle's most reliable troops would have marched upon them in these circumstances is very questionable. Alas, the situation was never brought to that point—the point that every revolution has to risk.

Let me emphasize again that all I have sketched out for you was perfectly possible. I write here of a reality that stared the French revolutionaries in the face. All that was necessary was for the workers to work the factories and turn their strike committees into factory committees. This decisive step was not taken; hence the people were not armed and the bourgeois system of property relations was not shattered. The Stalinists shrewdly deflected the revolutionary movement into political lines by calling for a Communist-Socialist coalition cabinet. Thus the struggle was channeled into an election campaign on strictly bourgeois grounds. For these reasons and others, the revolt receded and in so doing produced a "backlash" from the mass of people who were watching and waiting. These people might have been won to the revolution had it succeeded. They seemed to be standing by and saying; "Let's see what you can do." Once the revolt failed, however, they voted for de Gaulle. De Gaulle at least had reality; the revolution, on the other hand, bad been vaporized by failure.

How did the Maoists and Trotskyists, the "vanguard" Bolshevik parties and groupuscules, behave? The Maoists opposed every demand for workers' control. (Some of them, after the revolt receded, began to revise their views and are now called "anarcho-Maoists"!) Chairman Mao had opined that workers' control is anarcho-syndicalism—hence a "petty bourgeois deviation." The job of the workers, cried the Maoists, was to "seize state power." Thus, in the name of "Bolshevik realism," the only basis for a social revolution—the occupation of the factories—was subordinated to abstract political slogans that had no reality in the living situation. Let me give you an example: marching to the Billancourt plant of Renault, the Maoists carried a big banner which read "Vive the CGT!"—this at a time when the most revolutionary workers were carrying on a bitter struggle with the CGT and were trying to shed the bureaucratic apparatus with which the labor federation had saddled the workers. What the Maoists were saying was "put us in control of the CGT." But who the hell wanted *them?*

The Trotskyists? Which ones—the FER? The JCR? The other two or three splits? The FER played an overtly *counterrevolutionary* role at almost every decisive point, condemning all the street actions that led to the general strike as "adventuristic." The students had their hands full with them in the street-fighting before the Sorbonne, where they tried to get the students to go home, and in the barricade fighting on the night of May 10, when they denounced the students as "romantics." Instead of joining the students, they held a "mass meeting" at the Mutualité. All of this did not prevent the FER from politicking like mad in the corridors and assembly meetings of the Sorbonne—after the students had succeeded. As to the JCR, more often than not they dragged their feet and created a great deal of confusion in the Sorbonne assembly with their politicking. Toward the end of the May–June events, they held back the movement and accommodated themselves to the non-Stalinist electoral left.

What was "missing" in the May–June events? Certainly not "vanguard" Bolshevik parties. The revolt was afflicted with these parties like lice. What was needed in France was an awareness among the workers that the factories had to be *worked,* not merely occupied or struck. Or to put it differently, what the revolt lacked was a movement that could develop this *consciousness* in the workers. Such a movement would have had to be anarchic, similar either to the March 22nd Movement or the action committees that took over Censier and tried to help the workers, not dominate them. Had these movements developed before the revolt, or had the revolt lasted long enough for them to develop an impressive propaganda and action force, events might have taken a different turn. Anyway, the Communists combined with de Gaulle to deflect the revolt and finally destroy it.

In my opinion, these are the real lessons of the May–June events. In reading what I have written, it becomes very clear why Marxist-Leninists in America devote little discussion to the May–June events in France: the events, even the memory of them, challenge all their tenets, programs, and strategies.

Paris
July 1968

MARAT/SADE

Most of the articles that have been written thus far about the Marat/Sade play have been drivel and the tritest remarks have come from its author, Peter Weiss. A good idea can slip from the hands of its creator and follow its own dialectic. This kept happening with Balzac, so there is no reason why it shouldn't happen with Weiss.

The play is mainly a dialogue between Desire and Need—a dialogue set up under conditions where history froze them into antipodes and opposed them violently to each other in the Great Revolution of 1789. In those days, Desire clashed with Need: the one aristocratic, the other plebeian; the one as the pleasures of the individual, the other as the agony of the masses; the one as the satisfaction of the particular, the other as the want of the general; the one as private reaction, the other as social revolution. In our day, Marat and de Sade have not been rediscovered; they have been reinterpreted. The dialogue goes on, but now on a different level of possibility and toward a final resolution of the problem. It is an old dialogue, but in a new context.

In Weiss's play, the context is an asylum. The dialogue can only be pursued by madmen among madmen. Sane men would have resolved the issues raised by the dialogue years ago. They would have resolved them in practice. But we talk about them endlessly and we refract them through a thousand mystical prisms. Why? Because we are insane; we have been turned into pathological cases. Weiss, on this score, is only just; he places the dialogue where it belongs, in an asylum policed by guards, nuns and an administrator. We are insane not only because of what we have done, but also because of what we haven't done. We "tolerate" too much. We tremble and cower with "tolerance."

How, then, are we to act? How, following the credo imputed to Marat, are we to pull ourselves up by the hair, turn ourselves inside out, and see the world with fresh eyes? "Weiss refuses to tell us," says Peter Brook in an introduction to the script, and then Brook trails off into talk about facing contradictions. But this doesn't carry any conviction. The dialogue, launched by its literary creator and by its stage director, has its own inner movement, its own dialectic. At Corday's third visit, de Sade lasciviously displays her before Marat and asks: "...what's the point of a revolution without general copulation?" De Sade's words are taken up by the mimes and then by all the "lunatics" in the play. Even Brook cannot leave the answer alone. The ending of the play, equivocal in the script version, turns into a riotous bacchanal in the movie version. The "lunatics" overpower the guards, nuns, visitors and administrator; they grab all the women on the stage and everybody fucks like mad. The answer begins to emerge almost instinctively: the revolution that seeks to annul Need must enthrone Desire for everybody. Desire must become Need!

DESIRE AND NEED POLARIZED

Need—the need to survive, to secure the bare means of existence—could never have produced a public credo of Desire. It could have produced a religious credo of renunciation, to be sure, or a republican credo of virtue, but not a public credo of sensuousness and sensibility. The enthronement of Desire as Need, of the pleasure principle as the reality principle, is nourished as a *public* issue by the productivity of modern industry and by the possibility of a society without toil. Even the widely touted recoil of the flower children from the verities of consumption, drudgery and suburbia has its origin in the irrationalities of modern affluence. Without the affluence, no recoil. To state the matter bluntly, the revolutionary growth of modern technology has brought into question every historical precept that promoted renunciation, denial and toil. It vitiates every concept of Desire as a privileged, aristocratic domain of life.

This technology creates a new dimension of Desire, one that completely transcends the notions of de Sade, or for that matter of the French symbolists, from whom we still derive our credo of sensibility. De Sade's unique one, Baudelaire's dandy, Rimbaud's visionary, each is an isolated ego, a rare individual who takes flight from the mediocrity and unreality of bourgeois life into hallucinated reveries. In spite of its high, anti-bourgeois spirit of negation, this ego remains distinctly privileged. Baudelaire, one of the most unequivocal of the symbolist writers, expresses its aristocratic nature with bluntness in his notion of Dandyism. The Dandy, the man of true sensibility, he tells us, enjoys leisure and is untroubled by Need. This leisure is defined by the opposition of the Dandy to the crowd, of the particular to the general. It is anchored in the very social conditions that breed Marats and the *enragés* of 1793—the world of Need.

Dandyism, to be sure, asserts itself against the existing elites, but not against elitism; against the prevailing privileges, but not against privilege. "Dandyism flourishes especially in periods of transition," Baudelaire notes with acuity, "when democracy is not yet all-powerful and the aristocracy is just beginning to totter and decay. Amidst the turmoil of these times, a small group of men, *déclassés,* at loose ends, fed up—but all of them rich in determination—will conceive the idea of founding a new sort of aristocracy, stronger than the old, for it shall be based on only the most precious, the most indestructible factors, on those heaven-sent gifts that neither money nor ambition can confer." The truth, however, is that its gifts are not heaven-sent. This aesthetic elite floats on the surface of the social war, a richly ornamented debris that presupposes, objectively, the very aristocracy and bourgeoisie it repudiates in spirit.

What, then, of the revolutionary movement—the movement that seeks to reach below the surface of the social war into its very depths? For the most part it dispenses almost completely with a concrete credo of sensuousness. Marxism, the dominant project within the revolutionary movement, offers itself to the proletariat as a harsh, sobering doctrine, oriented toward the labor process, political activity, and the conquest of state power. To sever all the ties between poetry and revolution, it calls its socialism scientific and casts its goals in the hard prose of economic theory. Where the French symbolists formed a concrete image of man, defined by the specifics of play, sexuality and sensuousness, the two great exiles in England formed an abstract image of man, defined by the universals of class, commodity and property. The whole person—concrete *and* abstract, sensuous *and* rational, personal *and* social—never finds adequate representation in either credo.* This is tragedy in the Hegelian sense that both sides are right. In retrospect, it is only fair to add that the social situation of their time was inadequate for the complete fulfillment of humanity. Ordinarily the social period admits neither of the liberated personality nor of the liberated society; its doors are closed to the free expression of sensuousness and to the unfettered exercise of reason.

But the doors are never solid. There are moments when they, and indeed the entire house, are shaken to the foundations by elemental events.

* A sense of incompleteness haunts Western philosophy after Hegel's death and explains much of the work of Kierkegaard, Schopenhauer, Stirner, Nietzsche, the surrealists and the contemporary existentialists. For the Marxians merely to dismiss this post Hegelian development as "bourgeois ideology" is to dismiss the problem itself.

In such moments of crisis, when the senses of everyone are strained to extraordinary acuity by social emergencies, the doors break down and the people surge past the hanging portals, no longer as masses but as awakened personalities. These people cannot be crucified on theoretical formulas. They acquire their human reality in revolutionary action. The Paris Commune of 1871 represents precisely such a moment when neither aesthetic nor social theory adequately encompasses the over-all social situation. The Communards of the Belleville district in Paris, who fought the battles of the barricades and died by the tens of thousands under the guns of the Versaillese, refused to confine their insurrection to the private world described by symbolist poems or the public world described by Marxist economics. They demanded the eating and the moral, the filled belly and the heightened sensibility. The Commune floated on a sea of alcohol—for weeks everyone in the Belleville district was magnificently drunk. Lacking the middle-class proprieties of their instructors, the Belleville Communards turned their insurrection into a festival of public joy, play and solidarity. Perhaps it was foredoomed that the prose of bourgeois society would eventually digest the songs of the Commune—if not in an orgy of slaughter, then in the day-to-day compromises and retreats required by work, material security and social administration. Faced with a bloody conflict and nearly certain defeat, the Communards flung life away with the abandon of individuals who, having tasted of experience in the open, can no longer return to the coffins of daily routine, drudgery and denial. They burned down half of Paris, fighting suicidally to the very last on the heights of their district.

In the Paris Commune of 1871, we have the expression not merely of social interest, but of social libido.* It is hard to believe that the repression following the fall of the Commune—the mass shootings, the ruthless trials, the exile of thousands to penal colonies—owed its savagery strictly to class vengeance. A review of the memoirs, newspapers and letters of the time shows that the bourgeois directed his vengeance against his own subterranean humanity. In the spontaneous outburst of social libido which we call the Paris Commune the bourgeois saw the breakdown of all the repressive mechanisms that maintain hierarchical society. He recoiled with the horror and ferocity of a man who suddenly comes face to face with his unconscious drives.

* Is it any different in other great revolutions? Can we resolve the anarchic, intoxicating phase that opens all the great revolutions of history merely into an expression of class interest and the opportunity to redistribute social wealth?

THE SELF: MYTH AND REALITY

No one really learned from the Communards of the Belleville district, with the result that Desire and the revolutionary credo developed away from each other. In separating, both were divested of their human content. The credo of Desire evaporated into a misty subjectivism, far removed from all social concerns; the credo of revolution hardened into a dense objectivism, almost completely absorbed in the techniques of social manipulation. The need to round out the revolutionary credo with Desire, or Desire with the revolutionary credo, remains a pressing, perhaps the most pressing, problem of our times. Serious attempts to achieve this totality were made in the 1920s, when the surrealists and Wilhelm Reich tried to resynthesize Marxism and transcend it with a larger conception of the revolutionary project. Although this project did not succeed, it did not fail. All the issues were passed on to us, transformed by new dimensions of thought and by a new sense of immediacy produced by the technological advances of our time.

Ironically, the greatest single obstacle to fulfilling this project is the revolutionary credo itself. Leninism, and its various offshoots have refocused the revolutionist's attention from social goals to political means, from utopia to strategy and tactics. Lacking any clear definition of its human goals, the revolutionary movement, at least in its currently organized forms, has assimilated the hierarchical institutions, puritanism, work ethic and general characterology of the very society it professes to oppose. The goals of Marxism are largely contained in the demand for the *seizure* of power rather than the *dissolution* of power; the former implies the existence of hierarchy and the power of an elite over society as a whole.

Almost equally important as an obstacle to the project envisioned by the surrealists and Reich is the emergence of a crude, undifferentiated subjectivism that casts the rediscovery of man exclusively in terms of self-discovery—in the journey inward. What is basically wrong with this form of subjectivism is not its emphasis on the subject, on the concrete individual. Indeed, as Kierkegaard has emphasized, we have been overfed with the universals of science, philosophy and sociology. The error that vitiates this subjectivism is its operating principle that the self can be divorced completely from society, subjectivity from objectivity, consciousness from action. Ironically, this inner, isolated self turns out to be one of the most fictitious of universals, one of the most treacherous abstractions, a metaphysical concept in which consciousness, far from expanding, contracts into banalities and trivia. Philosophically, its ultimate state is pure being, a purity of experience and inner repose that adds up to nothing.* Its ultimate state, in short, is the dissolution of Desire into contemplation.

The fact is, the self cannot be resolved into an inherent "it," a cryptic "soul" covered and obscured by layers of reality. In this abstract form, the self remains an undifferentiated potentiality, a mere bundle of individual proclivities, until it interacts with the real world. Without dealing with the world it simply cannot be *created* in any human sense. Nietzsche reveals this feature of the Self when he declares "...your true nature lies not concealed deep in you, but immeasurably high above you, or at least what you call your self." Valid introspection turns out to be the conscious appropriation of a self formed largely by the world, and thus a judgment of the world and of the actions needed to reconstitute it along new lines. This order of self-consciousness reaches its height during our time in revolutionary action. To revolt, to *live* revolt, is the complete reconstitution of the individual revolutionary, a change as far-reaching and as radical as the remaking of society. In the process of discarding accumulated experiences, of integrating and re-integrating new experience, a self grows out of the old. For this reason it is idiotic to predict the behavior of people after a revolution in terms of their behavior before it. They will not be the same people.

If it is true that valid introspection must culminate in action, in a reworking of the self by experience with the real world, this reworking achieves a sense of direction only insofar as it moves from the *existent* to the *possible,* from the "what is" to the "what could be." Precisely this dialectic is what we mean by psychic growth. Desire itself is the sensuous apprehension of possibility, a complete psychic synthesis achieved by a "yearning for..." Without the pain of this dialectic, without the struggle that yields the achievement of the possible, growth and Desire are divested of all differentiation and content. The very *issues* which provide a concept of the possible are never formulated. The real responsibility we face is to eliminate not the psychic pain of growth but rather the psychic suffering

* My concern with this philosophical aspect of subjectivism stems from the fact that it is advanced not only by a salad of Hindu Cagliostros but also by serious thinkers such as Norman 0. Brown.

of dehumanization, the torment that accompanies the frustrated and aborted life.

The goal of crude subjectivism is stasis—the absence of pain, the achievement of undisturbed repose. This stasis yields an all-embracing placidity that dissolves anger into love, action into contemplation, willfullness into passivity. The absence of emotional differentiation means the end of real emotion. Confronted with the goal of insensate stasis, dialectical growth could justly demand any right to emotion—including the right to hate—to reclaim a real state of sensibility, including the ability to love selectively. The apostle of the undifferentiated type of sensibility (more precisely, sensation) is Marshall McLuhan, whose fantasies of integral communication consist entirely of kicks and highs. Technique, here, is degraded into ends, the message into the media.

THE DISINTEGRATING SELF

The fact remains, nonetheless, that there can be no meaningful revolutionary credo that fails to include the subject in its point of departure. We have passed beyond a time when the real world can be discussed without taking up in depth the basic problems and needs of the psyche—a psyche that is neither strictly concrete nor strictly universal, but both newly integrated and transcended. The rediscovery of the concrete psyche is the most valid contribution of modem subjectivism and existentialist philosophy to the revolutionary credo, albeit the rediscovered psyche is partial and incomplete, and often tends to become abstracted. In an era of relative affluence, when material immiseration is not the exclusive source of social restiveness, the revolution tends to acquire intensely subjective and personal qualities. Revolutionary opposition centers increasingly around the disintegration of the quality of life, around the anti-life perspectives and methods of bourgeois society.

To put this matter differently, the revolutionist is created and nourished by the breakdown of all the great bourgeois universals—property, class, hierarchy, free enterprise, the work ethic, patriarchalism, the nuclear family and so on, *ad nauseam.* From all of this wreckage, the self begins to achieve self-consciousness and Desire begins to recover its integrity. When the entire institutional fabric becomes unstable, when everyone lacks a sense of destiny, be it in job or social affiliations, the lumpen periphery of society tends to become its center and the *déclassés* begin to chart out the most advanced forms of social and personal consciousness. It is for this reason that any work of art can be meaningful today only if it is lumpenized.

The lumpen's self is permeated by negativity, a reflection of the overall social negativity. Its consciousness is satyr-like and its mockery is acquired by its distance from the verities of bourgeois society. But this very mockery constitutes the self's transcendance of the repressive ideologies of toil and renunciation. The lumpen's acts of disorder become the nuclei of a new order and his spontaneity implies the means by which it can be achieved.

Hegel understood this fact beautifully. In a brilliant review of Diderot's *Rameau's Nephew,* he writes: "The mocking laughter at existence, at the confusion of the whole and at itself, is the disintegrated consciousness, aware of itself and expressing itself, and is at the same time the last audible echo of all this confusion... It is the self-disintegrating nature of all relations and their conscious disintegration... In this aspect of the return to self, the vanity of all things is the self's own vanity, or the self is itself vanity...but as the indignant consciousness it is aware of its own disintegration and by that knowledge has immediately transcended it... Every part of this world either gets its mind expressed here or is spoken of intellectually and declared for what it is. The honest consciousness [the role that Diderot allots to himself in the dialogue*] takes each element for a permanent entity and does not realize in its uneducated thoughtfulness that it is doing just the opposite. But the disintegrated consciousness is the consciousness of reversal and indeed of absolute reversal; its dominating element is the concept, which draws together the thoughts that to the honest consciousness lie so wide apart; hence the brilliance of its own language. Thus the contents of the mind's speech about itself consist in the reversal of all conceptions and realities; the universal deception of oneself and others and the shamelessness of declaring this conception is therefore the greatest truth... To the quiet consciousness which in its honest way goes on singing the melody of the True and the Good in even tones, i.e., on one note, this speech appears as 'a farrago of wisdom and madness...'"[40]

Hegel's analysis, written more than a century and a half ago, anticipates and contains all the elements of the "absolute refusal" advanced so poignantly at the present time. Today, the spirit of negativity must extend

* Diderot takes the role of the virtuous man, the petty bourgeois, engaged in a dialogue with Rameau's nephew, a Figaro-like scamp and pimp.

to all areas of life if it is to have any content; it must demand a complete frankness which, in Maurice Blanchot's words, "no longer tolerates complicity." To lessen this spirit of negativity is to place the very integrity of the self in the balance. The established order tends to be totalistic: it stakes out its sovereignty not only over surface facets of the self but also over its innermost recesses. It seeks complicity not only in appearances but also from the most guarded depths of the human spirit. It tries to mobilize the very dream-life of the individual—as witness the proliferation of techniques and art forms for manipulating the unconscious. It attempts, in short, to gain command over the self's sense of possibility, over its capacity for Desire.

DESIRE AND REVOLUTION

Out of the disintegrating consciousness must come the recovery, the reintegration and the advance of Desire—a new sensuousness based on possibility. If this sense of possibility lacks a humanistic social content, if it remains crudely egoistic, then it will simply follow the logic of the irrational social order and slip into a vicious nihilism.* In the long run, the choices confronting the modern bohemian—hip or freak—are not between a socially passive subjectivism and a politically active reformism (the prevailing society, as it moves from crisis to crisis, will eliminate these traditional luxuries), but between the reactionary extremism of the SS man and the revolutionary extremism of the anarchist.

Bluntly, to drop out is to drop in. There is no facet of human life that is not infiltrated by social phenomena and there is no imaginative experience that does not float on the data of social reality. Unless the sense of the *merveilleux,* so earnestly fostered by the surrealists, is to culminate in a credo of death (a credo advanced with consistency by Villiers de l'Isle Adam in *Axel),* honesty requires that we acknowledge the social roots of our dreams, our imagination and our poetry. The real question we face is *where* we drop in, *where* we stand in relation to the whole.

* This is perhaps as good a place as any to emphasize that capitalism promotes egotism, not individuality or "individualism." Although bourgeois society loosened the hold of precapitalist unitary societies on the ego, the ego it created was as shriveled as the one it replaced. The tendency in modern state capitalism is to homogenize and massify the ego on a scale that can be compared only with the totalitarian societies of the archaic Oriental world. The term "bourgeois individualism," an epithet widely used by the left today against libertarian elements, reflects the extent to which bourgeois ideology permeates the socialist project; indeed, the extent to which the "socialist" project (as distinguished from the libertarian communist project) is a mode of state capitalism.

By the same token, there is nothing in the prevailing reality that is not polluted by the degeneration of the whole. Until the child is discharged from the diseased womb, liberation must take its point of departure from a diagnosis of the illness, an awareness of the problem, and a striving to be born. Introspection must be corrected by social analysis. Our freedom is anchored in *revolutionary* consciousness and culminates in *revolutionary* action.

But the revolution can no longer be imprisoned in the realm of Need. It can no longer be satisfied merely with the prose of political economy. The task of the Marxian critique has been completed and must be transcended. The subject has entered the revolutionary project with entirely new demands for experience, for re-integration, for fulfillment, for the *merveilleux.* The very character structure promoted by the revolutionary project in the past is now at issue in its most nuclear forms. Any hierarchical organization of human differences—sexual, ethnic, generational or physical—must now give way to the dialectical principle of unity in diversity. In ecology, this principle is already taken for granted: the conservation, indeed elaboration, of variety is regarded as a precondition for natural stability. All species are equally important in maintaining the unity and balance of an ecosystem. There are no hierarchies in nature other than those imposed by hierarchical modes of human thought, but rather differences merely in function between and within living things. The revolutionary project will always remain incomplete and one-sided until it recognizes the need to remove all hierarchical modes of thought, indeed all conceptions of "otherness" based on domination, from its own midst. Social hierarchy is undeniably real today in the sense that it stems from a clash of *objectively* conflicting interests, a clash that up to now has been validated by unavoidable material scarcity. But precisely because this hierarchical organization of appearances exists in bourgeois society at a time when the problem of scarcity can be solved, it must be eliminated completely from the revolutionary community. And it must be eliminated not only in the revolutionary organization, but in the outlook and character structure of the individual revolutionary.

To rephrase Pierre Reverdy's words, the poet now stands on the ramparts—not only as dreamer, but also as fighter. Stalking through the dream, permeating the surreal experience, stirring the imagination to entirely new evocative heights are the liberatory possibilities of the objective world. For the first time in history, object and subject can be joined in the revolutionary affinity group—the anarchic, revolutionary collectivity of sisters and brothers. Theory and praxis can be united in the purposive revolutionary deed. Thought and intuition can be merged in the new revolutionary vision. Conscious and unconscious can be integrated in the revolutionary revel. Liberation may not be complete—for us, at least—but it can be totalistic, involving every facet of life and experience. Its fulfillment may be beyond our wildest visions, but we can move toward what we can see and imagine. Our Being is Becoming, not stasis. Our Science is Utopia, our Reality is Eros, our Desire is Revolution.

New York
June 1967

References

1 G. W. F. Hegel, *The Phenomenology of Mind,* trans. J. B. Baillie, 2nd ed. rev. (Humanities Press; New York, 1949), p. 654.

2 Karl Marx and Frederick Engels, "The Communist Manifesto," in *Selected Works* (International Publishers; New York, n.d.), vol. 1, p. 227.

3 Raoul Vaneigem, "The Totality for Kids" (International Situationist pamphlet; London, n.d.), p. 1.

4 Guy Debord, "Perspectives for Conscious Modification of Daily Life," mimeographed translation from *Internationale Situationiste,* no. 6 (n.p., n.d.), p. 2.

5 Josef Weber, "The Great Utopia," *Contemporary Issues*, vol. 2, no. 5 (1950), p. 12.

6 Ibid., p. 19 (my emphasis).

7 Abraham H. Maslow, *Toward a Psychology* of *Being* (Van Nostrand; New York, 1962), p. viii.

8 Quoted in Angus M. Woodbury, *Principles of General Ecology* (Blakiston; New York, 1954), p. 4.

9 Robert L. Rudd, "Pesticides: The *Real* Peril," *The Nation,* vol. 189 (1959), p. 401.

10 E. A. Gutkind, *The Twilight of the Cities* (Free Press; Glencoe, N.Y., 1962), pp. 55–144.

11 H. D. F. Kitto, *The Greeks* (Aldine; Chicago, 1951), p. 16.

12 Karl Marx and Frederick Engels, *The German Ideology* (International Publishers; New York, 1947), p. 24.

13 Pierre-Joseph Proudhon, *What Is Property?* (Bellamy Library; London, n.d.), vol. 1, p. 135.

14 U.S. Congress, Joint Committee on the Economic Report, *Automation and Technological Change: Hearings Before the Subcommittee on Economic Stabilization,* 84th Cong., Ist session (U.S. Govt. Printing Office; Washington, 1955), p. 81.

15 Alice Mary Hilton, "Cyberculture," Fellowship for Reconciliation paper (Berkeley, 1964), p. 8.

16 Lewis Mumford, *Technics and Civilization* (Harcourt, Brace and Co.; New York, 1934), pp. 69–70.

17 Eric W. Leaver and John J. Brown, "Machines without Men," *Fortune,* November 1946.

18 F. M. C. Fourier, *Selections from the Works of Fourier, (*S. Sonnenschein and Co.; London, 1901), p. 93.

19 Charles Gide, introduction to Fourier, op. cit., p. 14.

20 Hans Thirring, *Energy for Man* (Harper & Row; New York, 1958), p. 266

21 Ibid., p. 269.

22 Henry Tabor, "Solar Energy," in *Science and the New Nations,* ed. Ruth Gruber (Basic Books; New York, 1961), p. 109.

23 Eugene Ayres, "Major Sources of Energy," American Petroleum Institute Proceedings, section 3, Division of Refining, vol. 28 III) (1948), p. 117.

24 Thomas Carlyle, *The French Revolution* (Modern Library; New York, n.d.), p. 593.

25 Friedrich Wilhelmsen, preface to Friedrich G. Juenger, *The Failure of Technology* (Regnery; Chicago, 1956), p. vii.

26 W. Warde Fowler, *The City State of the Greeks and Romans* (Macmillan & Co.; London, 1952), p. 168.

27 Edward Zimmerman, *The Greek Commonwealth,* 5th ed. (Modern Library; New York, 1931), pp. 408–9.

28 Karl Marx, "The Eighteenth Brumaire of Louis Bonaparte," in Marx and Engels, *Selected Works,* Vol. 2, p. 318.

29 V.I. Lenin, *The Threatening Catastrophe and How to Fight It,* The Little Lenin Library, vol, II (International Publishers; New York, 1932), p. 37.

30 Quoted in Leon Trotsky, *The History of the Russian Revolution* (Simon & Schuster; New York, 1932), vol. 1, p. 144.

31 V. V. Osinsky, "On the Building of Socialism," *Kommunist,* no. 2, April 1918, quoted in R. V. Daniels, *The Conscience of the Revolution* (Harvard University Press; Cambridge, 1960), pp. 85–86,

32 Robert G. Wesson, *Soviet Communes* (Rutgers University Press; New Brunswick, N.J., 1963), p. 110.

33 R. V. Daniels, op. cit., p. 145.

34 Mosche Lewin, *Lenin's Last Struggle* (Pantheon; New York, 1968), p. 122.

35 Karl Marx and Frederick Engels, *Selected Correspondence* (International Publishers; New York, 1942), p. 292.

36 Frederick Engels, *Herr Eugen Dühring's Revolution in Science (Anti-Dühring)* (International Publishers; New York, 1939),p. 323.

37 Marx and Engels, "The Communist Manifesto."

38 Karl Marx and Frederick Engels, *The Holy Family* (Foreign Languages Publishing House; Moscow, 1956), p. 102.

39 Paul Avrich, *Kronstadt 1921* (Princeton University Press; Princeton, N.J., 1970), pp. 172–73. For a different interpretation of the Kronstadt events see my introduction to Ida Mett, *The Kronstadt Uprising* (Black Rose Books; Montreal, 1971).

40 Hegel, op. cit. The passage cited here is quoted in Marx and Engels, *Selected Correspondence,* pp. 542–43.